Roasted Carrots with Harissa Aïoli and Dukkah. Plum Macaroon
Cake. Chaat Tostadas. Roasted Peaches with Glazed Sesame Oats.
Few food writers have such an insightful, intuitive understanding of
flavor—or a more eclectic and inspiring range of culinary influences
at work in their kitchen—than Tara O'Brady. Fewer still write with her
trademark warmth and thoughtful prose, which *Saveur* describes as
"like pulling up a seat at the table of an old friend."

Seven Spoons is O'Brady's remarkable and much-anticipated
debut. In it, she shares more than one hundred of her best and
most mouthwatering recipes—crowd-pleasing breakfasts like
Blackberry Buttermilk Whole Grain Scones, weeknight staples like
Everyday Yellow Dal, and terrifically inventive desserts like Roasted
Grapes with Sweet Labneh. These elegant, flavorful, and wonderfully
creative recipes, plus the show stopping photography, will have you
heading straight for the kitchen to get cooking.

SEVEN SPOONS

SEVEN SPOONS

My Favorite Recipes for Any and Every Day

TARA O'BRADY

appetite

by RANDOM HOUSE

TO SEAN, BENJAMIN, AND WILLIAM,
MY O'BRADY BOYS.

LIFESAVING
EQUIPMENT
FOR EMERGENCY ASSISTANCE CONTACT 9-1-1

CONTENTS

A PRACTICE OF COOKING

My first home with Sean, the man who would later become my husband, was a light-bathed, third-floor walkup just off the main drag of a decent-sized city in southern Ontario—the city where he was born, but a place I'd only visited. The apartment had a postage stamp for an entry, a sliver of a kitchen, a large living room, two bedrooms, one bath, and a balcony that ran the length of the place. Tall windows lined that same side, windows wider than my arms could stretch, with sills deep enough for a row of succulents to sit in matched white pots. My favorite seat in the house was at the end of a couch closest to those windows, through which a massive maple tree would stain the sunlight turmeric come autumn. I miss those windows.

From that apartment, we could walk to the grocery store, to the lakeshore, and to the coffee shop, and Sean could walk to work. It was a good neighborhood.

Our preferred pub was a block away, a smallish place that was decidedly British in its leanings. The room was perpetually dim. The deep banquettes were burgundy velvet with button-tufted backs, and the tables were glossy wood atop heavy iron bases. The walls were crammed, frame to mismatched frame, with horse racing, football, and royal memorabilia. It was the kind of place where on your second visit, the staff would remember you from your first. Besides fish and chips, bangers and mash, and a decent chicken tikka, that pub made the best burger around. It came charred on the outside and juicy at its middle, garnished with thick-cut bacon, cheddar, iceberg lettuce, and a generous slice of beefsteak tomato. Pickles were served on the side. I miss those burgers, too.

Choosing that apartment was probably one of the easiest, and smartest, decisions I've ever made. Aside from choosing the person I shared it with, of course. That apartment was where everything began.

For the first time in my life I felt like I was making a home rather than playing at it. In the domestic division of duties, I took over our kitchen. I was comfortable in the tiny galley space and found a specific sense of fulfillment in being in charge of it.

The trouble was, after furnishing it with pots and pans and crisp tea towels, I had no idea what to do in that room. I had no idea what to cook.

I knew *how* to cook. I grew up in what could only be called a food-loving family, after all; a family that discussed lunch at breakfast and planned road trip routes around where we wanted to eat along the way. My maternal grandmother, who stayed with us often, kept notebooks on the coffee table for scribbling down recipes from the cooking shows on PBS. My mother collected crockery. She and my father held unforgettable dinner parties, with Mum chic in pearls and wearing perfume. She'd have cooked for hours, and there was a bubbling excitement in the reveal of what she had made. Dad would fill up the ice bucket and polish the silver. Ours was *the* house, and *the* kitchen, at the center of celebrations with both friends and family.

My childhood was one without culinary boundaries. My parents had moved to Canada, specifically Montréal, only a handful of years before my older brother was born (I was born soon after). They were originally from India—my mother from the north, and my father from the south. From my birth to about when I was fourteen, we often journeyed back to India to visit. My mother's and my father's side each had differing culinary traditions; there was tandoori chicken, *idlis* and *sambar, rassam, chapatis, thali* meals, and *pani puri,* as well as shepherd's pie and Yorkshire puddings my maternal grandmother adored. (Through her my family has an Anglo-Indian connection, the particulars of which are unfortunately unknown.) When I was two years old, we moved from Québec to Ontario. Our next-door neighbors, the Roganos, had two daughters, and later a third, with the middle daughter my age and my best friend for all the years we lived side by side. They were Italian. And so, in between the masala dosas and sausage rolls at home, I'd be over at their house, asking for seconds of chicken scaloppini and licking Nutella off a spoon.

We were also a Canadian family. I knew that my hometown had the best bagels. Mum would make Buffalo chicken wings and egg drop soup, and one time she made a cheesecake crowned with a pile of cherries and a golden graham cracker crust that climbed all the way up the sides. I recall how the fresh, dairy tang of the cheese was set off by the tart fruit, lush and bathed in thick syrup. I thought no other dessert could be more beautiful. At Thanksgiving we'd have a proper roast turkey with all the trimmings *and* mutton pilau.

It was a childhood where cooking was part of our daily routine, and the kitchen was where we hung out.

I have cooked for as long as I can remember. The food I first made was often outside of my family's canon—I'd wager it was my way of feeling independent. I "invented" pizza sandwiches in elementary school and assembled casseroles with canned soup as the featured ingredient. I took on cookies and cakes in high school, and fine-tuned my Pavlova in university.

After university came the next stage of my adult life, the first I truly shared with another. And so I began to think about the food *we* liked. I wanted to establish the way I cooked, the flavors that intrigued *our* palates, and the recipes that might slowly become our regulars.

The idea of we, not me alone, was another thing altogether. At the time, Sean didn't like onions, the first ingredient in so many Indian recipes. I, on the other hand, held a years-old prejudice against mushrooms—one of his favorite foods. Sean's family has been in Canada for generations, with Irish and English roots, and the tastes to match. It was through the

Ralphs and O'Bradys that I was introduced to the nuanced merits of an exceptional butter tart, one with a pastry that's both sturdy and flaky, and the filling firm enough not to ooze. In their company I ate a particular pasta salad, ice cream sandwiches made with fresh waffles, and a cake that had sliced apples standing on end in concentric circles, like edible dominoes, in a clafoutis-like batter.

Sean brought an entire food history to our home, one drastically different from my frame of reference. However, as much as my upbringing shaped me, my way of cooking and my tastes weren't that of my parents, not exactly. Neither were Sean's that of his. Deciding *our* food would be an act of both negotiation and discovery.

I strode as confidently as I could into the uncharted wilds of our kitchen. I wanted to be able to improvise, to master the culinary witchcraft that allows a true cook to whip up something delicious from seemingly nothing, to tell if bread dough has enough flour by feel and if a loaf is properly cooked by sound, or to check if a cake is baked by eye, and to judge by the smell of butter that it is browned and not burnt—tricks only learned by doing.

I culled sources for advice on what should fill fridge and pantry; I compiled a catalog of equipment to keep on hand and ingredient combinations that worked together.

I started to cook. Not every day at first—that pub on the corner was still our usual reward on Friday nights, and the diner down the way was our destination come Sunday mornings—but I cooked a lot. I cooked from memory, advice, magazines, books, the Internet, and television shows.

I tried recipes printed on the backs of food packages and flour sacks and in promotional materials they gave away at the grocery store checkout. I made yogurt the way my mother did, leaving it overnight in the oven with the interior light on. I made peanut butter cookies to fill a jar on the counter, fiddling with the ratio of sugars and honey with each batch until I settled on the best combination of chew and crunch. I tested and tasted my tomato sauce until it was close to Mrs. Rogano's of my memory. I made cinnamon buns that were a spectacular bomb one Christmas morning. I volunteered a dish for every office party and potluck. We held our first dinner party.

Sean learned to like onions, and I came around to mushrooms.

At some point in that tiny kitchen, I fell in step with the rhythm of cooking. I learned which spices I wanted at arm's reach, which knife felt right in my hand, and the vinegars that were most useful. The kitchen shelves filled up. I made fewer lists, instead taking more notes. I noticed the way oil spreads and shimmers in a hot pan, how a fresh egg slips thickly from its shell. I didn't just cook; I became a cook.

One year into living in that apartment, I started a blog called *Seven Spoons*, so named for a number that seems to pop up in my life quite often and, well, spoons sounded nice with it. It would be my modern-day recipe file, a place to keep all the scraps of cookery knowledge I was collecting.

Seven Spoons was a chronicle of what was going on in our kitchen and, by extension, our lives. It granted me a space to work through the emerging opinions I was developing about food and cooking, and was my way of offering the newly established online food community a seat at our table.

These days, ten years from that apartment and since *Seven Spoons* began, my life is quite different. Sean and I bought our first house, and had our first son (Benjamin), then moved to our second house, and had our second son (William). There are a million and one directions in my waking hours, but I find there's a welcome habit in cooking, in the routines of the kitchen around which our lives revolve. It's what gets us going in the morning and brings us back together each night.

A COOKBOOK WRITTEN
AT THE KITCHEN TABLE

My cooking gained root in a commitment to good ingredients, treated well, and to their best potential. I am less about innovation and more about getting supper on the table, but doing so thoughtfully, and beautifully, too. I discovered my style through trial and error and not always easily, with the burns and scars to show for it. I am, as ever, devoted to the meals of my childhood, but am continually excited by the changing world of food.

In *Hot, Sour, Salty, Sweet*, Naomi Duguid and Jeffrey Alford say, "Markets breathe, they rest, they laugh, they yell. They absorb all the life around them and multiply it." I'll argue that today's kitchen does much the same—our pantry shelves, our table, are an illustration of the myriad influences of our day-to-day. It's thrillingly eclectic when you think deeply about it, but is nonetheless what we consider the norm.

By extension, how we use our kitchen reflects how we live our lives. How we cook, what we eat, and why we eat it is the story of who we are as a people, our heritage, priorities, and culture.

This book, like the site that shares its name, is a collection of favorite recipes. It is called *Seven Spoons* as a bookend; it is the culminated lessons of years of learning, bound up into a tidy volume. It is an honest account of the food that I crave, the food I eat, and the food I take pleasure in making. I cook seasonally, and am drawn to whole foods, yet I'm not a culinary purist by any stretch of the imagination. My tastes might vary from minute to minute. There are occasions when stripped-down simple is what is needed, and other times that warrant fancy; yet whatever the circumstance, I'm rarely indifferent.

In this book you will find dishes that suit each and every day, from staples such as a Seeded Boule to sublime scrambled eggs for unhurried weekends; from make-ahead snacks like energy-packed bars to a leisure-worthy lunch featuring tostadas by way of India; from a blessedly low-effort pasta dinner with lemons to a roast chicken accompanied by a relish a friend said could make a shoe palatable. It has sick days' comfort with Feel-Better Curried Soup with Crispy Chicken, and the winter holidays are covered with a cake that has me counting down to the annual arrival of blood oranges.

This book was written and photographed in my home, with images taken usually right before I sat down to eat. You will see plates and spoons repeated, and how the light changes with the seasons, so it is very much the real-time account of how these meals came to my table. I hope that seeing the recipes as they are truly served will help you envision how you might do the same.

A cookbook's value is only half on the page; the other half is in the action it inspires. My goal in sharing these recipes and lessons is for you to come away empowered to trust your instincts, to consider your own perspective and opinions, and to keep you well fed. I hope you find what follows to be a book comfortable on the nightstand, yet one that belongs in the kitchen.

Let's dig in.

HOW TO USE THIS BOOK

I wrote this book as my side of the conversation I imagine we'd have while cooking. It includes the chatty tidbits that are cookery's gossip, whether that is the backstory to a dish or why certain biscuits crumble and others flake.

I hope to share the experience of cooking with you as best I can through the page, and so there are times when recipes have ingredients or instructions that are purposefully left to your interpretation. Timelines are given as a map, and the sensory prompts are your signposts. My oven is different than yours, and ingredients vary, so poke, prod, sniff, taste, hear, and smell what's happening as you cook, and go from there.

And in all cases, trust your instincts. It is your meal, after all.

However, for some clarity:

If BUTTER is not specified as salted or unsalted in the recipe's ingredients list, use what you have on hand. There's some leeway when using small amounts. One standard stick of butter equals ½ cup.

A HANDFUL means a scant ½ cup. Herbs should be loosely packed.

A GOOD PINCH is ¼ teaspoon or so. A PINCH is ⅛ of one.

STOCKING THE PANTRY

I live in a red brick and wood house on a quiet street at the base of the Niagara escarpment. The house, built in just-past-the-middle of the last century, is a work in progress; we bought it from the original owner, and have spent the intervening years peeling off wallpaper, learning the intricacies of home plumbing repair, and reclaiming wood floors from carpeting the exact color of pea soup. There are blinds that need replacing, and a light fixture I need to finish refinishing, and I wish we could move the vegetable bed to the part of the garden that actually gets sun. But, I am wary about changing the kitchen. It is not that it is modern—it isn't—or that the appliances have all the bells and whistles— they don't—it is that the cupboards are exactly what I want. Not their looks, but their layout and their utility. Above the stove on one side is a skinny cabinet for spices; on the other side there's one tailor-made for oils; and across from there, a pantry cupboard, taller than me, with pull-out shelves. Those cupboards are part of what sold me on this house in the first place. That said, for all their ease and order, it took me a while before I figured out what should go in them; there were hits and misses, and boxes and bottles cast aside. It took living in our kitchen, cooking in it regularly, before I knew what I needed.

Setting up a kitchen is akin to building a wardrobe, or starting any sort of collection, whether snow globes, or baseball cards, or pottery (my weakness). You could go out and buy everything all at once in one store; but while the pieces might go together, they might not work together in a way that suits you.

Figuring out what you want and need in your kitchen, be it equipment or ingredients, is best achieved through trial, and accumulation over time. You might like one brand of pot, but another for pans; the grocery store's bread could be perfect, but the butcher shop may be your preference for your Sunday roasts. Maybe you go through paprika faster than cinnamon, and so matching-sized bottles don't suit, or you like a variety of honeys, one mustard, and a whole shelf reserved for hot sauces (in which case, we'll get along famously). Having a well-outfitted pantry creates the ability to experiment, switching in comparable ingredients and tailoring recipes to serve you best.

These are your decisions to make; I'm not in your kitchen, nor am I eating your food (though I'd accept the invitation). Your choices should make *you* feel good, full stop. My thoughts and the example of what I keep on hand are meant as exactly that—mine. The foods that follow should be a starting point rather than the finish. Remember, cooking is also my livelihood; the last thing I want is for you to feel compelled to go out and replicate my hoard.

So. I buy my food as locally as I can, but not without exceptions—or else I would be living a life free of avocados, mangoes, citrus, tea, coffee, and chocolate, and that is not a life I want to lead. I do my best to buy organic (both certified organic and from those who practice the methods without the paperwork), especially in the case of fruit and vegetables that I don't plan to peel. (For citrus when the zest is to be consumed I also look for unwaxed fruit, or give them a good, thorough scrubbing before use.) I choose ethically raised meats, poultry, and eggs; sustainable fish; and hormone-free animal products across the board.

I use these ingredients with care, trading better quality for consuming less. However, exceptional ingredients aren't necessarily expensive. At the farmers' market a dollar gets me enough green beans for a side at dinner, tortillas are sold there for less than at the store, and our CSA share is similarly cost-effective. I purchase most of our dry goods in small amounts from the bin section of our grocery. These staples—grains, pulses, flours, sugars, beans—are cheap, and in the case of specialty varieties, I only have to buy what we need.

It suits my schedule to do small, intentional shopping trips. I also find an understuffed fridge and shelves allows me to see what's there, making it that much easier to use things up. I like to clear the decks as much as I can before I fill them again, to minimize waste and spoilage. I try to preserve, pickle, and freeze what I can when there's plenty.

Whether a food is fresh, canned, or bottled, or something prepared, I seek out ones with the least amount of processing possible; if there is any processing, I favor a process that does not strip away nutrients and is not done to the detriment of the environment.

Beyond that, I won't go too deeply into the facets of each and every ingredient; there are countless resources for further information if you are so inclined, starting with the producers themselves, where possible. Good, workhorse staples may take consideration and effort in their sourcing, and on occasion a little more money, but they will return your investment tenfold.

DAIRY & ALTERNATIVES

Good-quality BUTTER is a personal vice, and it is rather nice to keep a European-style, cultured variety around for the times when only bread and butter will do. Buttercreams, butter-based sauces, and enriched pastries all benefit from some special consideration, but pick the times that are most worthy of a splurge. For day-to-day cooking, baking stacks of cookies, or even most cakes, a standard brand will do just fine. I keep or make GHEE (page 259) for cooking, as well.

I usually have COW'S MILK in the fridge and a NUT MILK (page 263) as well, along with homemade YOGURT (page 264), and a couple forms of CREAM—soured or crème fraîche (page 261) for garnishes and cooking, half-and-half for my husband's coffee, and heavy if I'm planning on baking. There's usually a can of COCONUT MILK in the cupboard.

I keep HARD CHEESES, such as cheddar and Parmesan or Pecorino, on hand always, and often a bit of something blue. I buy SOFT CHEESES like buffalo mozzarella, unripened chèvre, and goat's milk feta as they are needed and treat myself to a little chunk of whatever the cheesemonger had to taste that day.

EGGS

I am lucky to have access to a farmers' market where I can buy EGGS straight from a farmer who raises the birds without cages and with space for the chickens to do what chickens do. There are also a few farms a reasonable drive away that have eggs available, so if I miss market day, I will head in that direction. I consider the time spent worthwhile: not only does my money then directly support local farmers and their efforts, but also I am assured of the freshness of the eggs I use, which is of paramount importance when using uncooked eggs in things like mayonnaise (page 265). What's more, the eggs are beautiful, with plump, sunset-orange yolks that stand up like halved apricots.

If you are buying eggs at a grocery store, be sure to read labels and become familiar with the terminology and practices of larger-scale egg farming.

OILS

For oils, I choose those that have been pressed, rather than chemically extracted, and use refined oils as sparingly as possible. I save my pennies and use relatively inexpensive brands for whenever heat is involved, and spend on oils that are intended for no-heat preparations or that will be added as garnish.

My go-to olive oil for cooking is subtle, EXTRA-VIRGIN OLIVE OIL from my grocery store's house brand. I keep a couple of strapping, robustly flavored, bold extra-virgin varieties for finishing, certain condiments and dressings, and some baking. Olive oils will range in color and taste, from almost tawny to bottle green, from peppery to grassy, so it may take a few tries to find the one you like. Natural, extra-virgin COCONUT OIL is a sultry addition to a dish, but its undeniably tropical overtones do restrict its use to certain applications. You will see "neutral-tasting oil" mentioned on occasion in the ingredients lists, and for me that means an (almost) flavorless PEANUT OIL, not to be confused with more assertive unrefined and toasted ones. Quality SAFFLOWER, GRAPESEED, or CANOLA OIL can be used in its place.

TOASTED SESAME OIL is a last-minute addition to many of my dishes, once the heat has been turned off, and it shines in cold preparations, whereas an UNTOASTED SESAME OIL is more suited to heat. As AVOCADO OIL is becoming easily available, I find I'm using it with increased regularity. There is a specialty store I like that often carries small cans of interesting oils, like PISTACHIO, HAZELNUT, WALNUT, PUMPKIN SEED, and PECAN OIL—all have an affinity for steamed, sautéed, and roasted root vegetables, and they provide a flavor accent for rice salads especially well. I'll confess to hoarding a collection of these containers in my fridge, where they stay fresher longer, and using them judiciously.

VINEGARS

I think it was when I started to understand the importance of acidity in recipes that I became a better cook. Vinegars are, generally speaking, an economical way to add punch to a dish. They work like salt in their ability to amplify and revive characteristics of other ingredients. Beyond vinaigrettes, a spritz of vinegar enlivens a tray of hot, roasted vegetables or brings a needed edge to baking. I keep RED and WHITE WINE VINEGAR in the cupboard, neither anything special but ones that taste consistently good. RICE VINEGAR can be made from white, brown, black, or red rice, and is common in Asian cuisines. Slightly sweet and not as harsh as many other vinegars, it is used in stir-fries, dressings, and dipping sauces, with a seasoned white variety used for sushi rice. I keep a rotating selection on hand. White rice vinegar is the most common, but brown is my favorite. You can use either for the recipes in this book. I have MALT VINEGAR for fish and chips and butter tart pie (page 225). SHERRY VINEGAR and CHAMPAGNE VINEGAR are especially suited to salads. APPLE CIDER VINEGAR is, too, and its fruity, sour-sweetness really sings in pickles (page 271). There's the tiniest bottle of extraordinary BALSAMIC VINEGAR that I use discerningly because it easily grabs far too much of the spotlight.

SALT, SPICES, HERBS, CONDIMENTS & OTHER FLAVORINGS

Salt varies wildly in its flavor and texture among types and brands. Experiment to settle upon those you prefer. I don't use many in this book, but I do have them in my cupboard at home, so I include them in this list for the sake of thoroughness. I use a medium-grain kosher salt that is middle-of-the-road salty for most of my cooking; in the States I would recommend Diamond Crystal brand KOSHER SALT. I keep a FINE-GRAIN SEA SALT for most baking, except for those times when I want a pronounced, salty hit, as in the Basic, Great Chocolate Chip Cookies (page 215). FLAKED SEA SALT is great to have in a bowl on the kitchen counter or dinner table, so that the cook or diners can add it at the last possible moment; its appeal lies in its texture and clean, clear flavor. Maldon brand sea salt, with its distinctive, pyramid-shaped flakes, is my go-to. Gray salt is a moist and complex sea salt, and Himalayan pink salt is sharp in its minerality. SMOKED SALT varieties add another dimension to the mix.

I buy PEPPERCORNS whole, never ground. This way not only preserves freshness but also allows the freedom to choose the texture of pepper I want. A steak can take a coarse grind, whereas a fine dusting would be the thing for adding piquancy to a cocktail. Heat shouldn't be one-note when it comes to peppers, chiles, and the like, so I am also a champion of assorted CHILE POWDERS, such as sweet and smoked paprika, dried red pepper flakes, gochujaru (Korean red pepper flakes), cayenne, and Kashmiri chile powder. Each brings its own unique burn to a dish—some are strident, some floral, all are useful in their own way.

On the topic of heat, I use a few different HOT SAUCES: gochcharu (Korean fermented chile paste), sriracha, harissa (page 274), and thinner Mexican- and Louisiana-style hot sauces, such as Cholula and Tabasco.

Back to the spice cupboard, as with peppercorns, I try to keep mostly WHOLE SPICES and grind them as needed. In a stainless steel box called a *masala dabba* (spice box) my mother brought me from India, I store cumin seeds,

cardamom pods, fennel seeds, cloves, cinnamon sticks, star anise, black mustard seeds, and coriander seeds. There's a separate tin for whole nutmeg, and then some jars—ground turmeric (from my grandfather's house in Dehra Dun; thanks again, Mum), ground ginger, Chinese five-spice powder, and more than I will list here.

I don't use many DRIED HERBS and tend to buy them in small bundles for specific recipes. My only regulars are dried mint, thyme, sage, and oregano. I use FRESH HERBS most often, and consider myself prepared if I have a bouquet of chives, cilantro, flat-leaf parsley, thyme, and basil standing in a little jar of water in the refrigerator. Oregano, rosemary, and sage visit often.

I'm usually set with three types of MUSTARD on hand: Dijon mustard, a fiery English mustard (I have prepared Keen's and powdered Colman's), and something interesting, like a whole-seed German mustard. If ever you're in Toronto, go to St. Lawrence Market and visit the Kozlick's stall. They'll get you sorted.

Japanese MISO PASTES, from mild to pungent, white to deepest red, are fermented seasonings made from soybeans and other ingredients, including salt, a specific type of fungus, and sometimes barley or rice. The resulting pastes have an earthy quality, making them ideal for seasoning roasted meats and vegetables, and as a foundation for soup or a salad dressing. A good introductory miso is called *shiro miso*, or white miso, which is sweet and soft. Even with shiro miso, though, the quality can vary and some are exceptionally salty and pungent. I often suggest Eden Organic's shiro miso to start, if that brand is available to you.

SOY SAUCE, TAMARI, and FISH SAUCE have unmatched deep savoriness. Soy sauce and tamari are both by-products of fermented soybeans, but tamari is specifically a result of the process of making miso and is often gluten free (check the labeling if this is a concern). I use them almost interchangeably, with a slight preference to tamari as a condiment. San-J is a good brand for both. Fish sauce is used in Southeast Asian cooking, and is made from salted, fermented fish (often anchovies). The longer the fish are fermented, the milder and more balanced the fish sauce will be. Despite its assertive aroma, fish sauce is not overpowering when used—it gives an umami-rich base to stir-fries, curries, and dressings. Red Boat is an organic brand that is becoming increasingly available.

Jars of PICKLES! Keep them around, whether they are capers, skinny green beans (hello, Bloody Caesar), carrots, Indian chile or mango pickle, jalapeños (page 271), kimchi, cornichons, or good old sour dills. As with vinegars, pickles are brilliant in how they contrast with other foods—they are straight-to-the-point sharp against rich foods, and add brightness to mellow ones.

Whole VANILLA BEANS are best bought in bulk from a reputable source. Look for beans that are plump and pliable. Store them in an airtight container in a cool, dark place and air them regularly. So stored, vanilla beans can be kept for months, and as long as a year; dried beans can be reconstituted by wrapping in a damp paper towel and microwaving on low heat for a few seconds. Moldy beans should be discarded. Vanilla bean paste is a cost-effective compromise in between bean and extract. Use a good-quality, pure extract when the prettiness of vanilla seeds would be superfluous.

SWEETENERS

Since I bake often, I keep larger-than-probably-usual stores of sweeteners on hand. RAW, NATURAL CANE SUGARS, such as Demerara, Barbados (muscovado), and turbinado (Sugar in the Raw is an easy-to-find brand), are coarse grained and comparatively dry, making them ideal for sprinkling on baked goods before they go into the oven, or to finish. I use finer-grained TURBINADO SUGAR when I can in recipes, but in some cases GRANULATED WHITE contributes specific qualities to baking that cannot be achieved with less processed sugar. LIGHT BROWN SUGAR brings tenderness to cookies, while DARK BROWN SUGAR offers that, plus stronger molasses-like notes. I use CONFECTIONERS' SUGAR to decorate desserts, to make icings, and in some baked goods.

My father taps trees for his own MAPLE SYRUP—boiling just enough sap to keep the family spoiled for a year. (I mention his efforts not to boast, but because they deserve recognition.) Until I can convince him to take his distribution international, I suggest looking out for a Grade B pure maple syrup. It has a smoky, spicy quality that rounds out when cooked. I especially like it paired with the almost herbal tones of a nice olive oil and make use of the combination in my granola (page 47) and Chocolate Olive Oil Zucchini Bread (page 57). UNSULFURED MOLASSES is a must for gingerbread and my blood orange spice cake (page 238).

I like RAW, LOCAL HONEYS when I can get them, and use AGAVE NECTAR here and there—often in cocktails.

Now to the black sheep of the family, CORN SYRUP. This is not the high-fructose corn syrup boogeyman. I only use the old-fashioned corn syrup that home bakers have used for generations; Karo is a common example. Corn syrup contributes a characteristic texture in certain desserts, and while I do offer substitutions, those stand-ins will not produce identical results.

GRAINS, BEANS & LENTILS

I'll often finish off my weekend by cooking up some grains for the week ahead. I'll let them cool, then transfer some to containers for the fridge, and others to the freezer if I've made a large batch. They can be tucked into wraps (page 77) or used to add bulk to soups and salads.

Stubby BROWN RICE and BROWN and WHITE BASMATIS are my staples. The former is a good multipurpose rice, with medium weight and nuttiness, while basmati is the rice I grew up with, and its subtle perfume works equally well with curry as it does with vanilla and cardamom for rice pudding (page 230). A SUSHI RICE (usually brown) and one for RISOTTO (arborio or carnaroli) are also regularly tucked in the back of my pantry, too.

Other grains like BULGUR, BARLEY, QUINOA, FARRO, MILLET, and BUCKWHEAT are terrific to have on hand, and I usually do, in various forms, along with old-fashioned ROLLED and STEEL-CUT OATS. BROWN and FRENCH LENTILS are easy to cook and have countless uses. I keep RED (*masoor*), YELLOW (hulled mung), and GREEN (whole mung) LENTILS, and a small amount of WHITE (*urad*) on hand for Indian cooking. DRIED CHICKPEAS, SPLIT PEAS, BUTTER BEANS, BLACK BEANS, and CANNELLINI round out my collection.

FLOURS

While it doesn't win many nutritional rewards, unbleached ALL-PURPOSE FLOUR has its uses. It produces cakes with a light, airy crumb, and it makes pastry work easy. I also store some unbleached white BREAD FLOUR. I like swapping in WHOLE GRAIN FLOURS when I can and keep both whole wheat bread flour and whole wheat pastry flour for such opportunities. ATTA (also known as durum), a whole grain flour ground from semihard wheat, is one of my essentials for making chapatis, parathas (page 127), naan (page 124), and other Asian breads. Small bags of CHICKPEA (gram flour), RYE, TEFF, QUINOA, TAPIOCA, WHITE and BROWN RICE, and BUCKWHEAT FLOURS are usually on my shopping list for the bulk bins.

NUTS AND SEEDS

I keep nuts and seeds in the refrigerator or freezer, depending on the amount I purchased. There are ALMONDS in all forms, PISTACHIOS, PEANUTS, CASHEWS, HAZELNUTS, WALNUTS, PECANS, HULLED SUNFLOWER SEEDS, PEPITAS, POPPY SEEDS, BLACK and WHITE SESAME SEEDS, FLAXSEED, HEMP HEARTS, and CHIA SEEDS, all of which I turn to for crunch, flavor, and nutritional boosts. Also, I may be part squirrel.

CHAPTER 1

BREADS & BREAKFASTS

In times of stress, I make bread. I find a solace in the methodic following of steps, in the reliability of the results, and in the clear, neat edges of an activity with a beginning and a definite end. The process slows a hurried mind, and the kneading provides an outlet for nervous energy. Somehow, whatever the next day will bring, there's some protection offered by loaf of freshly baked bread. It grants a bolstering sense of capability.

Beyond that comfort, making bread is a lesson in all types of cooking, not only baking, as bread is one of those foods that does best when it's paid some attention; rising times and flour amounts can vary wildly depending on the weather, brand of ingredient, or temperature of the room. Your dough may turn out differently; it may be stickier or stiffer, rise especially fast or rather lackadaisically. It's best to trust how the dough behaves and looks, following those cues as to when and how to proceed. And the way to improve your bread is through practice.

So, beginning with bread seems fitting.

Now, in my humble opinion, breakfast food is the best food. There's something hopeful about starting out with a really enjoyable bite. It can be filling and hearty, like the take on huevos rancheros I make for my husband (page 39), it can be luxurious like the flaking bite of a bostock (page 41), or it can take on the virtuous form of a simple bowl of savory oats (page 45).

I should confess, I don't always have my breakfast first thing in the morning. But, I always have breakfast. It might be toast and a smoothie before dawn, soft-boiled eggs with cheese-fried toasts when I'm in need of some midday soothing, or peaches roasted with Chinese five-spice before bed—morning, noon, or night, the recipes in this chapter will hit the spot.

SIMPLE SANDWICH BREAD

This basic sandwich bread is just that: a white-flour loaf that is nice toasted and untoasted, with a tight, even crumb and a plainness of taste (meant in a way that's a compliment). This recipe is quick enough, with bread out of the oven in a little over two hours from start to finish; you can make a loaf easily after dinner for tomorrow's breakfast, or if you start mid-morning, it'll be ready for lunch. This recipe works nicely with a bowl and spoon, and uses only flour, water, sugar, yeast, and salt. It's almost as simple as it gets, and often that's more than enough.

.... *Makes 1 loaf* ....

1 tablespoon granulated or turbinado sugar

1½ cups (355 ml) warm water (105° to 110°F/40.5° to 43°C)

2¼ teaspoons (8 g package) active dry yeast

About 4 cups (510 g) all-purpose flour

1½ teaspoons medium-grain kosher salt

NOTE: 1 cup (130 g) of bread flour in place of the same amount of all-purpose flour will produce a denser, chewier loaf.

Grease a large bowl and an 8 by 4-inch (20 by 10 cm) loaf pan with butter and set aside.

Stir the sugar into the warm water in a large bowl, then sprinkle over the yeast. Leave undisturbed until the mixture is foamy, about 5 minutes. If after that time there are no bubbles, wait a minute more. If still nothing, discard the slurry and try again with fresh yeast and fresh water.

If everything's looking swell, give the mixture a good stir with a silicone spatula or wooden spoon. Use that same spoon to stir in the flour and salt. Keep stirring to form a rough dough. If the dough seems too sticky and isn't coming away from the sides of the bowl, add more flour, a tablespoon at a time, until it does. Turn everything out onto a lightly floured work surface. Now here's the work, because you'll have to knead the dough, which should take about 8 minutes.

One or two hands can be used to knead; these instructions are for two hands, because that's the easiest method to learn. Gather the dough up into a rounded lump. With the heels of your hands, gently push the center of the dough down and away from you in as fluid a motion as possible. Give the dough a quarter turn (to the left or right, it doesn't matter, just keep turning that same way as you continue). Get your fingertips under the far edge of the dough, and fold it back toward you, so the ends meet up. Using the heels of your hands again, press those ends together and push them into the dough and away from you. Turn the dough another quarter turn, and then fold it back again. Repeat this pattern of push, turn, fold. As you knead, the dough will change in texture, becoming elastic. If at any time it sticks, dust lightly with flour. You can tell the dough has been kneaded enough when it feels smooth and taut like the surface of an inflated balloon. Pressed with your knuckle, it should quickly spring back. Shape into a ball, with ends tucked underneath.

Place the ball in the greased bowl, rolling it over so it's slicked on all sides. Turn the dough right side up and cover loosely with greased plastic wrap or a lint-free kitchen towel. Set in a warm, draft-free spot to rise until doubled in bulk, 45 to 60 minutes.

Deflate the risen dough with a gentle punch. Turn the dough out onto a lightly floured work surface, with the smooth side down (the side that was face up in the bowl). Stretch the dough to form a rough 9 by 12-inch (23 by 30 cm) rectangle. From one of the short ends, roll the dough into a tight cylinder, pinching the roll together to seal. Bring the open ends up, and pinch them closed as well. Place the roll, seam side down, in the prepared pan; cover with greased plastic wrap or a lint-free kitchen towel and leave to rise again until almost double in size, 35 to 45 minutes.

About 10 minutes before the dough has finished rising, preheat an oven to 400°F (200°C) with a rack in the lower third of the oven. Remove the plastic wrap or towel from the pan. Bake for 35 to 40 minutes, or until golden brown. Immediately flip the bread out of the pan onto a lint-free towel. Use the towel to pick up the loaf and tap its underside with your knuckle—when properly baked, the bread will sound hollow. If needed, return the loaf to the pan and bake for 5 minutes more. Once fully baked, turn the bread out of its pan onto a wire rack. The loaf should be left right side up until it reaches room temperature before slicing—the crumb and crust will set as it cools. That said, because we rarely wait that long before tucking in, I can hardly decree that you must do so.

SEEDED BOULE

When I began baking breads regularly, I began with softer sandwich breads (page 26), then worked my way up to crusty boules made with pre-ferments (biga, poolish) and, finally, sourdough and levain.

Then came Jim Lahey's No Knead Bread recipe, published in the *New York Times* in 2006—it not only changed the way many people bake bread, but it also changed *who* baked bread. Lahey's method delivered gorgeous, crackling loaves, with little hands-on time, a long rise that could easily be scheduled for overnight, and the ingenious method of using a Dutch oven to create a moist environment for the bread as it bakes.

Since then, bakers and writers like Chad Robertson, Jeff Hertzberg, Zoë François, and Ken Forkish have continued to inspire and enlighten with their detailed, informative books on the subject of bread at home.

This seeded boule is the result of my abject thievery of those authors' knowledge, adapted to suit my preferences. My loaf is a bit larger than most because I like to bake enough to feed my family for a day, with some left to carry us over to the next. And, this larger batch of dough, while still manageable to handle, is enough to form two nicely sized loaves, in case the need for a bready gift arises. (Simply divide the dough in half and stretch, fold, and let rise each piece separately, then bake in two 4- or 5-quart [3.6 or 4.5 L] heavy ovenproof pots.) I use 30 percent whole wheat flour in this recipe, which seems to give us the balance of fractured crust and spongy interior that we like. To further emphasize the crust, the dough is rolled in seeds before baking, and their roasted smokiness is one of the most striking aspects of the bread, post bake. I love how they become welded to the crust. Sesame seeds are a standout, their singed nuttiness reminds me of Montreal's sesame bagels, straight out of the wood oven, tinged with char.

I recommend baking this bread covered, in an uncoated Dutch oven or cast-iron skillet. Either yields darker, crispier crusts than those baked in enameled cast iron, and are my preference.

The folding of the dough after mixing is entirely optional; it will improve the bread's flavor and final crumb structure, but if you don't want to wait around to perform the routine, it will still be very good. Between you and me, I often fall asleep before I get to folding.

Makes 1 large loaf

3½ cups (450 g) all-purpose flour

1¼ cups (140 g) whole wheat flour

1½ teaspoons fine-grain sea salt

¼ teaspoon active dry yeast

2 cups (480 ml) lukewarm water (around 95°F/35°C)

3 tablespoons mixed seeds (black and white sesame seeds, flaxseeds, poppy seeds)

... continued

Seeded Boule, continued

NOTE: Slashing or scoring the dough before it bakes helps the bread rise to its full height potential. In the method as written, the rough seams achieve the same effect, often with unexpectedly beautiful results—I once had a loaf emerge with a tear pattern in the shape of South America.

However, there is also the option to slash the loaves using a sharp, thin-bladed or serrated knife. To do so, place the dough smooth side down in the proofing basket. Once it is ready, flip the dough out onto a board as before, and use your selected knife to score the loaf. Cut deeply, say ¼ to ½ inch (6 mm to 1 cm) deep, with the blade in a vertical position, and the dough will rise equally on either side of the mark; if you make a ¼-inch (6 mm) deep cut at a shallow angle, the dough will rise more on one side than the other, and the bread will have a flap when finished. Scoring takes some practice, and with time, you'll gain an understanding of how the shape of cuts will affect how the loaves will bake.

In a large bowl that holds at least 2½ quarts (2.5 L), mix the flours, salt, and yeast. Pour in the water, then stir with wet hands or a damp silicone spatula to incorporate completely. Fold the dough onto itself a few times, so that it starts to feel a bit stiff, then flip the dough so the raggedy side is at the bottom. Cover the bowl with a lint-free towel or plastic wrap.

Either set the bowl aside for 12 to 18 hours, or, if still feeling up to some light work, come back to it after about 30 minutes. Uncover the bowl, use a wet hand to sweep down the interior of the bowl to the underside of the dough, leading with the side of your hand rather than fingertips. Pull one handful of the dough up from the bottom and over the top, so the dough is folded and stretched. Turn the bowl and repeat; continue to turn the bowl and fold the dough until you're back to where you started. Each fold will build tension, so by the end, it should hold together as a rounded lump. Flip the dough over, so it is smooth on top, then cover again. Repeat the process 2 more times, waiting 30 minutes in between each. After the last time folding, cover the bowl and let the dough rise at room temperature for 12 hours.

About 90 minutes before you want to bake, uncover the dough. Lift the edge of the dough up, stretching it, then let go, so it drops back in the bowl. Turn the bowl and repeat 4 to 6 times, so the dough deflates gently. Replace the cover on the bowl and set aside for 15 minutes.

Lightly dust a proofing basket or a large bowl with flour and one-quarter of the seeds. Flip the dough out onto a lightly floured board. Fold the dough in half 2 or 3 times, then knead briefly and quickly, so that it springs back when touched. Form it into a tight ball by tucking the ends under and rolling the rounded dough against the counter with cupped hands. Sprinkle most of the remaining seeds across the dough and board, then roll the dough around until it's coated with seeds on all sides. Place the dough in the prepared basket, seam side down. Sprinkle the last of the seeds on top of the dough, then cover with a lint-free towel and let rise for 1 hour.

About 45 minutes before baking, preheat the oven to 500°F (260°C), with a heavy, 6- to 8-quart (6 to 8 L) tightly covered Dutch oven on the rack in the lower third of the oven.

Pull the pot from the oven (taking care and wearing good-quality oven mitts—the pot will be ridiculously hot!). Turn the dough out onto a lightly floured work surface, so the seam side is now exposed. With utmost care, remove the lid from the pot. Take off the oven mitts. Slip your hands under the dough and lift it over the pot. Without getting your hands too close to the screaming-hot pot, quickly and decisively drop the dough into it. (Alternatively, flip the dough directly from the basket into the pot, but this can be tricky.) Put the oven mitts back on. If the dough didn't land evenly, give the pot a shake and it should right itself. Cover the pot with its lid, and pop it back in the oven. Immediately turn the heat down to 475°F (245°C). Bake for 30 minutes, then remove the lid, and bake until the bread is chestnut brown, 20 to 30 minutes more.

Tip the bread out of the pot (tilt the pot on a heat-safe surface with one hand, then catch the loaf with the other, protected with a lint-free towel) and cool on a wire rack. Baking wisdom says to let the bread cool completely, to fully establish the crust and set the crumb, but 15 minutes is usually my threshold of patience.

MY BEST BISCUITS

My definition of the perfect biscuit would be one that is tender at its middle and crisp at the edges, with pliant, defined layers. It should split cleanly and stand up to the weight of peach preserves, or country ham, or, on exceptional days, some of each. To achieve this Platonic ideal, I believe biscuits can't just be made, they must be built.

The texture of these biscuits owes equal due to ingredients and technique. The dough starts with baking powder and baking soda for leavening, then cold butter is worked into broad flakes by hand, rather than the roundish pebbly shapes yielded by pastry cutters and food processors. Finally comes the physical construction of layers. The method is similar to making a laminated dough—think croissants—and while it seems a complicated or lengthy procedure, it's not. It is hard to capture in words, however, and far easier to understand once your hands are involved. The dough is patted out, folded in half, then turned, flattened, and folded again. This routine is repeated until the shaggy mass is transformed into a smooth rectangle. Stacking the dough upon itself establishes strata of flour and butter, exponentially increasing in number with every fold, while pressure pushes the sheets of butter even thinner. When baked, the water in the butter evaporates and creates long pockets of steam, the thrust of which lifts the dough, and puffs the biscuits to towering glory.

I have found that round biscuits rise higher than square, but squares are quicker to make and result in fewer scraps. Keep in mind that unlike most baking, the ingredients needn't be at room temperature; fridge-cold yogurt, buttermilk, and eggs are preferred.

.... *Makes 12 biscuits* ....

4 cups (510 g)
all-purpose flour

1½ tablespoons aluminum-free baking powder

½ teaspoon baking soda

1¼ teaspoons medium-grain kosher salt

1 teaspoon granulated sugar or fine-grained turbinado for savory biscuits, 1 tablespoon for sweet

1 cup (225 g) unsalted butter, cold and cut into ¼-inch (6 mm) dice

½ cup (120 ml) whole milk yogurt (page 264)

½ cup (120 ml) well-shaken buttermilk (page 258), plus more as needed

2 eggs

Heavy cream or melted unsalted butter for brushing (optional)

Preheat an oven to 425°F (220°C) with a rack in the upper third of the oven. Line a baking sheet with parchment paper.

In a large bowl, whisk together the flour, baking powder, baking soda, salt, and sugar. Sprinkle the butter into the bowl, then use your fingers to toss the pieces into the dry ingredients. Press the butter into flakes by rubbing each cube between your fingers,

. . . **continued**

My Best Biscuits, continued

NOTE: Some people are sensitive to the taste of commercial baking powder; if you fall into that category, or just happen to be out of baking powder, make up small batch of homemade baking powder by combining ¼ cup (35 g) cream of tartar, 2 tablespoons baking soda, and 2 tablespoons cornstarch in a small, airtight container. Use as you would store-bought baking powder.

The eggs can be swapped for an additional ⅓ cup (80 ml) yogurt (page 264).

You can also use compound butter (page 260), sweet or savory, here.

keeping the flakes coated with flour. (Once all the butter is in wide shingles, the mixture can be held in the fridge overnight, covered.)

Use a fork to thoroughly mix the yogurt, ½ cup buttermilk, and the eggs together in a measuring cup until smooth. Dig a well in the middle of the dry ingredients, then pour the liquids into the center. Using a butter knife or the same fork as before, pull the dry ingredients into the wet to make a soft dough. Do not overwork. The liquid only needs to be incorporated; the dough shouldn't be smooth, and there will be flour loose in the bowl.

Turn everything out onto a board or work surface. It will look unpromising. With your hands, gently bring together all the wet clumps into the center, then pat to level. Scoop some of the loose flour onto the top of the doughy bits, then fold the dough in half to encase the flour, pushing down lightly to seal and spread the dough. Turn the dough 90 degrees, press more flour into the surface, fold, turn, and press again. Repeat the process until all the flour is incorporated and the dough is relatively smooth, 5 or 6 turns total. After the last turn, delicately work the dough to a generous ¾-inch (2 cm) thickness.

Cut the dough either into 12 squares with a knife or with a floured 2-inch (5 cm) biscuit cutter (round or square). In either case, try not to seal the edges of the biscuits, because this will inhibit the rise. For the knife, that means using a chopping (rather than slicing) motion; for the cutter, resist the urge to twist the cutter as it meets the board. Collect any scraps and gently form them into biscuity shapes; do not reroll. Place the biscuits upside down on the prepared baking sheet. If there is time, chill the cut biscuits for 10 minutes before baking.

Bake, without opening the oven door, for about 18 minutes, at which point the biscuits should be golden and well risen and feel light for their size. If desired, brush the tops of the biscuits with heavy cream or melted butter at the 16-minute mark. Remove from the oven, let cool until they'll no longer burn your mouth, then tuck in. The biscuits are best eaten the day they are made. Leftovers can be split and toasted, or rewarmed in a low oven.

DIPPER EGGS WITH CHEESE-FRIED TOAST SOLDIERS

It may seem odd to be particular about soft-boiled eggs and toast, given how basic a dish it is, but I am—as is my younger son. We want the yolk warm, still viscously liquid; the white set but tender; the bread dense, even crumbed, and cut into broad fingers to facilitate the impatient digging into egg cups. And, for the best toast soldier around, there has to be a layer of grated cheese, affixed with mayonnaise no less, applied to the toast before frying. Mayonnaise won't burn as easily as butter, so it allows the necessary time to get a resolutely lacy, deeply saline crust. The trick is to time your preparation so that the eggs and toast are ready simultaneously, so set your water to simmer just before you start preparing the toasts. Then the eggs should go into their pot when the bread starts to fry. Mind-blowingly good.

Serves 2

2 thick slices sturdy sandwich bread

1½ tablespoons mayonnaise (page 265)

¼ cup (30 g) finely grated Parmesan or Pecorino Romano cheese

About 1 tablespoon minced chives (optional)

2 to 4 eggs, depending on appetite

Flaky sea salt and freshly ground black pepper

Smoked paprika (optional)

NOTE: If you don't have egg cups, you can peel soft-boiled eggs, albeit carefully. Run them under cold water until cool enough to handle, rap the fat end against the counter, then peel. Place in a small bowl, split, and dip away.

Fill a heavy saucepan with water deep enough to later cover the eggs by 2 inches (5 cm). Bring the water to a simmer, then reduce the heat so that the water is only quivering.

Meanwhile, heat a cast-iron skillet over medium heat. On a board, spread one side of each slice of bread with a thin coating of mayonnaise. Sprinkle half the cheese over the slices, then press gently to secure the fleecy layer of cheese. Flip the bread over. Spread the second side with more mayonnaise and cover with the remaining cheese, patting down again. Fry the bread in the hot pan until evenly golden brown and crisp, 3 to 5 minutes per side. Sprinkle with the chives while hot, then set aside to keep warm if needed.

Meanwhile, once the water is at the proper temperature, use a strainer or slotted spoon to carefully lower the eggs into their bath. Cook for exactly 6 minutes, adjusting the heat as needed to maintain the barest simmer, with tiny bubbles just breaking the surface. When the timer dings, remove each egg with the slotted spoon and place in an egg cup. Lop off each top with a knife. Season with salt and pepper and paprika. Cut the toasts into strips and have at it. Be sure to keep seasoning the eggs as you devour them.

SOFT-SET SCRAMBLED EGGS

My mother's mother was born Enid, but she changed her name to Jaishri when she married my grandfather on her twenty-seventh birthday. She had family in India, England, and Canada, so for many years she would divide her time between the three.

She was, albeit briefly, a flight attendant in the 1940s. She once left a passenger behind on a trip, and the family joke was he'd annoyed her, and so she'd done it on purpose. Later, she was a teacher, which left her afternoons free to play cards and smoke cigarettes with her friends. She liked crossword puzzles, Persian Melon lipstick, a sip of wine with dinner, and watching tennis. I remember the day she took her hair, which was long and dark and worn in a low bun at the base of her neck, and cut it into a short bob, set in curls. I thought she looked like Queen Elizabeth.

She and I were close. She had a sharp wit, was competitive and encouraging, and had a talent in the kitchen.

Grandma made a fierce shrimp curry, her *puris* (Indian deep-fried flatbreads) were always puffed, and her croquettes were always tender. She had, to put it mildly, strong opinions on food. She was not afraid to call a recipe "absolute rubbish," or pointedly ask why I'd chosen to make one dessert over the one she prefered.

When her health began to decline in later years, the subject of food felt prickly as her appetite waned; not only was food something she loved, but it was also something we shared. When we'd talk on the phone, one of her first questions would be, "What did the boys have for breakfast?" and the conversation would end with, "And what are you making for dinner?"

My sons called my grandmother Gigi. I explained to them that the soft-set scrambled eggs they knew as "*dhanya*-and-onion-eggs" ("cilantro-and-onion-eggs") were really hers. We talked about how I especially liked her to make them for me when I was sick. I made her veal escalopes one night, then her clear chicken stew the next. In the steam and stirring, I summoned a childhood spent with my grandmother at the stove. I filled my sons up with her cooking, sharing her legacy, bite by bite.

Gigi passed away on July 24, 2012, two months shy of her 91st birthday. It was a Tuesday.

We had a family dinner in her honor, at my parents' house, the following Sunday. It was like so many Sundays had been for what seems forever—a midafternoon gathering with all of us together, my parents, aunts and uncles and cousins, my brother and his family, and then mine. There were samosas and *chana bhatura* with pickled vegetables, a standing rib roast, Indian sweets like *barfi, gulab jamun, jalebi,* all manner of *halvas,* and a raspberry trifle with thick, vanilla-specked custard. We opened the doors to everyone who knew her, and there was music and stories and photographs.

That was her celebration, but it wasn't a good-bye. I conjure Gigi every time I make one of her recipes, with her instructions and reminders clear in my head as I do so. She taught me to keep a wooden spoon in the pot so the dal doesn't boil over, and to always keep something on hand to offer guests, even if only a bag of potato chips and cold ginger ale.

Among so many other lessons, she taught me to make eggs.

Grandma's eggs never see a sizzle. They are not a dry and bouncy scramble; instead, they are a velvety emulsion barely coaxed into solid. I learned to make them in a double boiler, but I rarely have such patience nowadays. Instead, I cook the eggs gently, over low heat in a heavy saucepan, with an attentive stirring regime. Take note: The frequency and style of stirring determine how curds form as the eggs cook. For a texture close to polenta, use a whisk and move it almost constantly; infrequent folds with a spatula will produce luscious waves. My method falls in between, stirring with an angled wooden spoon as for risotto, and ending up with rumpled custard that has body to stand up, then slumps soon enough on the plate. Follow the process that achieves your ideal.

I serve these with Beet-Cured Gravlax (page 115) or a hulking slab of crusty, seeded bread (page 29), toasted, with a chunk of fresh goat's cheese on the side. I believe Gigi would approve.

.... *Serves 4* ....

8 eggs
¼ cup (60 ml) light cream or half-and-half
¼ cup (60 g) unsalted butter

Small bunch of tender herbs (such as chives, dill, mint, cilantro, parsley, or a mix), leaves and tender stems only, minced

Fine-grain sea salt and freshly ground black pepper

Stir the eggs and cream together in a heavy saucepan. The aim isn't to fluff the eggs, just to get the yolks and whites blended. Plunk in 3 tablespoons of the butter. Slowly warm the eggs over medium-low heat, stirring occasionally. Once the butter melts, start stirring at intervals for larger curds and constantly for small, simultaneously pulling the cooked eggs away from the sides and bottom of the pan as they set. When half of the eggs are in curds, half thickened liquid, stir in the last tablespoon of butter and the herbs. Continue to stir, until the eggs are almost finished, but still underdone; the residual heat will finish the job on the way to the plate. Season with salt and pepper and serve.

HUEVOS A LA PLAZA
DE MERCADO

My city has a farmers' market three times a week in a central square. My favorite seller for charctuerie and cheese is a tall gentleman with a black moustache, who always has a sample to offer across the blade of his small knife—some sausage that's new this week, or a cheddar of which he's particularly proud. There's another man from whom I'll buy huevos rancheros and tacos for that day's breakfast, and extra tortillas for the days when the market is closed. And those two men, plus the vegetable man with the stall across the way, are the ones I always visit first.

This recipe, a version of huevos rancheros, marries the ingredients of our market, in a gutsy, rustic stack of corn tortillas, eggs, and cheese, doused with a chile-kissed and paprika-stained tomato sauce. It is substantial and hunger slaying, and my secret hangover cure, in case you have an interest in such things.

.... *Serves 4* ....

SAUCE

Small bunch of cilantro, leaves and tender stems

2 shallots, chopped

1 clove garlic, smashed with the side of a knife

1 jalapeño, seeded, if desired, and chopped

1 can (15-ounce/425 g) whole tomatoes, preferably fire-roasted

1 teaspoon mild olive oil, plus more as needed

4- to 6-ounce (115 g to 170 g) piece cured sausage with some fat and spice, such as Spanish chorizo, diced

Medium-grain kosher salt and freshly ground black pepper

EGGS AND THEIR TOPPINGS

Mild olive oil or ghee (page 259), for cooking the tortillas and eggs

8 to 10 small corn tortillas

4 to 8 eggs

½ cup (60 g) queso fresco

2 avocados, peeled, pitted, and chopped

Chile Cream (page 102), Charred Green Onion Dressing (page 185), or sour cream

Mexican-style hot sauce

2 limes, cut into wedges

Pickled jalapeños (page 271)

To make the sauce, pluck the leaves from the cilantro and set aside. Chop the stems, then drop them into a blender with the shallots, garlic, and jalapeño. Pour in a quarter of the tomatoes and their liquid, then buzz the vegetables to make a puree. Add the rest of the tomatoes and process to your liking.

Warm the oil in a medium saucepan over medium heat. Tumble in the chorizo and cook, stirring often, until the sausage is crispy and golden on all sides and has released some of its juices, 3 to 5 minutes. Using a slotted spoon, transfer the sausage to an ovenproof plate and set aside.

... **continued**

Huevos a la Plaza de Mercado, continued

NOTE: I sometimes use
canned yellow tomatoes
but, of course, red ones
are just fine. Instead of
preparing on individual
plates, you can assemble
and broil the whole
gang of egg-and-sauce-
topped tortillas on a large
parchment-lined baking
sheet, then serve straight
from the oven, family style.

Tip the tomato puree into the hot pan with a generous pinch of salt and a few turns of pepper from the mill. Bring to a boil over medium-high heat, stirring often. Reduce the heat to a simmer and cook, stirring regularly, until the sauce is thickened and tastes cooked, around 30 minutes. Check for seasoning and keep warm.

Preheat an oven to 200°F (95°C), with ovenproof serving dishes placed on the rack in the upper third. Once the oven has reached temperature, tuck the crisped sausage in beside the dishes.

To make the eggs, in a large cast-iron or nonstick skillet, heat a thin film of oil over medium heat. Working in batches as necessary, warm the tortillas, flipping once, until they are heated through, tender, and starting to puff, 1 to 2 minutes per side. Move the tortillas to the plates in the oven as they are cooked. Once they're all done, use the pan to cook the eggs—sunny side up, over easy, scrambled, whatever. Pull all the dishes from the oven, including the one with the sausage, and preheat the broiler. Divide the eggs among the plates, then spoon some of the tomato sauce on top. Crumble the queso over all and place under the broiler until the tortillas char slightly, around 2 minutes. Make sure not to leave them unattended; it's a fine line between toasted and *en fuego*.

Serve right away, garnished with the sausage, avocados, Chile Cream, and the reserved cilantro leaves. Have hot sauce, lime wedges, and jalapeños on the table.

BOSTOCKS

Bostocks are slices of brioche bathed in orange syrup, slathered with almond cream, and then baked. In the oven, the syrup at the edge of the brioche candies, becoming thin and snappy, while the center turns custardy, an exact match to the consistency of the cream. It is all I could ever want in a pastry: not overly cloying, nuanced, and, dare I say, sophisticated.

Bostocks, like French toast (*pain perdu*), almond croissants (*croissants aux amandes*, see Variation on page 42), and bread pudding, are an ingenious way to use up old bread—although I occasionally let brioche go stale for the express purpose of making this recipe. If there is time, slice the brioche the night before, so it becomes dry through and through, ready to soak up as much orange syrup as possible. If that's not in the cards, lightly toast the brioche, so that the cut sides are crisp but without color.

Bostocks are best the day they are made, warm or at room temperature. I like them eaten out of hand, with a coffee, or served warm with roasted rhubarb, Pickled Strawberry Preserves (page 111), or Fresh and Twangy Blueberry Sauce (page 245). My preference is to garnish the almond cream only with sugar, to preserve that blissful oneness of texture. Flaked almonds do contribute by way of looks, so I include them as a topping suggestion.

Brioche can vary in both sugar and fat; the almond cream and syrup quantities here are suitable for a comparatively lean to middle-of-the-road loaf, one that is not markedly sweet or rich when eaten plain. (The humor of calling brioche "lean" is not lost on me.) If the bread you're using skews extravagant, pull back on the embellishment.

.... *Makes 8 to 10 pieces* ....

ORANGE SYRUP

¾ cup (150 g) granulated sugar

¾ cup (180 ml) water

1 teaspoon orange flower water

4 to 6 strips citrus zest (lemon, orange, yuzu), each 1 inch (2.5 cm) wide

ALMOND CREAM

½ cup (115 g) unsalted butter, softened

1 cup (115g) confectioners' sugar

1 cup (100 g) almond meal (see Note)

1 tablespoon all-purpose flour

Seeds scraped from a vanilla bean

2 teaspoons rum or brandy (optional)

Scant ¼ teaspoon almond extract

¼ teaspoon fine-grain sea salt

1 egg, lightly beaten

TO ASSEMBLE

8 to 10 slices stale brioche, each around 1 inch (2.5 cm) thick

Flaked almonds, for sprinkling (optional)

Confectioners' sugar, for dusting

... continued

Bostocks, continued

NOTE: To make the almond meal, finely grind 3½ ounces (100 g) blanched, whole almonds in the food processor. Since the processor is already out, the almond cream can be made using the machine; add the all-purpose flour to the bowl of the processor with the almond meal. Scrape in the butter and process until blended, about 1 minute. Sift in the confectioners' sugar, and pulse to incorporate. Scrape down the sides of the bowl and blade. Close the lid and pulse for 30-second intervals for 2 minutes, until quite fluffy. Pulse in the vanilla, rum, almond extract, and salt. Pour in the egg and process until smooth. Cover and store as above.

To make the syrup, stir together the granulated sugar, water, orange flower water, and zest in a small saucepan. Bring to a boil over medium heat, then lower the heat and simmer for 5 minutes. Set aside to cool. Cover and refrigerate overnight, or for up to 1 week. Remove the zest before using.

To make the almond cream, beat the butter in a bowl with a silicone spatula or a hand mixer until the butter holds a peak when the spatula is lifted. Sift in the confectioners' sugar, then fold to incorporate. Beat until fluffy, about 3 minutes. Scrape down the bottom and sides of the bowl. Sift in half the almond meal, stir to incorporate, then sift in the rest with the flour. Mix again, then stir in the vanilla, rum, almond extract, and salt. Pour in the egg and stir until creamy. Transfer to a bowl, then press a piece of plastic wrap against the surface to prevent it from drying out. Refrigerate until cold, about 2 hours, or up to 3 days ahead.

To assemble the bostocks, preheat an oven to 375°F (190°C). Line a baking sheet with parchment paper, then arrange the brioche on top. Brush syrup all over the slices until saturated. If any syrup remains, wait until the first soaking is absorbed, then brush again. Spread one cut side with almond cream, all the way to edges, then sprinkle with almonds. Bake until the cream is puffed and browned, and the brioche deeply toasted, 18 to 22 minutes. Let the bostocks cool for 5 minutes on their tray. Sift a light flurry of confectioners' sugar over all, then all that's left is the eating.

Almond Croissant Variation: Split 6 to 8 stale croissants in half horizontally. Brush with syrup, fill with almond cream, and sandwich. Glaze the tops with more syrup and smear on more almond paste, shower with almonds, and bake for 12 to 15 minutes. Dust with confectioners' sugar.

SAVORY STEEL-CUT OATS WITH CHEESE AND SPINACH

The general method I use for making steel-cut oats is from Ian Bishop via one of Nigel Slater's television programs. Bishop was the 2008 winner of the Golden Spurtle World Porridge Making Championship—a very real, annual event held in Carrbridge, Scotland, and one that sounds a rather good time.

My routine begins with toasting the oats in fat before adding any liquid, but from there, Mr. Bishop takes over. I've come to learn the constant stirring of oats as they cook is of utmost importance, as is salt—added at the right moment, and in a greater quantity than might be assumed. Those small lessons changed my oatmeal entirely, yielding a toothsome, cozy porridge of nubbled, creamy grains.

My children most often eat their porridge simply and sugared, with a puddle of cream, sliced bananas, a few blueberries, and the thinnest pour of maple syrup. But on a dark morning in deep winter when extra insulation against the world is needed, I'll bulk mine up with cheese and greens, and, often, preserved tomatoes or an egg. If you like congee, or the thought of a risotto to start the day appeals, do give it a try.

.... *Serves 4* ....

PORRIDGE

2 teaspoons butter or mild-tasting olive oil

1 cup (80 g) steel-cut (Irish) oats

3½ cups (840 ml) water

½ teaspoon fine-grain sea salt

SAVORY ADDITIONS

Pecorino Romano or Parmesan cheese

2 cups (115 g) fresh baby spinach leaves

Really nice extra-virgin olive oil

Flaky sea salt and freshly cracked black pepper

Soused Tomatoes (page 193), gently rewarmed in their oil (optional)

Snipped fresh chives

To make the porridge, in a heavy saucepan, melt the butter over medium heat. Add the oats and stir them around in the butter until they smell a bit nutty, 3 minutes or so. Pour in the water and bring to a boil, stirring all the while. When the oats start to bubble heavily at the edge, and the liquid looks thick, 15 minutes or so, sprinkle in the salt. Keep stirring for 5 to 7 minutes more, until the oats are distinct but creamy and tender. (Stop here for sweet variations; see instructions below.)

Divide the porridge among bowls. Grate over a bit of cheese—I like some to start, so it melts upon contact with the oats—then

... continued

Savory Steel-Cut Oats with Cheese and Spinach, continued

top with a handful of spinach leaves and a drizzle of olive oil. Season with salt and pepper. Gently lay one or two tomatoes on top of each serving, then sprinkle with chives (and more cheese, if so moved). Spoon away.

Sweet Variation: Stop following the above instructions after the first paragraph. While cooking, sweeten, if desired—I don't—with sweetener of choice (honey, pure maple syrup, sugar), then splosh on some whole milk or cream, and add caramelized bananas or apples, black currant or blueberry jam, or runny marmalade.

Fried Oatmeal Cakes: Let the plain porridge cool, then use wet hands to shape scoops into patties. Fry in olive oil. Top with an egg, cheese, and greens wilted with garlic.

Miso and Mushroom Oatmeal: Make the plain porridge as written, but season with about 2 teaspoons red or white miso and serve with mushrooms sautéed in soy sauce. Finish with toasted sesame seeds and snipped green onions.

NOTE: Toasting the oats gives another dimension to their flavor, and cuts down on the cooking time. To make a big batch, spread the steel-cut oats on a rimmed baking sheet and place in a 300°F (150°C) oven for 15 to 20 minutes, stirring a few times. Let cool, then store in an airtight container in the cupboard as you would untoasted oats. When using toasted oats in this recipe, add them, the butter, and water all at once to the pan. Add salt around the 10-minute mark, and then continue to simmer to desired tenderness, 3 to 5 minutes more.

FIG AND GINGER
CLUSTER GRANOLA

Everyone has a favorite recipe for granola, and here's mine. It has clusters. For those of us who are particular about our granola, clusters are a big deal. Often recipes that boast a rubbled, clumped texture use a lavish amount of fat to achieve the effect, or gloss the business with an egg white as glue. This recipe uses a slurry of sweeteners and the natural holding power of oats—as flakes and as flour—for its grip. In the end, the granola is light, yet crunchy, without a jaw-numbing workout. And, here's a discovery, granola can be made with different styles of oats, old-fashioned or quick-cooking, even in combination. Just don't use instant. The two oats will yield distinct results, with the larger flakes of old-fashioned rolled oats granting more chew, and the smaller, quick-cooking oats giving a crisper bite.

There are a lot of ingredients here. But it is the mix of all those bits and pieces that ensures every bite has some interest: there's the fat waxiness of the cashews, the snicker-snack snap of pecans, the leathered fruitiness of the figs, and the warmly humming, granular sweetness of candied ginger against the resinous depth of olive oil. Beyond a few minutes of chopping, the method is as straightforward as can be.

I tuck all the small bags of nuts, seeds, and dried fruit in one large food storage bag in the freezer next to the oats; that way, when the mood strikes, most of the ingredients are fresh and ready to go.

This recipe is my standard and is intended only as a starting point. By all means, add, substitute, or subtract ingredients (add ground nutmeg or ground ginger, or cardamom; take away the seeds and go heavy on the nuts; swap honey for the maple syrup, pistachios for pecans, or dried apricots and dried cherries for the figs) as long as the general guidelines are loosely followed.

Makes approximately 8½ cups (2 L)

¼ cup (60 g) unsalted butter

3 tablespoons extra-virgin olive oil

3 tablespoons pure maple syrup

½ cup (100 g) packed light brown sugar

½ cup (120 ml) water

1 teaspoon medium-grain kosher salt

1 teaspoon vanilla extract

5 cups (455 g) old-fashioned rolled or quick-cooking oats

1½ cups (140 g) nuts, chopped if large (I use an equal mix of sliced almonds, cashews, and pecans)

¾ cup (65 g) flaked coconut, sweetened or not

¼ cup (35 g) raw, hulled sunflower seeds

¼ cup (35 g) whole or ground seeds, such as chia seeds, sesame seeds, flaxseeds, or hemp hearts

¾ teaspoon ground cinnamon

½ cup (70 g) finely chopped candied ginger

½ cup (70 g) raw pepitas

1 cup (150 g) chopped dried figs

Candied Cacao Nibs (page 248) (optional)

... continued

Fig and Ginger Cluster Granola, continued

Preheat an oven to 325°F (160°C) with racks in the upper and lower thirds.

In a saucepan set over medium heat, melt the butter into the olive oil and maple syrup. Add the brown sugar, water, and ½ teaspoon of the salt. Cook, stirring often, until the brown sugar dissolves. Remove the saucepan from the heat, stir in the vanilla extract, and set aside to cool.

In a food processor fitted with the metal blade, grind 2 cups (180 g) of the oats into flour. Transfer this oat flour to a large bowl. Stir in the remaining 3 cups (275 g) whole oats, the remaining ½ teaspoon salt, and the nuts, coconut, seeds, and cinnamon. Pour the butter and sugar mixture over everything and stir to coat. Let stand for about 10 minutes, to give the oats the opportunity to lap up the sugar syrup.

Line 2 half sheet pans or standard baking sheets with parchment paper. Using your hands, drop the oat mixture in clumps onto the pans, then bake in the preheated oven until dry, light golden, and evenly toasted, 45 to 50 minutes, gently stirring and turning the granola with a large spatula every 15 minutes or so and rotating the pans once from top to bottom and front to back.

Remove from the oven and leave the granola on the pans. The granola will continue to crisp as it stands. After 5 minutes, stir in the candied ginger and pepitas. Once the granola has cooled completely, stir in the figs and the cacao nibs.

Transfer the granola to an airtight container and store at room temperature for up to 2 weeks.

ROASTED PEACHES WITH GLAZED SESAME OATS

Another way with oats, this time in a marginally sweet cereal that doesn't seem at all meager. These are oats made glistening with a thin, mapled, sesame seed–studded shellac. The sesame seeds, for which I like a mix of black and white, break up the texture of the oats, and their flavor is surprisingly, satisfactorily pronounced.

The peaches barely require a recipe. They get a brushing of their own allotment of maple syrup seasoned with Chinese five-spice powder and a vanilla bean, then are baked in a moderately hot oven. The fruit emerges fragrant and shining, retaining its shape but supple enough to give way to a spoon.

The recipe can be adapted to any manner of stone fruits and is special enough to make the move to after-dinner and dessert consideration. If possible, make the oats the night before; then the next day you're already ahead of the game.

.... *Serves 4* ....

GLAZED SESAME OATS

2 tablespoons pure maple syrup

2 tablespoons light brown sugar

¼ cup (60 ml) mild olive oil or melted coconut oil

2 tablespoons water

¼ teaspoon fine-grain sea salt

2½ cups (250 g) old-fashioned rolled oats

½ cup (45 g) sliced almonds

¼ cup (35 g) sesame seeds (black, white, or a mix)

PEACHES

4 firm but ripe peaches, halved and pitted

¼ cup (60 ml) pure maple syrup

¼ teaspoon Chinese five-spice powder

Seeds scraped from a vanilla bean or 1 tablespoon vanilla bean paste

SERVING OPTIONS

A yogurt that you like, Greek-style or regular (page 264), plain or vanilla, or fresh ricotta (page 264)

Hemp hearts, bee pollen, or hulled sunflower seeds

Preheat an oven to 375°F (190°C) and line a rimmed baking sheet with parchment paper.

To make the sesame oats, in a large bowl, stir together the maple syrup, brown sugar, olive oil, water, and salt. Fold the oats, almonds, and sesame seeds into the syrup mixture until coated. Scurry it all out onto the prepared baking sheet, patting to an even layer. Bake until the oats are golden and lightly toasted, 15 to 20 minutes, turning the pan once, and flipping and shuffling the oats around regularly. Cool on the baking sheet for at least 20 minutes before serving, or, once fully cool, transfer

... continued

Roasted Peaches with Glazed Sesame Oats, continued

to an airtight container for later use. (Store the oats at room temperature if made in advance.)

To make the peaches, preheat the oven 375°F (190°C), if needed. Line another rimmed baking sheet or large roasting pan with parchment paper. Arrange the fruit on the pan, cut sides up, with spaces in between each. If they cuddle up too close, they'll steam, not roast.

Grab a small bowl and mix together the maple syrup, five-spice powder, and vanilla seeds. Brush the peaches with about half the mixture—let some collect in the hollow left by the pit, but don't drown the flesh—and place the pan in the hot oven. Bake the peaches until they look soft, juicily bursting, and singed at the skin, 20 to 25 minutes. If you'd like to give the fruit a proper bronzing, place them under a hot broiler. Don't gamble and leave them too long, or they'll burn as soon as your back is turned. Remove the fruit from the oven and let cool a few minutes before serving with yogurt, a raining handful of the gilded oats, the rest of the spiced maple syrup, and a sprinkling of hemp hearts.

Eat straight away, or at room temperature, or chilled enough that the peaches are cold but the juices still loose and running.

BERRIED BREAKFAST BATTER-STYLE COBBLER

A cobbler for breakfast works surprisingly well. Made with a miserly amount of sugar and fat as far as cobblers go, this pillowy one resembles a French clafloutis in method, but ends up with the properties of a spoonbread or muffin with a nice crust on the sides.

This cobbler makes great use of gluten-free flours, but all-purpose flour can be used, and will make a slightly coarser-textured result.

The cobbler is hardly troublesome to get sorted, but can be made even less so by keeping a batch of the dry ingredients bagged in the freezer.

.... *Serves 4, heartily* ....

COBBLER

¼ cup (60 g) unsalted butter

½ cup (65 g) brown rice flour or (70 g) teff flour

½ cup (60 g) tapioca flour

½ cup (100 g) fine-grain turbinado or granulated sugar

1½ teaspoons aluminum-free baking powder

½ teaspoon medium-grain kosher salt

Finely grated zest from ½ orange

½ cup (120 ml) milk

1 egg

1 cup (140 g) blueberries, fresh or frozen

1 cup (100 g) cranberries, fresh or frozen

Coarse sugar, for sprinkling

TO SERVE

Greek-style yogurt, thinned with the juice of ½ orange

Toasted nuts and seeds (such as almonds, pepitas, hulled sunflower, sesame)

Honey or pure maple syrup

To make the cobbler, preheat an oven to 350°F (175°C). Spoon the butter into a 9-inch (23 cm) cast-iron skillet and set it in the hot oven.

In a large bowl, whisk together the flours, sugar, baking powder, salt, and zest. In a small bowl, beat the milk and the egg. Whisk the wet ingredients into the dry until just combined.

When the butter has melted, carefully remove the pan from the oven. Pour in the batter and, without incorporating the butter, coax the batter toward the edges of the skillet with the back of a spoon. (The batter will look like an inadequate amount; have faith it will be enough.) Scatter the berries over the top, followed by the coarse sugar. Bake until the batter browns, and the center of the cobbler springs back from a gentle poke, 25 to 30 minutes. Let cool for 10 minutes before serving with the toppings of your choice.

BLACKBERRY BUTTERMILK WHOLE GRAIN SCONES

My brother and sister-in-law once had a house with blackberry bushes that ran the fence line on one long side of the backyard. When I say, "ran the fence line," I could just as easily say "consumed the fence completely," because the bushes, deeply emerald and thick, obscured the metal that stood behind them, the branches inextricably interwoven with it. The garden gate was beside the hedge, so in spring you'd walk alongside a wall of blossoms, in summer past clusters of busy bees, then finally you'd no longer keep strolling but stop and pick jeweled berries, purple-black and finger staining. When they were preparing to sell that house, my mother and I arrived one evening armed with white plastic buckets, heavy gloves, and garden shears to clip cuttings from those bushes. I've got a few bushes in my yard now, but they've never flourished as they did there.

I will, most often, choose a scone over a muffin. Scones have the best qualities of a muffin, which is to say, all the qualities of a muffin's top. There's a greater proportion of crusted edge, and the crumb is slightly dry and not very sweet. I like that making scones requires a bit of hand-dirtying, but a light touch, so the making feels productive, but not particularly laborious.

Blackberries are my instinct for these, but blueberries, raspberries, cherries, or cranberries would not be considered a compromise. For richer scones, replace some of the buttermilk with an equal amount of heavy cream.

Makes 12 scones

½ cup (115 g) cold unsalted butter

1½ cups (150 g) old-fashioned rolled oats, plus more for garnish

1¾ cups (225 g) all-purpose flour, plus more for dusting

¼ cup (25 g) ground flaxseed or (30 g) buckwheat flour

½ cup (100 g) fine-grain turbinado or granulated sugar, plus more for garnish

1 tablespoon baking powder

1 teaspoon baking soda

1 teaspoon fine-grain sea salt

½ cup (70 g) sliced hazelnuts, plus extra for garnish

5 ounces (140 g) blackberries, sliced if large, dusted with flour

Finely grated zest of 1 lemon

About 1 cup (240 ml) well-shaken buttermilk (page 258), plus more for brushing

Preheat an oven to 400°F (200°C). Line a half sheet pan or rimmed baking sheet with parchment paper. Cut the butter into a small dice and keep on a plate in the freezer.

In the bowl of a food processor fitted with the metal blade, grind ¾ cup (75 g) of the oats to a fine meal. Add the all-purpose flour, ground flaxseed, sugar, baking powder, baking soda, and salt to the processor and pulse a few times to combine. Open the machine and scatter the remaining ¾ cup (75 g) whole oats, hazelnuts, and cold butter over the dry ingredients. Replace the cover and pulse quickly 5 to 7 times. Turn the mixture into a large bowl and sprinkle the blackberries on top.

Stir the lemon zest into the buttermilk with a fork. Pour half the buttermilk across the flour and butter mixture. With that fork of yours, start to work the liquids into the dry ingredients. Add most of what's left of the buttermilk, and stir again with brisk strokes. Take a look—the dough should be crumbly and light, but if squeezed, it should stick together. If it does, stop. If it doesn't, keep adding a few drops of buttermilk, stir once or twice, then check again.

Turn the dough out onto a lightly floured work surface. Give a nimble knead to bring the dough together. Divide the dough in half, then shape each piece into a 1-inch (2.5 cm)-thick round. Brush with buttermilk, then sprinkle with sugar and some more hazelnuts and oats. Use a floured knife to cut each round into 6 wedges. Space the pieces out on the prepared baking sheet.

Bake until the tops are nicely, evenly bronzed and the cut sides look flaky and dry, 20 minutes. When fully baked, the scones should feel light for their size and sound almost hollow when tapped on their bottoms.

Cool on a wire rack for at least 5 minutes. These scones are best served soon after baking, but they can be kept at room temperature, wrapped in plastic wrap or in an airtight container, for 3 or 4 days. Split or leave whole, then rewarm in a low oven before eating.

CHOCOLATE OLIVE OIL ZUCCHINI BREAD

I had some difficulty with this bread, not in its making but in its naming. While the sum of the parts is what we're all here for, each of those parts has an indispensable role to play.

I put the chocolate first because one glance at this quick bread, and there's no mistaking the presence of cocoa. Chopped semisweet chocolate mollifies the unfaltering darkness of that cocoa powder; the irregular shards melt into the bread so that here and there within the crumb are damp pockets of sweetness.

The olive oil is the surprise, tasting resiny and somehow green. The one I use most often makes me think of lemons and fields of newly mown hay, which feels right for something baked at harvest's height.

The zucchini is, of course, the main event, and so gets the glory of the final fanfare. There's a full 4 cups of it in the recipe, divided between two loaves. The pale shreds weave through the batter, so the resulting breads are gratifyingly bulging with bumps and crags.

All that said, I could have mentioned the walnuts. They're toasted, so that their fatty waxiness is made snappy, and their aromatic bitterness is amplified. Along with the olive oil, you've got a winner of a combination.

The buttermilk, too, could have been up there in lights because this bread would be so much less without the spring in the crumb, and the buttermilk's to thank for that. It, along with the whole wheat flour, steers the bread away from residence in the land of cake and clears the way for having some for breakfast.

. . . . *Makes 2 loaves or 18 large muffins* . . . .

1½ pounds (680 g) zucchini, stemmed

1½ cups (190 g) all-purpose flour

1½ cups (170 g) whole wheat flour

½ cup (45 g) cocoa powder

1½ teaspoons baking soda

1 teaspoon aluminum-free baking powder

1½ teaspoons medium-grain kosher salt

1 cup (115 g) chopped walnuts, toasted

8 ounces (225 g) semisweet chocolate, chopped

½ cup (120 ml) extra-virgin olive oil

1 cup (240 ml) well-shaken buttermilk (page 258)

2 eggs

1 cup (200 g) granulated sugar

½ cup (105 g) packed light brown sugar

2 teaspoons vanilla extract

... continued

Chocolate Olive Oil Zucchini Bread, continued

NOTE: If olive oil is not your thing, replace it with an equal amount of melted butter. The bread will be denser and sweeter because it will lack the mitigating edge of olive oil.

Preheat an oven to 350°F (175°C). Grease two 8½ by 4½-inch (21 by 10 cm) loaf pans with butter. Use a length of parchment paper to line the bottom and long sides of the pan, forming a sling, and lightly butter the parchment paper as well. Set aside.

Cut the zucchini to fit through the feed tube of your food processor, keeping the pieces as long and wide as possible. With the grating blade attached, shred the zucchini, resisting the compulsion to press down on the feed tube's plunger while the machine is running. As we want the bread to be damp but not sodden, scatter the resulting strands across a (lint-free) kitchen towel, then place another on top, patting it down gently. After 15 minutes or so, the zucchini will be ready to go.

In a large bowl, whisk together the flours, cocoa powder, baking soda, baking powder, and salt. Stir in the walnuts and chocolate.

In another bowl, whisk together the olive oil and buttermilk. Add the eggs, sugars, and vanilla and beat until smooth. Stir in the zucchini.

Pour the wet ingredients into the dry and stir until combined, taking care not to overmix. Divide the batter evenly between the 2 prepared pans and bake, rotating once, until a cake tester inserted into the loaf comes out almost clean, around 50 minutes. Cool the loaves in their pans on a rack for 20 minutes.

If you can wait long enough to cool them to room temperature before slicing, well done. But if you can't wait, and cut the loaves into ragged pieces while still warm, then I can't say I blame you.

Muffin Variation: I often bake half the batter as a loaf and half the batter as muffins. Line 9 wells of a standard muffin pan with paper liners, fill, and bake until a cake tester poked in the center comes out reasonably clean with only a few damp crumbs, about 18 minutes. Transfer the pan to a wire rack. Take the muffins out of the pan after they've cooled for 10 minutes, and then cool the rest of the way on the rack.

VANILLA ESPRESSO WALNUT BUTTER

I was a kid who liked the big-brand, super sugary peanut butters, with little to no interest in the kind from the health store. Even when my friend told me about a place where they ground it fresh ("there's a machine and you can watch!"), I was unimpressed. It wasn't my idea of peanut butter. It was grainy and stuck claustrophobically to the roof of my mouth.

With such intolerance, I have no idea what made me decide, come adulthood, to start making nut butters at home. Healthy-ish, not-that-sweet ones, even. The process is comedically easy in terms of the payout. This is more about a general idea than specifics, and hopefully will lead to some experimentation with the variations that follow.

Makes about 1 cup (240 ml)

1½ cups (175 g) raw walnuts

½ cup (30 g) raw, hulled sunflower seeds

2 tablespoons honey, agave syrup, or pure maple syrup

½ teaspoon fine-grain sea salt, plus more as needed

Seeds scraped from 2 vanilla beans, or 2 tablespoons vanilla bean paste, plus more as needed

½ teaspoon finely ground espresso beans, plus more as needed

Walnut, flaxseed, or other oil, as needed

NOTE: The butter can be made without roasting the nuts; while the finished butter might not be considered raw (since the nuts do get quite hot during processing), it is exceptionally creamy, with a true walnut flavor. Alternatively, the walnuts can be soaked before use, to remove some of the tannins and to increase nutritional value. Cover the nuts and seeds with water and leave overnight. Drain, and then dry thoroughly so they are crisp but without color, for about 6 hours in an oven set to the lowest temperature possible and up to overnight if using a dehydrator.

Preheat an oven to 325°F (165°C).

Scatter the walnuts and sunflower seeds on a rimmed baking sheet and roast for 20 minutes, tossing regularly to ensure even roasting. Let the nuts cool completely, or the finished butter will be overly greasy.

Tumble the nuts and seeds into the bowl of a food processor fitted with the steel blade; process to a paste. Stop the machine and scrape down, especially around the blade. Add the sweetener, salt, vanilla, and espresso beans and run the machine again, until the butter is truly smooth, 7 to 10 minutes. Check for seasoning, look for any bits that have gone unblended, and gauge consistency. Adjust the salt, vanilla, and espresso beans, and drizzle in the oil, if any is needed, in which case blitz for 1 minute more. Scrape the butter into a jar. Let cool to room temperature before storing, tightly covered in the fridge, for up 2 months.

Variations:
Pistachio + cardamom + melted white chocolate
Almond + cinnamon + orange zest
Pecan + nutmeg + ground ginger
Hazelnut + melted dark chocolate

CHIA PUDDING WITH FRUIT AND GOLDEN HONEY ELIXIR

This pudding takes advantage of how chia seeds can gel a liquid (because of their soluble fiber); it's a bit creamy, with an understated vanilla note. I put up a batch in the evening, and it is ready for me come breakfast. I serve it with fruit, seeds and nuts, and sometimes toasted oats, but truly, the star of this recipe is the turmeric-infused honey I pour over the top—somewhat cheekily christened Golden Honey Elixir. Turmeric root, unmistakably ochre and persuasively astringent, is often used in Ayurvedic medicine for its antibacterial, anti-inflammatory, antioxidant, and antiseptic properties. It is believed to help with brain function, digestion, and heart disease. For the elixir it is combined with honey, apple cider vinegar, and ginger, all healing and preventive powerhouses on their own. The idea behind this potent slurry comes from two sources: the turmeric paste prescribed for myriad of ailments in alternative medicines, and Golden Milk, a traditional restorative sip made with milk, ginger, and turmeric.

Even if you don't go to the trouble of making the chia pudding, do try the elixir, which works perfectly well as a topping for yogurt, as a drink (stirred into hot, not boiling, water, or gently heated and stirred into milk), as the base for salad dressings (especially ones with root vegetables), in smoothies, and even on vanilla ice cream.

Serves 2

PUDDING

¼ cup (60 ml) Greek-style plain or vanilla yogurt

2 to 3 tablespoons chia seeds, depending on desired firmness

¾ cup (180 ml) unsweetened milk (dairy or nondairy both work)

1 tablespoon agave nectar or honey

Generous ½ teaspoon vanilla extract or vanilla bean paste

Fine-grain sea salt

SERVING OPTIONS

1 cup (240 ml) Greek-style plain or vanilla yogurt

2 to 4 tablespoons Golden Honey Elixir (recipe follows)

Pinch of fine-grain sea salt

Fresh fruit, such as sliced peaches, sliced strawberries, or red currants

Chopped nuts, such as pistachios or almonds

To make the pudding, in a bowl, whisk the yogurt and chia seeds until smooth. Slowly add the milk, followed by the sweetener, vanilla, and a pinch of salt, stirring all the while. Cover and refrigerate overnight. Stir again before serving.

When ready to serve, stir the pudding, then fold in the 1 cup (240 ml) yogurt once or twice. Drizzle the Golden Honey Elixir and salt on top, then fold once more. Divide between plates, along with your toppings of choice. Eat straight away.

. . . continued

GOLDEN HONEY ELIXIR

Makes about 1 cup (240 ml)

¾ cup (180 ml) honey, preferably raw

3 tablespoons grated fresh ginger

2 tablespoons apple cider vinegar, preferably raw and unfiltered

Zest of 1 lemon

1 tablespoon plus 1 teaspoon ground turmeric

About ⅛ teaspoon freshly ground black pepper

Stir all the ingredients together in a jar until smooth. Let stand for at least 30 minutes before using, or cover and refrigerate. Use within 1 week.

NOTE: Chia pudding made with whole seeds has a texture similar to that of tapioca pudding—that is to say, gelatinous spheres suspended in weighty liquid. Use ground chia for a smoother consistency, if desired.

If you happen to have frozen raspberries, they're pretty spectacular as an addition. Bash them in a sealed storage bag with the bottom of a sturdy glass, so they're in bits but not pulverized. The icy nubs burst like pomegranate seeds when eaten and streak the yogurt in fuchsia ripples.

BLURRY SUNRISE SMOOTHIE

This tie-dyed smoothie sounds a little like it belongs on a Tiki bar menu instead of as a breakfast offering. Still, the moniker, inspired by how the golden and fuchsia layers blend into each other, amuses my children and me, so there's that.

If raw beet isn't appealing, go ahead and steam, roast, or even microwave it until barely tender, then chill before using here. The aim is to soften the flavor of the beet, without cooking the life out of it. For extra color and kick, include a spoonful of Golden Honey Elixir (page 62) when buzzing the carrot.

If you don't have a high-powered blender, the beet and carrot may be need to be grated rather than chopped.

.... *Serves 2* ....

2 navel oranges, peeled

1 red beet, scrubbed well and chopped

1 cup (105 g) fresh or frozen raspberries

1-inch (2.5 cm) piece ginger, peeled and chopped in half

Very cold water, as needed

1 cup (185 g) fresh or frozen chopped mango

1 carrot, scrubbed well and chopped

Break 1 orange into segments and add to the carafe of an upright blender. Puree. Add the beet, raspberries, and 1 piece of ginger, and blitz again. Add cold water to get the blade moving if necessary. Divide between 2 glasses.

To the same blender, add the remaining 1 orange in pieces, followed by the mango, then the carrot, and the second piece of ginger. Puree, once again adding cold water as needed. Tilt one of the filled glasses and carefully pour half of the carrot smoothie over the top the beet (this will give a slant to the layers). Do the same with the second serving, then use a straw or chopstick to swirl the layers. Sip away.

DEFAULT SMOOTHIE

I don't consider this a green smoothie, even though it's inarguably kelly green, because the color isn't its defining characteristic. This is a more full-figured sip, with banana as its base. It is substantial enough to consider a meal, without cumbersome heaviness.

I like this, as is, in the morning. In the afternoon I'll often add ½ cup (10 g) baby arugula or handfuls of fresh flat-leaf parsley or cilantro, or a shot of lemon juice for a pick-me-up.

For the liquid, apple juice makes a lighter, slightly sweeter smoothie, whereas nut milks add body and creaminess. If none of those are available, use very cold water instead.

Serves 2

1 smallish navel orange or a fattish clementine, peeled and split into segments

1 crisp apple (such as Honeycrisp, Gala, Granny Smith), stemmed and cut into chunks (the core and seeds are fine)

1 banana, peeled

2 cups (135 g) stemmed, torn kale, packed (about ½ a bunch)

1 heaping tablespoon nut butter

½ cup (120 ml) filtered apple juice or plain nut milk, plus more as needed

Combine all the ingredients in an upright blender and process until liquefied. If the smoothie is too thick, carefully incorporate more liquid as needed, slowly through the feed hole on the lid with the motor running. Pour into glasses and drink right away.

Pineapple Coconut Smoothie Variation: Use 1 cup (240 g) fresh or frozen pineapple instead of the apple and orange, and use light coconut milk for the liquid.

CHAPTER 2

LUNCHES

For an embarrassingly long time, I failed at lunch. If it had been a school assignment, I would have been sent to detention, if not the principal's office, and recommended for tutoring. The strange thing was, I had a good start in the subject, coming home every day during those first years of elementary school for minestrone soup, or cauliflower-stuffed parathas, or Mum's peanut butter and jelly sandwiches, which included salted butter as well. (She maintains that peanut butter is not actually butter, so it would be illogical to skip the proper stuff.) It was when I was put in charge of my own lunch, in the high school cafeteria, and later in university and then at work, that lunch became a chore. It was one of scrimping and saving or a busy-with-other-things annoyance, leading to shared cafeteria sandwiches, cereal bars, and later a habit of leftovers from the night before, hastily packed into boxes in the midst of that morning's rush.

I may be a late study to the lunchable arts, but I'm catching up. The remembered lesson—that lunch can be, and should be, the welcomed break in our day to recoup and recharge—changed how I approach it entirely. The recipes that follow are my crib notes for a master class in midday meals: a killer, miso-boosted burger that takes 10 minutes to make, collard wraps with herbed yogurt that pack well, and salads that bear repeating.

FATTOUSH WITH FAVA BEANS AND LABNEH

Fattoush is a Lebanese chopped vegetable salad with bread, seasoned with sumac. That dusted maroon, provocatively sour spice electrifies everything it touches with a vividly citric bite. Some fattoush recipes have yogurt or buttermilk in the dressing; this one is laid atop a bed of unadulterated labneh. The result is astoundingly refreshing; it is a natural, equal partner to barbecued meats, lentil koftas (page 151, without the sauce), or feta, fresh or baked.

.... *Serves 4* ....

1 lemon

½ cup (120 ml) extra-virgin olive oil

1 clove garlic, minced

1 tablespoon ground sumac, plus more for garnish

1½ teaspoons dried mint

Medium-grain kosher salt and freshly ground black pepper

2 cups (455 g) tomatoes, about 3, but a mix of sizes and varieties is lovely

8 ounces (225 g) podded fresh or frozen fava beans, blanched

1 English cucumber, cut lengthwise and thinly sliced

2 green onions, white and light green parts only, thinly sliced

2 radishes, sliced wafer thin

Bunch of flat-leaf parsley, leaves and tender stems

Small bunch of mint

2 pita breads, split into layers and toasted on low until dry

2 cups (480 ml) labneh (page 262) or Greek-style yogurt

Smoked paprika, for sprinkling (optional)

In a small bowl, finely grate the zest of half the lemon on top of the olive oil. Squeeze in most of the juice from the lemon, about 3 tablespoons. Whisk in the garlic, sumac, and mint and season with salt and pepper. The vinaigrette should be quite sharp; add more lemon juice if it's warranted. Set aside.

Cut the tomatoes into reasonably bite-size pieces, in chunks, quarters, or in halves for smaller varieties. A combination of shapes adds to the rustic visual charm of the salad, as well as textural interest. Tumble the tomatoes, favas, cucumber, green onions, and radishes into a large bowl. Pick the small leaves off the parsley and mint, and keep to one side. Coarsely chop the remaining leaves and add to the bowl. Drizzle most of the dressing over the salad and toss. Check for seasoning, adding dressing by the tablespoon as needed, then toss again. Tear most of pita into the bowl and give a few gentle folds to incorporate. Let the salad marinate for 10 minutes.

Divide the labneh among 4 serving plates or spread across a large platter. Drizzle with any remaining dressing, then turn the fattoush out over the top with the reserved herbs and the last of the pita. Sprinkle with more sumac and the paprika. Dig in.

MESSY BISTRO SALAD WITH SPANISH-FRIED EGG AND CRISPY CAPERS

I have a bad habit of reading while eating lunch when left to my own devices. I will sometimes eat at my desk, or our kitchen table, or I'll stand at the counter, but always with a book.

My typical lunches are the sort I can eat unthinkingly, using a fork or a spoon, with no knife required. I go for one-bowl affairs, with not much to divide my attention from flicking through pages as I chew. Salads work well for that, and here is one that's hardly an exception. It is a haphazard collection of ingredients that borrows heavily from the Mediterranean pantry. First it pulls from a French bistro, for its big, rustic croutons and the tender bite of bitter lettuce; then there's a skip over to Italy for crackling shards of golden pancetta. Then it's westward again for a lacy-edged, oozingly yolked egg that is fried by bathing it in hot olive oil, which I was once told is the Spanish way of doing things. The Manchego is Spanish, too. The final flourish is a few frilled, briny capers that have been fried as well, but I'm not sure to whom I owe thanks for that.

This is a rough-and-tumble, satisfying salad, full of textures and flavors, all of which can be messily speared with a fork. For me, that equals lunchtime perfection.

.... *Serves 2* ....

⅓ cup (80 ml) plus 1½ tablespoons (23 ml) mild olive oil

4 slices pancetta or Serrano ham

2 thick slices crusty bread

½ teaspoon Dijon mustard

1 heaped teaspoon honey

1 tablespoon minced mixed fresh tender herbs, such as chives, tarragon, chervil, and parsley

1 tablespoon champagne vinegar

Medium-grain kosher salt

2 tablespoons extra-virgin olive oil

2 eggs

Freshly ground black pepper

2 tablespoons capers, rinsed if packed in salt, drained if in brine

About 1 pound (455 g) frisée, light green and white parts only, separated into small pieces

About 3 ounces (85g) Manchego, Grana Padano, or a similar hard cheese

Over medium heat, heat ½ tablespoon of the mild olive oil in a pan with sloped sides. Lay the ham in the pan and cook until crisp, around 3 minutes, turning as needed. Tear the bread into irregular chunks. Remove the ham from the pan and set aside. Add the bread to the hot pan, with another 1 tablespoon of the olive oil. Fry, turning, until the bread is golden all over, 5 to 8 minutes. Transfer the croutons to a large bowl.

. . . continued

Meanwhile, stir together the mustard, honey, herbs, vinegar, and a generous pinch of salt in a small bowl. In a slow, steady stream, whisk in the extra-virgin olive oil. Check for seasoning and set aside.

Wipe out the pan, then raise the heat to medium-high, and pour in the remaining ⅓ cup (80 ml) mild olive oil and let it get nice and hot. Crack one egg into a small bowl. Tip the frying pan so that the oil collects into a pool and carefully slide the egg into the oil. Keeping the pan still slightly tilted, use a spoon to bathe the egg in hot oil, until the egg has a golden crust and the white is set, 60 seconds or so. Remove the egg to a plate lined with paper towels and season with salt and pepper. Repeat with the second egg.

When the eggs are cooked, use the same pan to cook the capers. Add the capers to the remaining oil and fry, stirring often, until the capers go crisp and open up like blossoms, approximately 45 seconds. Use a slotted spoon to remove the capers to the plate with the eggs.

To assemble the salad, spoon some of the vinaigrette over the torn bread and toss the pieces to coat. Divide the croutons between 2 plates, and then set an egg on top of each. Using the same large bowl as before, dress the frisée with a thin coating of the vinaigrette, then distribute it over the bread and eggs. Use a vegetable peeler to shave over the Manchego, top with ham, and garnish with the fried capers. Drizzle over any remaining vinaigrette and serve immediately.

SALAD ROLLS

As soon as hot weather hits, salad rolls, also known as spring or summer rolls, take their place as our seasonal standby—not only for their heat-beating coolness, but also for the fact that one box of rice paper wraps contains enough to last a few months, and keeps well in the cupboard. Thus, salad rolls are a boon for spontaneous, undeniable hunger, or those times when you're so busy that you forgot to shop. After an inventory of what's in the crisper drawer or the CSA basket, and whizzing up a few dipping sauces, the meal is pretty much taken care of.

For the sauces, having two feels extra special, but one will more than suffice. The first is a creamy Japanese *goma* style, with toasted sesame seeds, mayonnaise, and lip-smacking amounts of rice vinegar. The second is a case of stirring together some staples—tamari, ginger, garlic—and is the one I make most often, especially when pressed for time, or the inclination to cook.

So you know, I rarely take charge of constructing the wraps; rather, I lay out all the bowls of fillings on the table, set up a soaking station at one end for the rice paper, and leave everyone to fend (that is, stuff and roll) for themselves. If you're into the glorious chaos of a crab boil, go for it. It isn't as messy as you'd think, and then everyone can munch as they work—instant gratification. For a more restrained meal, fill and shape before the lunch bell rings.

.... *Serves 4* ....

SESAME DRESSING

½ cup (70 g) sesame seeds, white or black, or both

½ cup (120 ml) mayonnaise, preferably Japanese

3 tablespoons unseasoned rice vinegar, plus more as needed

1½ tablespoons toasted sesame oil, plus more as needed

1 tablespoon tamari or soy sauce, plus more as needed

2 teaspoons natural cane sugar

TAMARI DIPPING SAUCE

2 tablespoons tamari or soy sauce

2 tablespoons Thai sweet chili sauce

2 teaspoons peeled and grated fresh ginger

1 clove garlic, grated

2 green onions, white and light green parts, cut thinly on the bias

ROLLS

8 to 12 round rice paper wrappers

4 to 6 large lettuce leaves (Boston, leaf, Bibb)

½ small head napa cabbage, shredded

1 carrot, peeled and julienned

1 large avocado, peeled, pitted, and sliced lengthwise

½ English cucumber, peeled or not, julienned

1 cup (30 g) fresh pea shoots

6 ounces (170 g) enoki mushrooms, cleaned and trimmed

Handful of cilantro and mint leaves

. . . continued

Salad Rolls, continued

NOTE: You can use nuoc cham (page 136) as one of the dressings.

To make the sesame dressing, roast the sesame seeds in a heavy skillet over low heat. Once the seeds start popping and smell toasted, which should take 3 to 5 minutes, transfer to a blender or mortar and pestle. Let the seeds cool for a few minutes, then grind them until they're fairly fine. Add the mayonnaise, vinegar, sesame oil, tamari, and sugar and blend. Check the balance of flavors, adding more sesame oil, vinegar, or tamari as needed; add water if the sauce is too thick to get moving. Buzz again, then cover and refrigerate. The dressing can be made up to 5 days in advance.

To make the tamari dipping sauce, stir together the tamari, chili sauce, ginger, garlic, and green onions in a bowl. I like it strong because the salad rolls can carry a good amount of seasoning, but if too intense, thin with a judicious amount of water. Chill until needed, but don't make too far in advance—I usually make mine right before I get on with the rolls.

To assemble the salad rolls, fill a large bowl with water that's hot but still comfortable to touch. Dunk one rice paper wrapper for 4 to 5 seconds, then lay on a work surface (a large cutting board works well; lay a kitchen towel underneath to catch any drips). The paper might still be stiff, but will continue to soften as it sits. Tear a piece of lettuce so it is slightly smaller than the roll, and place on top of the wrapper. Arrange a thin bundle of cabbage horizontally across the bottom third of the wrap. Stack some carrot, avocado, cucumber, pea shoots, enoki, and herbs. I usually let some of the filling peek over one side. Pull the bottom of the roll up to enclose the filling tightly. Fold one side over, and continue to roll, keeping things as snug as possible in their swaddling. Repeat with the remaining wrappers and fillings until all are used up.

Serve the rolls soon after they are made, with the sauces on hand for dipping.

COLLARD WRAPS WITH HUMMUS AND QUICK-PICKLED VEGETABLES

There is a deli I try to visit when I can. . . . Well, it's really a country store, if we're being specific, and they make a hummus and vegetable sandwich that uses every vegetable, sprout, and salad leaf they have on offer. The sandwich sings loudest when you make sure to snag a sour pickle for its partner. Its vinegared bite cleaves the fulsome richness of the hummus and spruces up the vegetables.

I follow that example with these wraps, by quick-pickling beets and carrots, then marrying those with a fennel and herb salad and herbed yogurt. With both hummus and quinoa as the foundation, this is not a meal of deprivation, but rather one of generosity.

The herb- and shallot-speckled yogurt called for here will invariably find its way into all manner of snacks and meals. A looser rendition is surprisingly effective spilled onto skinny wedges of cantaloupe or similar melon. Hide a smear under a poached egg and snip some fresh red chiles over the top. Spread a thick version on brown bread with sliced radishes or swathe around roasted potatoes.

I use a spiralizer—a handy-dandy hand-crank contraption that turns hard vegetables into long, noodle-ish strands, sold online or in Asian kitchen or food shops—for the vegetables. Or really, my children do. Not only does it free me from one job, but it gets my sons involved in the kitchen and makes them that much more eager to include said vegetables in their respective rolls. I've listed quinoa here, but I make these with whatever cooked grains I have on hand, or sometimes leave the grains off entirely, and swap in some cubed, browned tofu; cooked lentils; or beans. Truth be told, most of these ingredients are interchangeable with others—cooked or marinated vegetables, sprouts, sesame seeds, almonds, walnuts, and whatever dressing catches your fancy.

You can also feel free to squash your filling between a folded naan (page 124) instead of the collards. Heaven knows we do often enough.

Serves 4

3 beets, trimmed and peeled, cut into matchsticks or cut on a spiralizer

3 carrots, trimmed and scrubbed, cut into matchsticks or cut on a spiralizer

½ cup (120 ml) white wine vinegar, plus more as needed

2 tablespoons sugar

½ teaspoon medium-grain kosher salt, plus more as needed

A few drops toasted sesame oil

1 small fennel bulb, trimmed and shaved

Handful of fresh flat-leaf parsley leaves, torn

Handful of fresh cilantro leaves, torn

Freshly ground black pepper

4 to 8 collard leaves (see Note)

1 cup (240 ml) hummus (page 112)

1 cup (185 g) quinoa, cooked or sprouted

1 small red onion, peeled and sliced wafer thin

4 radishes, sliced wafer thin

¼ cup (70 g) hazelnuts, toasted and coarsely chopped

1 cup Herbed Yogurt (recipe follows), made with labneh (page 262) or plain Greek-style yogurt

. . . continued

Collard Wraps with Hummus and Quick-Pickled Vegetables, continued

NOTE: In an optional step, to soften the taste and texture of raw collards, blanch them (submerge for 45 seconds or so in boiling water, then plunge into a bowl of ice water). Dry well before stuffing.

Put the beets and carrots in separate small bowls, then divide the vinegar, sugar, and salt between them. Add a few drops of sesame oil to the carrots. Toss each bowl's contents to combine, then leave at room temperature for 30 minutes.

In another bowl, toss the fennel, parsley, and cilantro with 1 teaspoon vinegar, then season with salt and pepper. Set aside.

To prepare the collards, trim the stem, then with your knife parallel to the work surface, shave the remaining stalk flush with the leaf. If your collards are large, 1 leaf per roll might be enough. With smaller leaves, use 2, laying one in each direction horizontally on a work surface and overlapping in the middle, to make 1 large wrap. Or, make 2 rolls per person.

To assemble each wrap, spread some hummus across a collard leaf (2 to 4 tablespoons, depending on how many rolls you are making). Divide the quinoa among the rolls, followed by the beets and carrots. Top with the fennel and herbs, then the onion, radishes, and hazelnuts. Spread a dollop of Herbed Yogurt to one long side of the filling—this will act as glue in a moment. Fold one or two of the short sides of the collard wrap over to encase the filling, then lift the long side opposite the yogurt over, tucking the filling in as tightly as possible, then roll. Serve immediately, or wrap well in plastic wrap and refrigerate for up to 6 hours.

HERBED YOGURT

Makes about 2 cups (480 ml)

½ lemon

1 shallot, minced

2 cups (480 ml) whole milk or low-fat yogurt (page 264), regular or Greek-style, not nonfat

Small bunch of flat-leaf parsley, chopped

Small bunch of dill, chopped

A few chives, minced

Fine-grain sea salt and freshly cracked black pepper

Extra-virgin olive oil, for drizzling

Finely grate some lemon zest into a medium bowl. Squeeze the juice from the lemon half onto the zest and stir in the shallot. Set aside for 5 minutes. Fold in the yogurt, parsley, dill, and chives, then season with salt and pepper and fold in a few drips of olive oil. Use right away, or cover and store for up to 2 days.

GLAZED EGGPLANT WITH ROASTED SHALLOTS AND GREENS

This is hardly work: only some stirring, brushing, and a bit of a fry up, and yet, here's lunch. The trifling effort yields plush, honeyed eggplant snuggled up with singed shallots and wilted greens. (You'll note that in the photograph at left, I use baby bok choy, which I chose to slice that day.) I love to serve this atop grains—cooked barley, quinoa, farro, or whatever I have in the refrigerator. Simple and splendid.

.... *Serves 4* ....

4 large shallots, peeled

1½ tablespoons toasted sesame oil

Fine-grain salt and freshly ground black pepper

4 Asian eggplants, about 1½ pounds (680 g) total

2 tablespoons mirin

1 tablespoon orange juice

2 tablespoons yellow or white miso

1 tablespoon strongly flavored honey, such as buckwheat

Sesame seeds, white or black, or a mix

1 tablespoon untoasted sesame oil

3 cups (10 to 12 ounces/ 285 to 340 g) stemmed and coarsely chopped sturdy greens, such as Chinese broccoli (kai-lan), Swiss chard, bok choy, or Tuscan kale

Tamari

Preheat an oven to 400°F (200°C).

Depending on their size, cut the shallots into halves or quarters through the root. Pour 1 teaspoon of the sesame oil onto a rimmed baking sheet. Toss the shallots around in the sesame oil and season with salt and pepper. Slice the eggplants in half lengthwise, through the calyx and stem (they look pretty, but don't eat either). With the tip of a paring knife, score the surface of the eggplant flesh at ½-inch (1.3 cm) intervals, without going all the way down to the skin. Brush the eggplant with a thin coating of sesame oil on all sides. Arrange, cut side down, alongside the shallots. Roast until the eggplant is soft, with some color (turn it over to check), 25 to 30 minutes.

Meanwhile, whisk together the mirin, orange juice, miso, honey, and remaining sesame oil in a small saucepan and bring to a boil over medium-high heat. Boil for 2 minutes, then pull from the stove and set aside. When the eggplant is ready, flip the halves to sit face up. Brush the cut sides with half the glaze. Rustle the shallots around, then return to the oven for 5 to 7 minutes more, until the vegetables are truly tender. Brush the eggplant with a second coat of glaze, leaving a little left in the

. . . continued

Glazed Eggplant with Roasted Shallots and Greens, continued

pan. Transfer the shallots to the saucepan with the glaze, gently turning them around to coat.

Preheat the broiler to high and blast the eggplant until scorched in places, 1 to 2 minutes. Set aside.

In a medium, heavy nonstick skillet or cast-iron pan, roast the sesame seeds over medium-high heat until darkened in color and smelling toasted, around 3 minutes, then remove to a bowl. Add the oil to the skillet and, when hot, add the chopped greens. Season lightly with salt and pepper and cook until wilted but still keeping some bright color, 5 to 7 minutes, depending on the greens.

To serve, transfer the shallots, greens, and eggplant to a serving dish. Add a few dashes of tamari to any leftover glaze, then drizzle over the eggplant. Sprinkle with the sesame seeds and serve.

BAKED EGGS,
NORTH INDIAN-STYLE

There is a Punjabi hard-boiled egg curry that is one of my pantry heroes, requiring only the gentlest of assists from the crisper drawer. Anyone who has ever added curry powder to their egg salad understands the alchemy that occurs when spice meets yolk. With the spirit of that egg curry still in mind, I borrow from the Italian classic, Eggs in Purgatory, and cook my eggs to tender perfection in a cumin and chile-flecked tomato sauce. It is everything I crave in a heartening meal: unwaveringly savory, sour, fiery, and filling.

There will be a lot of sauce—intentional, because it is meant to share the spotlight with the eggs. Still, its quantity is something to keep in mind for smaller groups or appetites. If concerned, scoop out some sauce before the yogurt is added and freeze for another day. Also, if your pan cannot accommodate enough eggs to feed your crowd, divide the sauce between two pans, or deploy an army of oven-safe dishes instead. I serve this with cooked bulgur, brown basmati rice, white beans, chickpeas, or naan (page 124)—but nearly any starch will do.

Serves 4 to 6

FOR THE EGGS AND SAUCE

2 tablespoons clarified butter or ghee (page 259) or mild olive oil

1 teaspoon cumin seeds

2 onions, peeled and diced

Bunch of cilantro

3 cloves garlic, minced

Medium-grain kosher salt

1½ teaspoons garam masala

1 teaspoon ground coriander

½ teaspoon ground turmeric

¼ teaspoon Kashmiri chile powder or dried red pepper flakes

4 pounds (1.8 kg) fresh tomatoes, cored and chopped, or 2 (28-ounce/870 g) cans whole tomatoes, crushed

2 bay leaves

⅓ cup (80 ml) plain Greek-style yogurt, not nonfat

4 to 8 eggs, depending on appetites

Freshly ground black pepper

SERVING OPTIONS

Toasted almonds

Fresh Green Chutney (page 133)

Baby spinach, baby kale, or pea shoots

Minced fresh chile

Lime wedges

Fresh dill, roughly chopped

To make the eggs and sauce, in a large, ovenproof skillet over medium-low heat, melt the clarified butter. Sprinkle the cumin seeds into the pan and sauté, shaking the pan often, until the cumin is fragrant, about 1 minute. Stir in the onions and cook until golden brown, 10 to 12 minutes. Meanwhile, pick the leaves from the cilantro and set aside. Discard the tough bottoms of the stems and finely mince the tender parts. When the onions

. . . continued

Baked Eggs, North Indian–Style, continued

NOTE: I prefer the way the sauce thickens up in the oven, but the whole shebang can be kept on the stove top. Once the eggs are added, cover the pan with a lid and leave to simmer for 5 minutes or so.

To crush canned whole tomatoes, pulse them in a food processor, or add their liquid to the pan and then squish each tomato by hand as they go into the pot. The equivalent amount of canned, crushed tomatoes will work quite nicely, delivering a more robust sauce.

are cooked, add the cilantro stems and garlic. Give a good turn with a spoon and cook for 2 minutes. Add the garam masala, coriander, turmeric, and chile powder, and stir constantly as you toast the spices for 30 seconds. Pour in the tomatoes and their juices and add the bay leaves. Raise the heat to bring to a boil, then lower the heat to a simmer. In about 20 minutes, with occasional stirring, everything should be soft and the sauce will look to have split—an oily layer will rise to the top of the gravy, a vital marker in a lot of Indian cooking. Season with salt.

Preheat an oven to 375°F (190°C).

Dollop the yogurt onto the sauce, then use the spoon to marble the two together slightly. Crack one egg into a small bowl. Use the edge of the bowl to clear some room in the sauce, and carefully slip the egg into the gap. Do the same for the other eggs. Once all have been thus added, season each with salt and a miserly amount of pepper.

Move the pan to the hot oven and bake, uncovered, until the eggs have reached your preferred set. For a guideline, it will be about 12 minutes for the whites to be opaque but the yolk still oozing. Serve immediately, showered with the reserved cilantro leaves and any garnishes, alongside your grain or starch of choice.

CHAAT TOSTADAS

I believe Indian snacks may be the cuisine's best-kept secret. *Chaat*, as they are collectively known, are most often sold from carts and roadside stands and usually include multiple components, in permutations of steamed, boiled, or fried starches (often more than one per dish) and an abundance of garnishes. *Papri chaat*—a plate of chickpeas, chiles, crisp wafers, potatoes, and yogurt—is cold, hot, crunchy, soft, sour, spicy, salty, and fresh. In other words, perfectly addicting. Because such a snack invariably turns into a meal, I call it lunch.

As the production of making chaat could be considered marginally excessive for every day, here's the most unfussy way to check those same boxes that I know. Make the sour-sweet chutney ahead, or purchase it from some grocery stores and most Asian groceries. Using corn tortillas means there's no dough to make, although they still require some preparation. A fried tostada shell will have a snappier texture than one that's been baked. Still, each has its merits, especially from a health perspective. In both cases, slightly stale tortillas work best.

From there, the chickpeas need a warming up in a skillet, and then it is simply a case of putting the pieces together. For the sake of simplicity I forgo the potato, but if in that mood, I renounce the tortillas and use these garnishes on baked russets or sweet potatoes (one per person), and call it dinner.

Makes enough for 4

CHICKPEAS

¼ cup (60 ml) neutral-tasting oil

2 cloves garlic, peeled and bruised with the side of a knife

½ teaspoon cumin seeds

¼ teaspoon Kashmiri chile powder, or a generous pinch each of sweet paprika and cayenne

2 cups (400 g) cooked chickpeas, rinsed if canned

Medium-grain kosher salt and freshly ground black pepper

TO SERVE

8 to 12 corn tortillas

1 cup (240 ml) plain yogurt, Greek-style or regular (page 264)

2½ cups (360 ml) Tamarind Chutney (recipe follows)

1 cup (240 ml) Fresh Green Chutney (page 133), with a handful of mint leaves added before blending

Chaat masala, or an equal mix of ground cumin, chile powder (Kashmiri or cayenne), and ground coriander

1 small red onion, minced

A couple handfuls of sprouts (such as alfalfa, mung bean, broccoli, chickpea, or radish)

Sev (crisp fried Indian noodles; optional)

Leaves from 1 small bunch of cilantro

Lime wedges

To make the chickpeas, pour the oil into a large skillet over medium-high heat. Add the garlic, cumin, and chile powder. Stir until you can smell the spices, 30 to 60 seconds. Turn the chickpeas through the hot oil until coated. Continue to cook until the chickpeas are crisped, 7 to 10 minutes. Season well with salt and pepper, then set aside.

... continued

Chaat Tostadas, continued

While the chickpeas cook, prepare the tostadas. Either shallow-fry the tortillas in hot oil, turning as needed, until crisp, about 1 minute over medium-high heat. Make sure the oil comes back to temperature between tortillas and drain them on paper towels when done. Or, brush tortillas lightly with oil and bake on a tray in a 400°F (200°C) oven for 5 to 6 minutes. I usually prepare the tortillas while the chickpeas cook.

To serve, divide the tostada shells among the plates, then top with the spiced chickpeas, followed in order by the yogurt, tamarind chutney, green chutney, chaat masala, onion, sprouts, sev, and cilantro. Assemble all at once or let guests garnish their plates at the table. In whichever scenario, spritz lime on at the last moment, and eat right away.

TAMARIND (*IMLI*) CHUTNEY

Makes about 2½ cups (590 ml) . . . .

8 ounces (230 g) seedless tamarind pulp

2 cups (480 ml) hot water, plus more as needed

½ cup (230 g) jaggery (see Note), palm sugar, or dark brown sugar, packed, plus more as needed

1 teaspoon Kashmiri or cayenne chile powder

1 teaspoon cumin seeds, toasted, then ground

½ teaspoon black salt (see Note)

½ teaspoon fine-grain sea salt

NOTE: Jaggery is an unrefined sugar made from sugarcane or dates and is used in many south Asian cuisines. It is found in the international aisle of some grocery stores, and in most Asian food stores. Black salt has a distinctive, sulfurous flavor and should also be available at an Asian grocer. Alternatively, use extra sea salt in its place.

Break the tamarind pulp into thumb-sized pieces and drop them into a bowl. Pour the hot water on top and set aside for 20 to 30 minutes, mashing and turning the tamarind regularly.

Push the tamarind pulp through a fine-mesh strainer into a heavy saucepan, and discard the fibers left behind. Crumble in most of the sugar, and set over medium heat. Bring to a boil until the sugar dissolves and the mixture is the consistency of thick honey. Pull the pan from the heat. Add the chile powder, cumin, black salt, and sea salt. Add more water if the mixture seems too thick. Taste. There should be a distinct tang, but a good sweetness and savory depth, and the spices should have a noticeable presence. Adjust the seasonings accordingly. Cool, then cover and refrigerate for up to a couple of weeks. Serve with chaat or samosas, or use as a glaze for chicken on the grill.

MUSHROOMS AND GREENS WITH TOAST

The title alone sells this one. Part Welsh rarebit, part fondue, and totally crave-worthy. The measurements need not be exact and, so you know, chunks of leftover roasted winter squash or other hearty vegetables also take well to such treatment, and can stand in, or be added to accompany, the mushrooms and greens.

On the topic of the mushrooms, I like to tear the mushrooms into reasonable bite size; it is quick enough work, and somehow meditative in its repetition, plus I think many mushrooms look best when spared the blade. Chanterelles, shiitake, and oyster mushrooms, for example, are especially attractive in rough pieces that preserve their natural shape. If pressed for time, slice or chop the mushrooms instead, but still let them be a bit irregular if you can.

.... *Serves 4* ....

3 tablespoons unsalted butter

1 tablespoon extra-virgin olive oil, plus more as needed

1½ pounds (680 g) mixed mushrooms, cleaned and trimmed

2 thick slices from a large, crusty boule

2 cloves garlic or 1 shallot, minced

1 tablespoon white wine vinegar

1 fresh red chile, stemmed, seeded, and minced

Medium-grain kosher salt and freshly ground black pepper

6 ounces (170 g) chopped greens such as kale, chard, spinach, or nettles

9 ounces (255 g) good melting cheese, thickly sliced (see Note)

NOTE: The cheese doesn't have to be one kind in particular. The point of this is using what's around— anything from a young chèvre to a robust, oozy blue. As long as it melts well, it's fair game. Fresh mozzarella or burrata, Taleggio, and Fontina are specifically good.

Melt the butter in the olive oil in a large, heavy skillet over medium-high heat. Tear the mushrooms into bite-size pieces and add to the pan. Cook, stirring regularly, until the mushrooms have given off their water and started to turn golden brown, 8 minutes or so.

Meanwhile, grill or toast the bread.

Once the mushrooms look nice, add the garlic and cook, stirring constantly, for 1 minute. Still stirring, drip the vinegar around the pan. Add most of the chile and season with salt and pepper. If using hearty greens that need some cooking, dump them in now. Move them around until wilted. After around 5 minutes, rip the bread into irregular croutons and push them into the vegetables. Lay pieces of cheese atop everything. Turn the heat down to medium-low, pop on a lid, and let the cheese melt, maybe 5 minutes, depending on the cheese. Sprinkle with the rest of the chile, hand out forks, then bring the pan to the table.

A BURGER TREATED LIKE A STEAK

I love a proper burger. Full stop.

For me, a burger made with pride offers one of those rare moments of true, greed-allaying, glorious pleasure.

The logic for this sandwich is that since a burger is chopped-up steak, it should be treated accordingly, which is to say, cooked in butter and not much else.

So, here there's just beef, pepper, and butter blended with white miso. The funked-up butter bastes the burger in salty richness, seeping through the patties and browning in the pan. The collected milk solids then cling to the meat and contribute to its chestnut-colored crust. It's not fancy—rather unabashedly unrefined, actually—and, it's gorgeous.

When choosing my beef I look for fat content first, aiming for 20 percent fat. As far as cut, chuck and brisket are great, and so is short rib, especially when mixed with some sirloin. Start with fresh ground meat from a reputable butcher or grind your own, then you can cook the beef to your liking. Prepackaged beef should always be cooked through, registering 160°F (70°C) in the middle (before resting).

The recipe only reads longish because I'm chatty. Make it once and you'll be a pro.

.... *Serves 4* ....

BURGERS

1⅓ pounds (600 g)
ground beef

2 tablespoons (30 g)
unsalted butter

1 to 2 teaspoons white miso,
depending on strength
and brand

Freshly cracked black pepper

4 banana shallots or 1 sweet
onion, peeled and thinly sliced

TO SERVE

4 small burger buns or
English muffins

Flaky sea salt

Thin slices Pecorino Romano
or Gruyère (optional)

Lettuce leaves

House Burger Sauce
(recipe follows)

To make the burgers, on a baking sheet, divide the beef into 4 equal portions. Use gentle, cupped hands to form into patties, each ⅔ inch (1.7 cm) thick and 4 inches (10 cm) wide, with a divot in the center to compensate for swelling as the patties cook. The beef should barely hold together, and crags are character. Cover the meat with plastic wrap and refrigerate until you are ready to cook, up to 1 day.

In a small bowl, mix 1½ tablespoons of the butter with the miso.

Get a 10- to 12-inch (25 to 30 cm) cast-iron skillet completely hot over medium-high heat. Liberally season the patties with

. . . continued

NOTE: For a change, switch in Hot Honey Butter (see Bee-Stung Fried Chicken, page 167) for the miso version here, reducing the honey to 2 teaspoons and then leaving off the House Burger Sauce. Of course you can use whatever additional toppings you'd like. I like sharp mustard, or pickled jalapeños (page 271).

pepper on both sides. Place the patties in the skillet along with the remaining ½ tablespoon butter. Cook until deeply browned and beginning to char, 3 to 4 minutes. After the first minute, or once they've firmed up, the patties can be shifted to ensure even cooking. If they stick, use a thin spatula to carefully pry them from the pan. Don't worry if the surface tears; adding texture will help form a layered crust. Flip, then spread one-quarter of the miso butter on top of each burger. Cook, shuttling as needed, until the meat is cooked to your desired doneness, 4 minutes or thereabouts for medium. Turn the burgers a few times in the butter so they are glazed and shining, then transfer to a warmed plate.

Turn the heat under the pan to medium and add the shallots. Let them go beautifully soft, stirring regularly for 10 minutes, more or less. There shouldn't be need to season with salt because there will be loads of flavor in the pan, but I like a little more cracked pepper.

To serve, split and toast the buns or English muffins. With a fork, pile on the shallots. Place a burger on top, add a miserly sprinkle of salt for crunch, and brush on some of the butter left in the shallot pan. Top with the cheese, then the lettuce. Spread the second half of the buns with House Burger Sauce, then press them down firmly to complete the burger. Feast.

HOUSE BURGER SAUCE

Makes enough for 4 burgers

½ cup (120 ml) mayonnaise, quality store-bought or homemade (page 265)

1 tablespoon ketchup

1 teaspoon dried mustard powder (or prepared yellow mustard)

2 teaspoons minced bread and butter pickles, plus ½ teaspoon of their brine

⅛ teaspoon sweet or smoked paprika

Freshly ground black pepper

Mix all the ingredients in a small bowl before you start with the burgers. Cover and refrigerate, so the flavors have a chance to get chummy. Chilled, it will keep for 4 days.

FENNEL AND CHARD PUFF

This is either a frittata with extra pouf, or a soufflé with a little less work. The contrast between the silky, caramel-touched vegetables and the muscular greens against the richness of egg, cream, and cheese is gratifying, comforting, and indulgent.

·· *Serves 4* ··

2 teaspoons almond meal (see Note)

1 tablespoon butter

1 pound (455 g) small fennel bulbs, trimmed and cut into small wedges, fronds reserved

2 shallots, peeled and cut into small wedges

1 tablespoon honey

Fine-grain sea salt and freshly ground black pepper

Bunch of chard, leaves torn and tender stems minced

1 lemon

4 eggs

½ cup (120 ml) crème fraîche

6 ounces (170 g) aged goat cheese, grated

1 tablespoon cornstarch or rice flour

2 teaspoons minced fresh herbs (parsley, chives, thyme)

NOTE: If you do not have almond meal to coat the casserole, buzz some nuts in a food processor—walnuts, pecans, and of course, almonds are good—or use additional cheese for dusting.

For personal servings, divide the batter among four small, shallow bowls, which have been given the same butter and almond meal treatment as above. Adjust the cooking time accordingly.

Preheat an oven to 400°F (200°C) with a baking sheet set on a rack in the upper third of the oven. Butter a shallow 8-inch (20 cm) round casserole and dust with the almond meal, tapping out any excess.

In a large skillet set over medium-high heat, melt the butter. Tumble in the fennel and shallots, making sure there's space in between. Leave them, undisturbed, for 4 minutes. Drizzle in the honey. Flip and let the second sides caramelize for another 2 minutes, then season with salt and pepper. When the vegetables are tender and almost cooked through, scatter in the chard stems and half of the leaves. Cook, stirring, until the greens wilt, about 1 minute. Add the remaining leaves. Deglaze with the juice of half the lemon. Stir until almost dry, then set the vegetables aside.

Separate the eggs, placing the yolks in one bowl and the whites in another. Stir the crème fraîche into the yolks. Sprinkle with the cheese, then the cornstarch, then beat to combine. Stir in the herbs and some lemon zest. Season with salt and pepper.

Beat the egg whites until stiff. Fold one-third of the egg whites into the yolk mixture, combine, then add the rest of the egg whites. Fold in most of the vegetables, then gently pour most of the batter into the prepared dish. Arrange the reserved vegetables on top, then partially cover with the rest of the egg mixture. Carefully place on the preheated baking sheet and bake until puffed and set, 18 minutes. Serve immediately.

AVOCADO TOAST

While a recipe for avocado toast might seem wholly unnecessary, it is the technique here that warrants recording. My avocado toast is an affair of mashed and sliced (or spooned) avocados on charred bread; since avocadoes can be bland, the mash ensures every bite is seasoned, while the large pieces are smooth and cool and meaty. This combination of textures and the balance of fat, heat, and astringency is remarkably habit-forming.

By the by, although brine from pickled jalapeños (page 271) sounds odd as an ingredient, it can take the place of the lemon juice for extra piquancy. Or, channel Jackson Pollock, and splatter toasts with Shaken Sesame Dressing (page 268).

·································· *Serves 2 for lunch, 4 as a snack* ··································

2 to 4 slices bread (see Note)

1 small clove garlic (optional)

2 large, ripe avocados

Fresh lemon juice or white wine vinegar, as needed

Fine-grain sea salt and freshly ground black pepper

2 teaspoons shimichi togarashi (hot Japanese spice mix), gochugaru (Korean ground red pepper powder), or crushed red pepper flakes

A few handfuls of sprouts or cress

Extra-virgin olive oil, for drizzling

NOTE: Quantities depend on the size of the avocados and the size and type of bread. For the bread, you want something with a closed crumb so that the avocado mash doesn't fall through. With a compact, grainy sandwich bread you might need four slices, whereas with a big, crusty boule you might need only two. For a baguette, I'll leave you with the math.

Heat a cast-iron griddle pan over medium-high heat. Grill the bread on each side until well marked, maybe 3 minutes per side, depending on your pan. Slice the garlic in half and rub one cut side on each slice of bread. (The bread can be toasted, too.)

Cut one avocado in half, remove the stone, and scoop the flesh from one half into a bowl. Season generously with lemon juice and a good pinch of salt and pepper. Mash the avocado coarsely with the back of a spoon, then check for seasoning—it should be pretty punchy. Slice or scoop the remaining flesh from the first avocado, and then cut, seed, and slice or scoop the flesh from the second. Spread the mashed avocado on the toasts, and arrange the slices on top. Shower over salt and shimichi togarashi and garnish with sprouts, a few more drops of lemon juice, and olive oil. Eat.

CHAPTER 3

SOUPS, STARTERS & SNACKS

I was never a Girl Scout, but I appreciate their motto to "always be prepared." I say this because I have pledged my allegiance to snacks. And snacks, good snacks, the snacks that save you from standing in front of the fridge eating jam with a spoon, *those* snacks call for planning.

While it requires that you think ahead, a snack strategy doesn't have to be complicated. Making sure to keep a jar of pâté and some pickles and cheese in the fridge means that a ploughman's lunch is never too far off; one batch of candied nuts will satiate a week's worth of afternoon hunger pangs; gougères can be prepped, then frozen and baked on demand; and a pot of gazpacho gets better as it sits. A modest investment at the outset can yield great dividends, as the small bites in this chapter prove, by bridging the gap between meals, beginning feasts, or becoming the feast itself.

ESQUITES AND YELLOW TOMATO GAZPACHO

You're most likely familiar with *elote*, grilled corn on the cob slathered in a mixture of mayonnaise, chile powder, lime, salt, and cheese, which is popular in Mexico. One summer dinner when we had more than the expected number at the table and not enough cobs for one per person, I stripped the corn into one big bowl and served from there. That was the night I learned about *esquites*, the Mexican street snack of boiled or sautéed corn kernels, finished like elote. Esquites not only makes corn go further, but also makes the eating neater, if that's a concern, and easier for those who have trouble with biting from the cob. (Parents with children of teeth-losing age, bookmark this page.)

Here, I take those flavors and whizz them into a cool gazpacho. The soup is vividly bright and refreshing, yet lush on the spoon. It suits the heat of high summer, on both the nights when you feel you can swim through the humidity and those that bake you dry. The corn, tomatoes, peppers, and onion create a layered sweetness, and then the vinegar dives straight through it all.

I prefer this soup without a burn; the poblano cream continues the vinegar's twang, with the emphasis on the fruity qualities of the pepper rather than its fire. The production is low effort, and the result is as irresistible as its predecessors.

.... *Serves 6* ....

SOUP

4 ears yellow or bicolor corn, husked and snapped in two

1¼ pounds (570 g) yellow tomatoes, stemmed

1 small sweet onion, chopped

2 cloves garlic, minced

1 yellow bell pepper, stemmed, seeded, and chopped

2 slices hearty white bread, ideally stale, each 1 inch (2.5 cm) thick, crusts removed

¼ cup (35 g) blanched almonds

1 tablespoon white wine vinegar, plus more as needed

Medium-grain kosher salt and freshly ground black pepper

2 to 3 tablespoons extra-virgin olive oil

CHILE CREAM

1 poblano chile

Small bunch of cilantro, leaves and tender stems chopped, plus a few sprigs left whole for garnish

1 ounce (30 g) cotija or feta cheese, crumbled

⅓ cup (80 ml) crema or sour cream

Medium-grain kosher salt and freshly ground black pepper

TO SERVE

1 lime

1 shallot, minced

1 avocado

Cayenne or smoked paprika (optional)

To make the soup, fill a biggish bowl with cold water and ice. Bring a large pot of water to a boil over high heat. Salt the water liberally. Plunge the corn into the pot and cook for 2 minutes. When the time's up, submerge the cobs in the ice water for 3 minutes, then transfer to a rimmed baking sheet. While the corn cools, keep the pot of water at a boil. With a paring knife, cut a small cross into the bottom of each tomato. Carefully drop the

NOTE: A word on breaking the cobs of corn in half: doing so will allow a smaller pot for boiling, and will give a flat base for removing the kernels later.

For those who look for pep in their chiles, use 2 to 3 jalapeños instead of the poblano in the cream. And in regard to that cream, it can instead be made with a pestle and mortar or by cutting by hand, yielding a brawny variation on the theme.

tomatoes into the boiling water and let them bob for 20 seconds. Lift the tomatoes from the pot and plunge into the ice water. Once cool, peel, core, and chop the tomatoes.

In a blender, process the onion, garlic, and bell pepper into a paste. Scrape down the sides of the carafe, then add the bread in chunks, followed by the almonds, and process again.

Slice the corn kernels from the cobs. Set aside approximately ¾ cup (180 ml) kernels for garnish, then add the rest of the corn to the blender, along with the chopped tomatoes. Puree the vegetables until absolutely velvety, about 3 minutes. Pour in 1½ teaspoons of the vinegar, a generous pinch of salt, and some pepper. Process again. With the motor running, add most of the olive oil in a thin, steady stream through the hole in the blender's lid. Pop the lid's stopper back into place and let the machine run for a good while, maybe 2 minutes more, until the liquid is silky and emulsified. Stop the blender, taste, adding more of the remaining 1½ teaspoons vinegar, salt, or oil, as needed. The flavors will dull when chilled, so they should be more than convincing now. Flip the motor on for another 30 seconds, then pour the soup into a serving bowl or pitcher. Cover and refrigerate for at least 2 hours, and up to overnight.

About an hour before you're looking to eat, make the chile cream. Char the poblano over a gas flame or under a broiler, turning regularly until blackened on all sides, 7 to 10 minutes. Transfer to a bowl and cover with plastic wrap. Leave to steam for about 20 minutes. Stem, peel, seed, and chop the chile, and add to a blender or food processor with the cilantro and cheese. Blitz to a fine green and white confetti. Scrape down the sides, pour in the crema, add a few grinds of pepper, and blend again. Taste, then season as needed with salt and pepper. Cover and refrigerate until needed.

To serve, in a small bowl, squeeze the juice from half the lime over the shallot. Sprinkle in some salt and pepper and leave at room temperature for 5 minutes, stirring now and again.

Right before serving, peel, seed, and dice the avocado. Fold the avocado into the pickled shallot. Ladle the chilled soup into bowls, top with the reserved corn, avocado, chile cream, cilantro leaves, and cayenne powder. Cut the remaining lime half into wedges and place in a bowl on the table. Eat.

CELERIAC SOUP WITH GREEN HORSERADISH OIL

While the preceding soup is almost frothy in its lightness, this puree is just as smooth but with a welcome, belly-filling warmth. Celeriac has a fragrant minerality and takes well to roasting. Here, the gnarled, knobbly root is trimmed to reveal the ivory interior, then cut into cubes to be paired with onions and celery, which have their own version of that same mineral quality. The soup is rich without adding any cream, but don't let that stop you from doing so, if moved in such a direction.

.... *Serves 4 to 6* ....

SOUP

1 good-size celeriac, about 1 pound (455 g), peeled and cut into 1-inch (2.5 cm) dice

2 sweet onions, chopped

2 cloves garlic, peeled and left whole

2 tablespoons mild olive oil

Medium-grain kosher salt and freshly ground black pepper

2 tablespoons butter

2 slices bacon, diced

2 stalks celery, chopped

1 russet potato, peeled and cut into 1-inch (2.5 cm) dice

4 cups (1 L) chicken stock or vegetable broth, plus more as needed

2 bay leaves

1 piece Parmesan rind, about 2 inches (5 cm) square

Crème fraîche or heavy cream (optional)

GREEN HORSERADISH OIL

Handful of flat-leaf parsley, leaves and tender stems

2 tablespoons fresh oregano

1 tablespoon freshly grated horseradish, or to taste

Finely grated zest from ½ lemon, plus juice as needed

1 clove garlic, peeled

Medium-grain kosher salt and freshly ground black pepper

¼ cup (60 ml) extra-virgin olive oil

SERVING OPTIONS

Finely grated Parmesan cheese

Toasted walnuts or roasted chestnuts, peeled and coarsely broken

To make the soup, preheat an oven to 375°F (190°C).

On a half sheet pan or in a shallow roasting pan, roll the celeriac, onions, and garlic around in the olive oil. Season with salt and pepper, then rustle the vegetables until they are in an even layer. Roast in the hot oven, turning periodically, until the vegetables start to turn golden, around 25 minutes.

Melt the butter in a large, heavy saucepan over medium heat. Add the bacon and cook, stirring, until the bacon is touched with color and starts to release some of its fat, 5 minutes or so. Add the celery to the pan with a generous pinch of salt and sauté until softened, 8 to 10 minutes, stirring often. Scrape the roasted vegetables into the pot, followed by the potato and stock. Give a good stir, raise the heat to high, and bring to a boil. Lower the heat, pop in the bay leaves and Parmesan rind, then cover the pan, and let it bubble at a gentle simmer until the potato is tender when speared through its center with the tip of a knife, around 20 minutes. Fish out the bay leaves and Parmesan rind.

Off the heat, use an immersion blender to buzz the soup until smooth, or alternatively, in an upright blender, working in batches as necessary. (When pureeing hot liquids in an upright blender, remove the stopper from the lid and cover with a folded lint-free tea towel that you don't mind getting dirty. This will help with the release of pressure and steam.) If the puree is too thick, thin by stirring in more stock or water, or heavy cream or crème fraîche. Check for seasoning, then place the pan back over low heat and keep warm.

To make the horseradish oil, use a pestle and mortar to pound the parsley, oregano, horseradish, lemon zest, and garlic into a paste, along with a generous pinch of both salt and pepper. Stir in the oil, then taste and season, adjusting the levels of salt, pepper, or lemon juice. Err on the side of spirited for the seasoning; the mild soup can carry it.

Serve the soup, passing around the horseradish oil and garnishes, so guests can dress their bowls as they'd like.

FEEL-BETTER CURRIED SOUP
WITH CRISPY CHICKEN

I have a whole catalog of soups that fall under the "Feel-Better" title. Differing in particulars of complexity and execution, most start with a potent base of ginger, garlic, and chiles. When I am sick or tired, I'm drawn to aggressive flavors—I require freshness, vigor, and vitality. I've included an array of dried chiles here, the spiciest being the small Thai chiles, which are quite feisty and can be omitted if you're sensitive to heat.

Thailand's well-known soup of noodles in a curried broth, *khao soi* (also called Chiang Mai Curry Noodles), provided inspiration for this bowlful of life-affirming goodness. My curry paste is a streamlined homage to the tradition; my broth is thinner, plus there's more of it, and there are additional vegetables. I roast chicken pieces until dried and densely chewy, and the skin is turned to cracklings, taking the place of the usual fried noodle garnish—sick or well, you'll fight over them.

Serves 4 to 6

CURRY PASTE

4 large dried chiles (Guajillo, California, New Mexico, or a mix)

1 or 2 dried Thai chiles (optional)

2 teaspoons coriander seeds

Seeds from 2 black cardamom pods or from 4 green pods

3 shallots, quartered

Small bunch of cilantro, leaves reserved for garnish, tender stems chopped

2-inch (5 cm) knob of ginger, peeled and cut into slices across the grain

6 cloves garlic, peeled and left whole

2 teaspoons ground turmeric

1 teaspoon Indian curry powder

CHICKEN

4 chicken thighs (about 1½ pounds/680 g), bones discarded and skin removed and reserved (see Note)

Medium-grain kosher salt and freshly ground black pepper

SOUP

1½ tablespoons neutral-tasting oil

2 (14-ounce/400 g) cans coconut milk

3 cups (710 ml) good-quality chicken stock, plus more as needed

1½ tablespoons fish sauce, or more as needed

2 teaspoons tamari or soy sauce, or more as needed

2 teaspoons light or dark brown sugar, or more as needed

Medium-grain kosher salt

8 ounces (225 g) rice noodles (or substitute udon, wonton, or Chinese egg noodles)

TO SERVE

Cilantro leaves

Thai basil leaves

Fresh Thai chiles, sliced, or Sichuan chili oil

Red onion, peeled and sliced into thin half-moons

Enoki mushrooms, trimmed of roots

Bean sprouts

Baby bok choy, separated into leaves, other similar greens, or pickled mustard greens, rinsed, and sliced

Lime wedges

... continued

Feel-Better Curried Soup with Crispy Chicken, continued

NOTE: It is quite simple to pull the bone from a chicken thigh. Remove the skin with your hands, then flip the thigh over. Working in small, shallow strokes, use the tip of a knife to cut the bone away from the meat. Free one long side, then the other, then finally slip the knife beneath the bone completely. Alternatively, ask the butcher to prep the chicken, making sure to get the skin.

To make the curry paste, snap the stems off the dried chiles and remove the seeds. Place in a heatproof bowl and cover with water from a recently boiled kettle and soften for 15 minutes.

Meanwhile, to make the chicken, preheat an oven to 425°F (220°C). Rub oil on a rimmed baking sheet.

Place the chicken thighs flesh side down on the prepared baking sheet, and season with salt and pepper. Flip and season again. Stretch the chicken skin out on the baking sheet and season as well. Bake in the hot oven until the skin is crisp and gnarly and the chicken is opaque throughout and its juices run clear when pierced with a knife, 30 minutes. The skin may be done earlier than the meat, so keep an eye on that. Remove the chicken from the oven and dry the skin on paper towels.

While the chicken is roasting, finish the curry paste. Toast the coriander and cardamom seeds in a large, heavy pot over medium heat. Once fragrant, 45 to 60 seconds, transfer to a mortar. Cool, then use the pestle to crush the spices into a powder. Add the soaked chiles (reserve the soaking liquid), shallots, cilantro stems, ginger, garlic, turmeric, and curry powder and carefully pound to a paste, adding some of the chile soaking water to help work the ingredients smooth. (Alternatively, make the paste in a small food processor fitted with the metal blade.)

To make the soup, in the same pot as before, heat the oil over medium heat. Fry the curry paste in the oil, stirring constantly, until darkened without burning, about 4 minutes. Add 1 cup (240 ml) of the coconut milk and boil, still stirring, until the fat separates from the liquid, 2 to 3 minutes. Repeat the process with another 1 cup (240 ml) of coconut milk, then add the remaining coconut milk and stir in the stock. Bring to a boil, then lower the heat and simmer, partially covered, for 20 minutes.

While the soup bubbles, prepare the noodles according to the package instructions. Once ready, drain them and rinse with cool water. Set aside. Chop the chicken into bite-size pieces. Sort the remaining garnishes and set everything out on the table.

Stir the fish sauce, tamari, and brown sugar into the soup. Add more stock if the broth is too thick. Taste and adjust the seasoning; it should taste savory and slightly sweet, with heat. Divide the noodles among the serving bowls, then ladle in the soup. Guests can dress their bowls as they'd like.

PICKLED
STRAWBERRY PRESERVES

I first had pickled strawberries at a restaurant in New York City. They were luminously scarlet, lacquered in juice, and daintily presented on top of sweet, sticky rice cakes.

This is a jammier but punchy take on those berries, which I serve most often with cheeses or dried meats. That said, the fruit can be used on toast, biscuits, or yogurt.

················· *Makes 1 to 2 pints (475 to 950 ml), depending on the fruit* ·················

1 lemon

1 teaspoon black peppercorns, plus more in the peppermill

½ teaspoon coriander seeds

2 bay leaves

2 pounds (910 g) strawberries

1⅓ cups (270 g) granulated sugar

¼ cup (60 ml) champagne vinegar (see Note)

⅛ teaspoon medium-grain kosher salt

½ teaspoon salted butter

NOTE: Red or white wine vinegars, and even apple cider vinegar, can be used instead of the champagne vinegar—since they're not as sharp, adjust the quantity accordingly.

Squeeze the juice of the lemon into a large nonreactive bowl. Fish out the seeds, and add them to a self-fill tea bag or doubled piece of cheesecloth. Bundle up with the peppercorns, coriander seeds, and bay leaves and close the bag. Give the bag a few whacks with something heavy, then add the bag to the juice. Cut the juiced lemon into chunks and drop those in, too.

Hull the strawberries and leave whole if tiny, or cut into pieces if larger. The aim is for all the berries to be of similar size, and that size to be a juicy mouthful. Place in a bowl. Pour the sugar over the fruit, followed by the vinegar and the salt. Toss to combine. Cover and let sit at room temperature for 3 hours, or overnight in the fridge. Stir occasionally.

Set a colander over a wide, heavy nonreactive pot. Give the berries and juice a stir, then slip everything into the colander, scraping out any straggling juice or sugar. Tip the fruit back into the bowl. Add the lemon peels and spice bag to the juices, along with the butter. Bring to a boil over medium-high heat. Cook, stirring, until the juices are clear, darkened, and beginning to thicken, around 7 minutes. Add the berries and continue to cook, shaking the pan now and again, until the fruit is plump but not falling apart, 8 to 10 minutes more. Discard the peels and bag. Fold a few grindings of pepper into the preserves, then pour into jars. Seal and cool to room temperature, then refrigerate for up to 1 month.

HUMMUS WITH WHITE MISO

I am mad for the combination of white (shiro) miso and tahini. The unapologetic salinity and fermented, umami-rich edge of the miso teases the sesame paste's mild, rich roundness into standing upright, while the tahini in turn balances out the miso's oomph. I love nothing more than this spread, flamboyant with garnishes, with some warm naan (page 124), and a cold, cold glass of white wine. That's my idea of cocktail hour.

Misos will vary in intensity among brands, so the amount may need to be adjusted accordingly.

Makes about 2½ cups (600 ml)

¼ cup (60 g) blanched almonds

2 cups (450 g) cooked chickpeas or 1 (15-ounce/425 g) can

¼ cup (60 ml) well-stirred tahini

¼ cup (60 ml) white (shiro) miso

2 cloves garlic, smashed with the side of a knife

¼ teaspoon crushed red pepper flakes

Juice from ½ lemon, approximately 2 tablespoons, plus more as needed

About ½ cup (120 ml) ice water

Fine-grain sea salt and freshly ground black pepper

Toasted sesame oil (optional)

SERVING OPTIONS

Extra-virgin olive oil

Flaky sea salt

Coriander seeds or cumin seeds, roasted and cracked

Ground sumac or za'atar

Toasted sesame seeds, white or black, or pine nuts

Minced fresh flat-leaf parsley and chives

Assorted sprouts (such as mung bean, broccoli, alfalfa)

Fried shallots

In a food processor fitted with the metal blade, process the almonds into a fine meal. Add the chickpeas and run the machine again, stopping and scraping down the sides occasionally, until the beans are crumbly and light. Pour in the tahini, miso, garlic, red pepper flakes, and lemon juice. Blend again for 2 minutes or so, then scrape down the sides of the machine. Switch on the motor and start drizzling in enough water so that the hummus billows up, aerated and fluffy. Depending on the beans, you may not use all the water, or you might need more. Let the machine go for 2 to 3 minutes after the consistency seems right. Taste and check for seasoning. For a roasted accent, drip in some toasted sesame oil.

Let the hummus sit for 30 minutes at room temperature before serving, or refrigerate in a covered container for up to 3 days. Serve with the garnishes of your choosing.

BLITZED RICOTTA
WITH PEAS

This is the type of no-cook snack that once you make it, you're thinking about when you can make it again. It starts with a pea pesto, flecked with mint and basil, which is then folded into a mound of ricotta and yogurt. It is at times mild and milky in its eating, other times energetically herbal, and other times all ripened sweetness. Use as a spread on bread and crackers, a dip for fresh vegetables, and a sauce for cooked ones. Since the peas are raw, only use fresh if you are planning on shelling them yourself. For frozen peas, petits pois are perfect.

Makes about 3 cups (710 ml)

2 cloves garlic, peeled and left whole

2 ounces (60 g) Pecorino Romano or Parmesan cheese, cut into chunks

¼ cup (35 g) pine nuts, toasted, plus more to serve

4 ounces (115 g) sweet small peas, fresh or defrosted if frozen

1 cup (30 g) pea shoots, loosely packed, tough stems trimmed

Handful of fresh basil leaves, about 1 ounce (30 g)

Handful of fresh mint leaves, about 1 ounce (30 g)

Grated zest from ½ lemon

Fine-grain sea salt and freshly ground black pepper

¼ cup (60 ml) extra-virgin olive oil, plus more for drizzling

2 cups (475 ml) whole-milk ricotta (page 264)

1 cup (240 ml) labneh (page 262) or plain Greek-style yogurt, not nonfat

1 small fresh red chile, stemmed, seeded, and minced (optional)

Drop the garlic, cheese, and pine nuts into the bowl of a food processor fitted with a metal blade. Grind with short pulses until a fine rubble. Turn off the machine, and add the peas, pea shoots, basil, mint, lemon zest, and a generous pinch each of salt and pepper. Process into a coarse paste. Turn off the machine and scrape down the sides of the bowl. Turn the machine back on and drizzle the olive oil through the feed tube in a thin, steady stream, stopping and scraping the blade and sides of the bowl as needed. Check for seasoning, then spoon the pea mixture into a small bowl, and set aside.

In the same, uncleaned processor, whip the ricotta, labneh, and a pinch of salt until fluffy. Layer the ricotta and peas in a serving bowl. Fold gently with the tip of a spoon to swirl. Coarsely chop the reserved pine nuts and add to the bowl. Drizzle with olive oil, scatter with chiles, and serve.

BEET-CURED GRAVLAX

Gravlax is the easiest introduction to curing fish, and this beet-dyed version is a particular looker. All it takes is a mixture of sugar and salt, some seasonings, and time. Science takes care of the rest, so in days, the flesh becomes dense, as its liquid is drawn out. Using salmon is traditional, while Artic char has a milder taste. Either way, choose the freshest fish possible.

··· *Serves 8 to 10* ···

GRAVLAX

2 pounds (910 g) Arctic char or salmon fillet, scaled but skin on

2 tablespoons (30 ml) gin, aquavit, or vodka

½ cup (100 g) granulated sugar

¼ cup (65 g) fine-grain sea salt

Finely grated zest of 1 lemon

1 bunch dill, coarsely chopped

3 beets, scrubbed well and grated

SERVING OPTIONS

Small greens or sprouts (such as radish, watercress, or alfalfa)

1 cup (240 ml) sour cream, stirred with 2 teaspoons grated horseradish, finely grated zest from 1 lemon, and black pepper, to taste

2 avocados, pitted and scooped into pieces from the skins with a spoon

Lemon wedges

Small loaf pumpernickel bread

Fennel pollen, toasted and ground fennel seeds, or dill fronds, for garnish (optional)

NOTE: Since gravlax keeps quite well in the fridge, I am happy to make a large amount. Still, if leftovers are a worry, halve the recipe.

To make the gravlax, lay the fillet skin side down on a board, and check for bones. Brush the fish with the gin. Line a rimmed sheet pan or roasting pan with a double layer of plastic wrap and place the fillet on the wrap.

In a bowl, mix together the sugar and salt, then coat the flesh of the fish in the mixture. Layer the lemon zest, dill, and beets on top. Pull the plastic wrap up and over the fish, binding tightly. Place another pan or a cutting board on top, then weight it down with cans, or something similarly hefty. Refrigerate for 2 days, pouring off any liquid every 12 hours, then weighting down again.

Remove the weights from the gravlax and discard the liquid. Unwrap the fish and carefully push away the seasonings. Use a long, thin-bladed knife to cut the gravlax into the thinnest slices possible, leaving the skin behind. (A generous half of one fillet serves 4 people nicely.) Wrap any remaining salmon tightly in clean plastic wrap, and store in the refrigerator for up to 10 days.

To serve, arrange the greens, a bowl of sour cream, avocado, lemon wedges, bread, and gravlax on a large board or platter. Let guests make their own open-faced sandwiches (tartines), sprinkled with additional pepper and fennel pollen.

CHICKEN LIVER PÂTÉ

India triggers a collection of Proustian food associations for me: *idlis* and *sambar, chikus,* guavas, Thumbs Up! Cola, thali meals and *pani puri,* carrot juice at my grandfather's house, and sweet milk tea. The pâté sandwiches we'd pack for train rides, and eating them, on the upper bunk of those sleeper cars with the light turquoise walls. We'd chew, while swaying with our progress across the tracks. The whipped texture of the pâté melded into the softness of the bread, and both stuck to the back of my front teeth.

Whenever I put out pâté for guests, it is usually one of the first things to go; yet, despite that popularity, I don't know if it is often thought of as something to make at home. That's a shame, because not only does a homemade version allow you to tailor the pâté to your tastes, but it is also dead simple to make. This one is mild and crowd-pleasing, with the warmth of a bit of booze, and an indistinct herbal backnote. Before seasonal entertaining is upon you, make a few crocks' worth, and once those festive times arrive, you are free to entertain in blithe ease.

Serve the pâté with cornichons, capers, or pickled onions, and mustard with bread, toasted or not. As you may have guessed, the pâté is also great in sandwiches.

Serves 8

PÂTÉ

1 tablespoon extra-virgin olive oil

2 shallots, minced

Fine-grain sea salt and freshly ground black pepper

1 pound (455 g) fresh chicken livers, cleaned and trimmed

½ cup (115 g) unsalted butter

A few sprigs of fresh thyme, leaves stripped and stems discarded

A couple of sage leaves

2 tablespoons brandy

2 tablespoons heavy cream

BUTTER CAP (OPTIONAL)

½ cup (115 g) unsalted butter

Small, short thyme sprigs and/or sage leaves, for garnish

Peppercorns, cracked or whole

To make the pâté, in a large, heavy skillet over medium-low heat, warm the olive oil. Add the shallots and sauté until translucent, 5 minutes. Season with salt and pepper. Tumble in the livers, ¼ cup (57 g) of the butter, and the thyme and sage. Raise the heat to medium-high and cook, stirring often, until the edges of the livers start to brown and the centers are still quite pink, 5 minutes or so. Off the heat, pour in the brandy; flame if desired, or carefully place back on the heat and let bubble until reduced by half, about 1 minute (keep a snug lid for the pot nearby, in case the alcohol does catch unexpectedly).

Scrape the mixture into a blender or food processor fitted with the metal blade. Pulse the livers to a coarse puree. Scrape down the carafe and blade of the blender, then run the machine again. Once mostly smooth, add the remaining ¼ cup (57 g) butter in chunks through the feed tube, followed by the cream. Scrape down again, check for seasoning, and quickly blitz once more.

Press the pâté through a fine-mesh sieve into a bowl, then pack into a serving bowl or wide glass jar. Smooth the top, wrap tightly with plastic wrap, and refrigerate—if not finishing with a butter cap—for 2 to 4 hours, depending on the depth of the bowl. If capping, 30 minutes or so should be sufficient.

To make the butter cap, melt the butter in a heavy saucepan over low heat with whatever herbs you're using. Gently simmer, so that the butter's milk solids collect at the bottom of the pot and foam rises to the top. Take off the heat, skim off the foam, and let stand for a moment. Unwrap the pâté. Pull the herbs from the butter and arrange on the surface of the pâté, then strew some peppercorns around attractively. Carefully spoon on enough butter to cover, holding back the milk solids. Return the pâté to the fridge until the butter is firm, 30 minutes. Then cover and refrigerate for 2 hours more. If undisturbed, the pâté can be kept for up to 2 weeks; once cracked, or if not capped, it should be eaten within 5 days.

PLOUGHMAN'S LUNCH

A *ploughman's lunch* is an English term referring to a meal of cheese, chutney, and bread, oftentimes with pickles, cold meats, and beer. The term originated in an advertising campaign by the country's cheese bureau in the 1950s and was adopted by their milk marketing board in the following decade, but it has a far longer cultural history. A ploughman's lunch is one of my husband's favorite kinds of meals, and mine, too, the sort that is based on assembly and grazing, and just enough of all the things you like best. The pâté (page 116), paired with pickled strawberries (page 111), an oozing wedge of Brie or Shropshire Blue, and some crusty bread (page 29) would make a fine spread.

HARD CIDER GOUGÈRES

I was once tasked with making an outrageous number of nibbles for a work event. Searching for something easy to produce in great numbers, I decided upon an old standby—gougères, the little choux pastry cheese puffs, for their simplicity and adaptability. Before the evening of the event, I piped and baked the golden bites, then popped them in the freezer, to be rewarmed en masse once needed. On the night of, they were a rousing success, gone in a flash.

I like making gougères in one pan and using only a spoon, but the eggs can be incorporated using a stand mixer fitted with the paddle attachment to avoid the arm workout, which is a boon if making these in bulk.

Makes about 4 dozen puffs

½ cup (120 ml) hard cider

½ cup (120 ml) water

6 tablespoons (85 g) unsalted butter, diced

¾ teaspoon fine-grain sea salt

1 cup (130 g) all-purpose flour

4 eggs

4 ounces (115 g) Comté or Gruyère cheese, grated (about 1 cup)

¼ cup (30 g) finely grated Grana Padano or Parmesan cheese

1 teaspoon minced fresh thyme

Generous pinch of cayenne, paprika (smoked or hot), or dried English mustard powder

1 egg yolk beaten with 1 tablespoon water, for glaze

Preheat an oven to 450°F (235°C). Line 2 baking sheets with parchment paper.

In a large, heavy saucepan over medium-high heat, heat the cider, water, butter, and salt until the butter melts. Add the flour all at once, stirring vigorously with a wooden spoon to make a dough. Continue stirring; the dough will become smooth and pull cleanly from the pan. Keep going, stirring and cooking the dough, until it is no longer sticky and smells faintly toasted, 2 to 3 minutes more. (Cooking out any extra moisture now helps make crisp puffs later.) Remove the pan from the heat and set aside to cool for 2 minutes. Stir regularly.

Slip the eggs into the pot, one at a time, mixing well after each. Stir in the cheeses, reserving about 1 tablespoon of the Grana Padano. Follow with the thyme and cayenne.

Using a piping bag fitted with a ½-inch (1.3 cm) plain tip, a 1½-ounce (45 g) spring-loaded ice cream scoop, or two spoons, form walnut-sized mounds on the prepared baking sheets, using about 1 tablespoon for each and leaving about 2 inches (5 cm) in between. Carefully pat down any peaks with a damp finger.

(At this point the portioned dough can be frozen on the sheet until hard, then transferred to an airtight container and kept in the freezer.)

Brush the formed dough balls with the egg wash and sprinkle with the reserved cheese. Bake for 10 minutes, then lower the heat to 350°F (175°C) and continue to bake until the gougères are golden all over and feel light for their size, 15 minutes more. (Add a few minutes if baking from frozen.) If they are browning too quickly, turn off the oven and let the puffs dry in the diffusing heat. Remove from the oven, turn off the heat, and use a thin-bladed knife or skewer to puncture each puff in an inconspicuous spot (say, a place where it's cracked). Return to the oven for 5 minutes.

Eat straight away or cool to room temperature, then rewarm in a low oven later on. Or, once again freeze as before, on trays, then move to a sealed container and reheat when needed.

Fresh Goat Cheese Variation: Use 1 cup (240 ml) milk instead of the cider and water, fresh goat cheese instead of the Comté, and chives instead of the thyme.

HALLOUMI IN CHERMOULA

I love halloumi for its squeaking rubberiness, and because it is much more forgiving to cook than feta, even though it still has a similar saline hit. It seems to last forever in the fridge, so with a package of halloumi in one hand and a collection of herbs in the other, there's the makings of a memorable starter—warm slices of cheese draped in earthy chermoula, a North African dressing.

Serves 4 to 6

1 fresh red chile, seeded, if desired, and chopped

4 cloves garlic, unpeeled and left whole

1 teaspoon coriander seeds

1 teaspoon cumin seeds

1 teaspoon smoked or sweet paprika

1 cup (25 g) fresh flat-leaf parsley, chopped

1 cup (25 g) fresh cilantro, chopped

Grated zest and juice from ½ lemon, wedges from ½ lemon

3 tablespoons extra-virgin olive oil

Fine-grain sea salt and freshly ground black pepper

1 pound (455 g) halloumi, cut into ¼-inch (6 mm) slices

In a large, well-seasoned cast-iron pan or heavy nonstick skillet over medium heat, dry roast the chile and garlic until toasted on all sides, 2 to 3 minutes. Set aside. In the same pan, toast the coriander and cumin until fragrant, stirring often. It should take about a minute. Process the spices in a grinder or mortar and pestle, then transfer to a medium bowl with the paprika. Pile the herbs, garlic, chile, and lemon zest on a board and chop into fine flecks. Rake the mix into the bowl with the spices. Stir in the oil and lemon juice and season with salt and pepper.

Wipe out the skillet and heat over medium-high heat. Fry the halloumi in the dry skillet, in batches if needed, until golden, a minute or so on each side. As they're ready, add the pieces to the chermoula. Once all the halloumi is golden and bathed, tip everything out onto a serving plate, being sure to rescue any sauce that lingers in the bowl. Tuck the lemon wedges in and around the cheese. Serve.

NAAN

My preferred naan are those made with a sourdough starter, then cooked in a tandoor; they are tender, but with texture. Blistered black here and there, pale elsewhere, these pita-like breads are best left to the talents of professionals.

I do make naan at home, sadly without a tandoor, in a version that requires less skill yet still meeting the requirements of char, chew, and pillowy doughiness. I favor a slow rise, using a small amount of yeast for lift. That said, baking powder and soda make for a quick leavening when time isn't on my side (see the variation at right). In either case, a heavy cast-iron or nonstick pan stands in for the tandoor; go for one that will heat evenly and hold on to that fire. When the wetted dough is placed in the pan and a lid goes on, it makes a stove-top steam oven. The combination of dry and wet heat browns, puffs, and cooks a naan in mere minutes; then it's on to the next one.

.... *Makes 8 pieces* ....

1 tablespoon melted ghee (page 259) or butter

½ teaspoon active dry yeast

1 teaspoon sugar

½ cup (120 ml) warm water

2 cups (255 g) white bread flour (see Note)

1 cup (130 g) all-purpose flour, plus more for dusting

1½ teaspoons medium-grain kosher salt

¾ cup (175 ml) plain whole-milk yogurt (page 264)

Nigella seeds, poppy seeds, cumin seeds, sesame seeds, or chopped garlic (optional)

Chopped fresh cilantro leaves, for garnish

Grease a large bowl lightly with ghee.

In a small bowl, stir the yeast and a pinch of the sugar into the water. Set aside for 3 to 5 minutes, at which point the mixture should look foamy. If it isn't, wait for another minute, and if it is still without activity, start again with fresh yeast.

In a bowl, whisk together the flours, salt, and remaining sugar. Make a well in the center of the dry ingredients, as if making a small volcano. Whisk the yogurt into the yeast mixture, then pour the yeast-water mixture into the middle of the dry ingredients (or crater, to continue the metaphor). With a fork, slowly bring the walls of the well into the liquid a little at a time, until all the liquid is incorporated but some loose flour remains. Turn the whole bowl out onto a clean work surface. Knead the dough until it is a satiny lump, 5 to 8 minutes. If the dough is too sticky to handle at any point, dust with flour.

Place the dough in the ghee-slicked bowl and cover with a damp, lint-free kitchen towel to rest at room temperature until doubled in bulk, 3 to 4 hours. (At this point, the dough can be covered in plastic wrap and refrigerated for up to 2 days. Take chilled dough out of the fridge 30 minutes before using.)

Preheat an oven to 200°F (95°C) with an ovenproof serving dish on the rack set in the middle.

Turn the dough out onto a work surface. Divide the dough into 8 equal portions. Shape each piece into a tight ball by rolling between your cupped hand and a work surface. Re-cover with your towel and leave the dough to relax, at least 5 and up to 10 minutes.

Preheat a large cast-iron skillet or nonstick pan over medium-high heat. Take one piece of dough and place in the center of a lightly floured work surface, keeping the rest of the balls covered. Use a rolling pin to flatten the dough into a round approximately ⅛ inch (3 mm) thick. If desired, pull on one side of the circle to form the traditional teardrop shape. If ever the dough resists rolling and springs back, move on and shape another ball of dough, then return to the first when finished. Once shaped, brush the dough with water and, if using, press any desired seasonings into the surface. Set the dough into the hot pan, wet side down, and brush the now-exposed dry side of the dough with a little water. Cover and cook, undisturbed, until bubbles form on the top of the dough, and the underside is speckled and brown, 2 to 3 minutes. Flip the naan and press with a folded kitchen towel to flatten any large bubbles. Replace the lid and cook until the underside is as browned as the top, 1 to 2 minutes more, then flip back over and brush with melted ghee.

Keep the naan warm in the oven as the remaining dough is shaped and cooked. The naan are best eaten right away but can be stored at room temperature for 1 day. Rewarm in a low oven, wrapped in foil. Garnish with the cilantro.

Quick-Rise Naan: Omit the yeast. Stir ¾ cup (175 ml) milk with the yogurt instead of using water. Whisk together the flours, salt, and sugar as above, adding 1 teaspoon baking powder and a generous ¾ teaspoon baking soda to the mix. Stir the wet ingredients into the dry ingredients to form a dough. Knead, cover with a damp kitchen towel, and let rest at room temperature for 1 hour before shaping and cooking as above.

GARLIC AND CILANTRO
LACCHA PARATHA

Parathas are Indian flatbreads that have fat in the dough and are fried in more fat on a griddle called a tava. (In comparison, chapatis are made and cooked without fat.) Parathas can be simply rolled; coiled and flattened, resulting in the flaky, layered effect here; or stuffed with hearty fillings like potatoes, cabbage, and cauliflower (imagine a thinner Jamaican patty, or Salvadoran pupusa). Those stuffed paranthas can be quite bulky and are eaten as a main dish with raita, ghee, or pickles, while the first two are used for sopping up dal (page 155) and curries (page 151).

If at any time the dough springs back when rolling, cover and move on to another piece for a few minutes, then return to the first.

.... *Makes 8 pieces* ....

Small bunch of cilantro, roots trimmed

4 green onions, roots and tough green parts trimmed

2 cloves garlic, peeled but left whole

1 fresh red or green chile, stemmed and seeded

1 cup (130 g) all-purpose flour

1 cup (95 g) atta (durum) flour or whole wheat pastry flour, plus more for rolling

1 teaspoon medium-grain kosher salt

1 teaspoon cumin seeds, toasted, cooled, and finely ground

¼ cup (60 ml) melted ghee (page 259) or unsalted butter

¾ cup water, plus more as needed

Chop the cilantro, green onions, garlic, and chile together in the center of a board until minced. Divide the mixture evenly between two bowls, one small and one large. Cover the small bowl and refrigerate (this will be used when shaping the parathas).

Into the large bowl with the second half of the herb mix, dump in the flours, salt, and cumin and whisk to combine. Pour in 1 tablespoon of the ghee and the water. Using your hands, slowly bring the dry ingredients into the wet until mostly combined. Add more water if needed, a teaspoon at time, to make a tender dough. Start kneading in the bowl, then turn out onto a lightly floured work surface and work until the dough is smooth, shiny, and not at all sticky, about 5 minutes. Rub a bit of ghee on the palms of your hands for the last few kneads. Return the dough to the bowl and cover with a damp, lint-free kitchen towel. Let rest for at least 30 minutes and up to 6 hours.

Divide the dough into 8 equal portions and shape each into a ball on a lightly floured work surface. Take one ball, dip both sides in flour, and use a rolling pin to roll it into a round as thin as possible without tearing, at least 7 inches (18 cm) in diameter.

... **continued**

Garlic and Cilantro Laccha Paratha, continued

Dust with a thin coating of flour and then flip over. Brush the clean side with some of the remaining ghee, then sprinkle with some of the reserved cilantro mixture from the fridge followed by more flour. Starting at one side, fold the edge over ¼ inch (6 mm). Lift the edge and fold back to form a pleat. Continue with the accordion fold, as if making a paper fan, to make a strip of stacked pleats. Stretch and compress the stack to set the pleats as they are formed. Starting at one end, wind the stack around itself into a tight coil, again stretching with each turn. Once rolled, tuck the loose end under the coil to secure. It will look like a cinnamon bun. Cover again with the towel and repeat the shaping with each ball until all the dough is used. About half the ghee should be left over.

Move the first coil back onto the work surface. Dip in flour on both sides, then flatten with your hands. With the rolling pin, roll into a 6½-inch (16 cm) circle. Cook the first paratha while you roll out the next.

Preheat a *tava*, cast-iron skillet, or heavy nonstick skillet over medium-high heat. Once hot, place the first paratha in the skillet and cook until bubbles start to appear on the surface, about 1 minute. Flip and brush with ghee. Cook 1 minute more, then turn again. Cook for about 2 minutes this time, then flip again, at which point the paratha should be spotted with char in places, and look dry and opaque all over. Let the second side cook, then remove to a dry, lint-free kitchen towel. Scrunch the paratha from all directions, pushing toward the center from top to bottom, then from left to right, to accentuate the layers. Brush with more ghee, if desired. Stack and cover the parathas as they are cooked. Serve as soon as all are cooked.

Scallion Variation: Use toasted sesame oil instead of ghee and add 2 more green onions to the cilantro mix for a snack similar to Chinese scallion pancakes. Sprinkle with toasted sesame seeds before serving with a dash of tamari.

Za'atar Variation: Combine ½ cup (15 g) flat-leaf parsley leaves, ¼ cup (7 g) mint leaves, and 1 shallot, all chopped together, and use this mixture in place of the cilantro and chiles. Add 1 teaspoon za'atar or sumac to the dry ingredients and use olive oil instead of ghee. Serve with hummus (page 112).

MASALA PEANUTS

Masala, an Urdu word, refers to both the spice mixtures and to dishes that have been spiced. It is sort of the subcontinental equivalent of deviled. *Chaat masala* is a particular type, used to season snacks (chaat, page 87), and it usually includes cumin, coriander seed, ground chile powder, amchoor (green mango), asafetida (hing), ajowan (carom), and a slew of other spices. It's one spice mix I'm happy to buy at our local Asian grocery, or with increasing availability in the international aisle at chain supermarkets. (It is also available online.) Here, it flavors a super-speedy dish of roasted peanuts with onions, cilantro, fresh chile, and lime—ideal for last-minute entertaining. Your guests can bring the beer.

Makes a generous 3 cups (500 g)

3 cups (425 g) raw peanuts, skinned

1 red onion, finely diced

Small bunch of cilantro, leaves and tender stems, chopped

1 green chile, seeded and minced (optional)

1 teaspoon chaat masala, or an equal mix of ground cumin, chile powder (Kashmiri or cayenne), and ground coriander

½ teaspoon Kashmiri chile powder or smoked paprika

Flaky sea salt

1 lime

Set a wok or heavy skillet over medium-high heat. Add the peanuts and dry roast, turning often, until lightly browned, 3 to 5 minutes. Off the heat, toss the peanuts with the onion, cilantro, green chile, chaat masala, chile powder, and a few pinches of salt. Squeeze on the juice from half the lime, then toss again. Check for seasoning, then serve immediately, with the rest of the lime in wedges alongside.

PAKORA
(INDIAN VEGETABLE FRITTERS)

These battered vegetable fritters were one of the reasons that ours was the most popular house on our street for after-school snacks when I was in elementary school.

My grandmother and mother generally made our pakoras with onions or sliced potatoes and only sometimes with cauliflower. Us kids, meaning my brother and me, and usually a gaggle of friends, would watch in shuffling anticipation as Mum submerged vegetables into the chickpea flour slurry, then raised them back up, letting most of the coating fall away, before finally lowering them into bubbling oil. The mounds of batter and veg would dance around in the *karahi* (Indian wok), the batter puffing and sputtering as it fried. Once golden all over, the fritters were drained, then brought to the table for immediate, salivating consumption.

Most of the kids ate their pakoras with plain tomato ketchup. My brother and I liked to cut our ketchup with hot sauce, and my grandmother and mother went for green chutney, straight. In those few spots where the batter collected, those pakoras were soft and fluffy; where the batter was thin, they'd fracture and splinter.

Now I make pakoras with almost any and all vegetables I have around. Onions are still my favorite, but Asian eggplant is very good; the batter crunchily contains the velvet meltingness of the flesh within. Sturdy greens, such as kale and peppery mustard, are a revelation, because the coating is thin enough for the leaves to crisp through and through. Potatoes, sweet potatoes, Jerusalem artichokes, beets, carrots, and skinny green beans are all ones to consider, too.

.... *Serves 4* ....

Approximately 2½ pounds (a generous 1 kg) mixed vegetables, cleaned and trimmed

1 cup (85 g) chickpea flour (gram flour, also called *besan* in Indian specialty stores)

1 to 2 small fresh red chiles, seeded and minced, or 1 dried red chile, crushed

1 tablespoon minced fresh cilantro

½ teaspoon fine-grain sea salt, plus more as needed

Oil, for deep-frying (peanut, vegetable, or canola)

SERVING OPTIONS

Flaky sea salt

Lime wedges

Fresh Green Chutney (recipe follows)

Tomato ketchup

Hot sauce, such as Sriracha

Prepare the vegetables. For onions, peel and slice them into thin rings horizontally. Potatoes, sweet potatoes, eggplants, and Jerusalem artichokes should be kept unpeeled, cut into ¼-inch (6 mm) slices. Cut beets into ⅛-inch (3 mm) slices or into halves or quarters lengthwise, in which case, parboil the pieces until

. . . continued

Pakora (Indian Vegetable Fritters), continued

barely tender when poked with the tip of a knife, then drain and dry well. Carrots can be left whole if skinny, or cut on the diagonal into slices around ¼ inch (6 mm) thick if not. Break the cauliflower into florets and blanch. Green beans can be left whole. Break sturdy greens into individual leaves. Set all the vegetables aside while you make the batter.

In a bowl, stir together the flour, chiles, cilantro, and salt. Slowly stir in enough water to bring the mixture to the consistency of heavy cream. Beat the batter well, until it is lightened and foamy at the edges. Set aside.

Line a baking sheet with a double layer of paper towels, then set a cooling rack upside down on top (so its feet are in the air). In a heavy pot on the stove or in a deep-fryer, pour in enough oil to come about 5 inches (12.5 cm) up the side (or follow the manufacturer's instructions with a deep-fryer). Heat the oil to 350°F (175°C).

If using onions, separate the slices into individual rings and drop them into the prepared batter, stirring gently to coat. Using a fork, pick up a clump of onion rings and allow the excess batter to drip back into the bowl. Carefully lower the clump of onions into the oil and fry until lightly golden on one side, 30 to 40 seconds. Flip the fritter and cook until crisp on the other side, 20 to 30 seconds more. Remove from the oil and drain on the prepared cooling rack. Season with salt.

Repeat, frying a few at a time, until all the onions are used. For the remaining vegetables, dip each piece in the batter, then lift out the vegetable, shaking off excess. Carefully add the vegetables to the oil without crowding. Turn the fritters now and again to ensure even cooking. When the fritters are golden brown all over and cooked through, transfer them to the rack. Timing will depend on the vegetables used, with harder vegetables taking a few minutes. Continue frying, draining, and salting until all the vegetables and batter are used.

Enjoy immediately, or keep pakoras warm in a low oven until everything is ready. Serve with a squeeze of lime juice, with additional wedges available. Offer both the green chutney and a condiment of ketchup blended with hot sauce for dipping.

NOTE: You can tailor the chutney to your taste. Replace the apple with more cilantro, or a mix of cilantro and fresh mint leaves, for an intense chutney. Or, combine a bit of chutney into yogurt (page 264) for a cooling one.

Use this chutney in place of chermoula (page 122), to finish a steak (page 172), or to accompany roast chicken (page 162).

FRESH GREEN CHUTNEY

Makes about 1 cup (240 ml)

1 Granny Smith apple

2 teaspoons water

2 teaspoons peeled, grated fresh ginger

2 cloves garlic, peeled and left whole

2 green chiles

¼ teaspoon natural cane or light brown sugar

1 teaspoon medium-grain kosher salt, plus more as needed

2 big handfuls of fresh cilantro leaves and tender stems, about 1½ cups (90 g), loosely packed

1 to 2 limes

Core the apple and chop the flesh into small chunks, leaving the peel on. Toss into an upright blender with the water and process until the apple is liquefied. This may take a few minutes of running the machine, stopping and scraping down the sides of the carafe, then running it again. Stop the machine. Scrape down the sides of the blender and add the ginger and garlic. Puree until smooth. Chop the green chiles into chunks and add, with seeds if you like heat, to the blender along with the sugar and salt, then process again. Add the cilantro and the juice from 1 lime, and puree. Scrape down the sides of the carafe, process again, and taste for seasoning, adding more lime juice or salt as needed.

Use immediately or cover and chill overnight in the fridge, keeping in mind that as the chutney sits its flavor will mellow, and it will lose some of its color.

FLAT POTATOES

These potatoes started out as a side dish but evolved into a favorite pre-dinner snack, almost like a hot version of chips and dip, best served alongside cold beers and in the company of friends. By pressing the potatoes between two heated, heavy pans while they are cooking, they come out of the oven compact and outrageously crisp. Here you'll find the best aspects of American potato chips (thin and shattering) and British pub style-chips (fat fries with fluffy insides), all in one.

Dunk them into either salsa verde (page 269), or blue cheese dressing (page 268), or Harissa Aïoli (page 199). Or, for those times when you don't want much interfering with the starchy, crunchy pleasure of a crusty potato, add some minced garlic to the parsley before tossing.

For the most consistent results, try for potatoes that are all around the same size, preferably 2 to 3 inches (5 to 7.5 cm) long.

·· *Serves 4* ··

1½ pounds (680 g) fingerling potatoes, larger ones sliced lengthwise

1½ tablespoons melted clarified butter (page 259) or mild olive oil

Flaky sea salt and freshly cracked black pepper

A small bunch of flat-leaf parsley, chopped

Preheat an oven to 400°F (200°C), with one heavy, rimmed sheet pan on the rack in the middle position and another heating below.

In a large bowl, tumble the potatoes with the butter, salt, and pepper. Once the oven comes to temperature, let the pans continue to heat for 5 minutes more. Remove the pan on the middle rack and place the potatoes, cut side down, on that pan, arranging them with spaces in between. Return the pan to the hot oven and put the second pan on top of the first. (So they now sandwich the potatoes, as arranged on the middle rack.) Bake until the potatoes are deeply golden and absolutely crisp, 25 to 30 minutes. While hot, season again and toss with the parsley. Eat as soon as your fingers can handle them.

VIETNAMESE-INSPIRED SAUSAGE ROLLS

I often crave Vietnamese food; I think what I crave is its intensely salivating balance of succulent meats with enough salt and sharpness to save them from their own unctuousness. With inspiration from a traditional *banh mi*, this is a quick pork sausage, sweet with shallot and apple; seasoned with soy, chile sauce, fish sauce, cilantro, and basil; then parceled up in butter pastry. Once baked, the crackling layers of pastry contrast with the tender filling. Serenity and moxie in one bite.

.... *Makes 24 pieces* ....

2 tablespoons mild olive oil

3 shallots, minced

1 small apple, peeled, cored, and finely diced

3 cloves garlic, minced

¼ cup (15 g) packed cilantro leaves and tender stems, minced

¼ cup (15 g) packed basil leaves, preferably Thai, minced

1½ tablespoons sweet Thai chile sauce

2 teaspoons fish sauce

1 teaspoon soy sauce

1 teaspoon cornstarch

1 pound (455 g) ground pork, preferably not lean

1 pound (455 g) all-butter puff pastry, thawed per package instruction

Flour, for the work surface

Sriracha, gochujang (Korean hot pepper paste), or prepared hot mustard (Chinese or English)

1 egg yolk, beaten with 1 teaspoon water

Poppy or sesame seeds (white or black) or both, for garnish

TO SERVE

Nuoc cham (recipe follows)

Pickled jalapeños (page 271)

NOTE: If you don't want to make the nuoc cham, serve rolls with Sriracha-swirled (preferably Japanese) mayonnaise or gochuchang mixed with honey, or prepared hot mustard.

In a medium skillet, warm the olive oil over medium-low heat. Cook the shallots for 2 minutes, stirring, then add the apple and garlic. Continue to cook, stirring now and again, until the shallots are quite soft and the apple is tender, 8 minutes more. Scrape the mixture into a large bowl with the cilantro, basil, sweet chili sauce, fish sauce, soy sauce, and cornstarch. Stir with a fork and then set aside to cool completely. With clean hands, mix the ground pork into the cooled shallot and apple mixture. If possible, cover and refrigerate for a few hours to let the flavors get to know one another.

Preheat an oven to 400°F (200°C). Line a half sheet pan or rimmed baking sheet with parchment paper.

If not already portioned, divide the puff pastry in half. On a lightly floured work surface, roll one piece of the pastry to

... continued

Vietnamese-Inspired Sausage Rolls, continued

a square measuring about 10 by 10 inches (25 by 25 cm). Cut the square in half horizontally with a sharp knife or pizza wheel. Spread a thin smear of sriracha ¼ inch (6 mm) away from the long side closest to you, going all the way from end to end. Take a quarter of the pork and arrange in a sausage-like shape on top of the sriracha. Brush the near pastry edge with beaten yolk, then roll the pastry over to encase the meat tightly, pressing to seal with fingers or the tines of a fork. Trim to neaten the seam side, if desired. Place the roll on the prepared baking sheet. Repeat, using a third of the remaining meat for the other half of the rolled pastry, then continue with the second block of pastry and the remaining filling. Keep the egg wash for glazing later. Place the rolls in the freezer for 10 minutes to firm up, then move the rolls back to the work surface. Brush the rolls with the egg wash, slash decoratively (optional), sprinkle with sesame seeds, and cut each large roll into 6 portions. Arrange the pieces on the baking sheet with a bit of room in between.

Bake in the preheated oven until deep bronze and hot through and through, 25 minutes. Eat straight away, with nuoc cham. Serve the pickled jalapeños alongside.

NUOC CHAM

Makes about 1¼ cups (300 ml)

¾ cup (180 ml) water

¼ cup (50 g) natural cane or granulated sugar

Juice from 1 lime

3 tablespoons fish sauce

1 clove garlic, peeled and left whole

2 Thai bird chiles, stemmed and seeded

Mix the water, sugar, and lime juice in a small bowl. Taste, and adjust until the sweet and sour is balanced. Stir in the fish sauce and set aside.

In a mortar and pestle, crush the garlic and chiles into a paste. Scrape the paste into the lime mixture and stir well. Let stand for 20 minutes before serving, or store, covered and refrigerated, for up to 2 days.

SPICED CANDIED NUTS

These are quick to make and perfect for gifting, or for nibbling throughout the day (which is my tactic). With their distinctive combination of sweet, heat, and spice, these candied nuts satisfy as a snack and add more than just gilding to a scoop of vanilla ice cream. It will look as though there is too much glaze as the nuts go into the oven—don't fret. As they bake the syrup will thicken and gather around the nuts. By the time they're done, the pan will be almost dry.

.... *Makes about 1½ pounds (680 g)* ....

1 teaspoon fine-grain sea salt, plus more if needed

½ teaspoon ground cumin

½ teaspoon ground cinnamon

½ teaspoon ground ginger

¼ teaspoon cayenne or smoked paprika

1 pound (455 g) raw mixed nuts (such as almonds, pecans, hazelnuts, walnuts, or cashews)

1½ cups (300 g) granulated sugar

¼ cup (60 ml) water

1 spring of fresh rosemary, leaves only

NOTE: While the ingredients list specifies raw nuts, I've used roasted, salted ones in the past. If you use raw nuts, they are a bit sweeter in the end; if you use roasted salted nuts, they'll be more savory.

In a small bowl, stir ½ teaspoon of the salt with the cumin, cinnamon, ginger, and chile powder. Preheat an oven to 350°F (175°C). Line a standard rimmed baking sheet with parchment paper or a silicone liner. Spread the nuts out across the pan and roast until aromatic and lightly toasted, 5 to 7 minutes, stirring halfway through. Remove from the oven and set aside.

Meanwhile, in a large, heavy skillet, stir the sugar with the water and remaining ½ teaspoon salt. Bring the mixture to a boil over medium-high heat, without stirring (you can swirl the pan a bit to distribute the sugar, but do not stir or the syrup will crystalize). Continue to cook until the sugar turns a medium amber color. Working carefully and quickly, stir in half the spice mix and all of the nuts.

Tip the nuts back out onto the still-lined sheet pan and spread out as evenly as you can with a fork. Sprinkle with a bit more spice mixture. Bake for 15 to 20 minutes, stirring and flipping the nuts with a pair of forks every 5 minutes or so, to keep the nuts coated in the caramel and breaking up any large clumps, and sprinkle again with the spice mix. The last time you stir the nuts, add the rosemary and additional fine-grain sea salt, if desired. You'll know the nuts are done when the glaze looks thin and shiny (it will start out quite thick).

Allow the nuts to cool completely on the baking sheet, then break up any remaining large clusters. Store in an airtight container for up to 1 week.

TRAIL MIX SNACK BARS

These bars are my go-to for hikes, bike rides, and long trips in the car. They're even good on days when I don't know whether and when I'll stop for lunch. They are easily adaptable (keep dates as the base and change the other fruits and nuts), and I like to make these before the weekend, in a few varieties, then keep them in my freezer for when a need arises.

.... *Makes 9 bars* ....

1 cup (140 g) shelled, raw peanuts

¼ cup (30 g) hulled sunflower seeds

1 packed cup (150 g) plump, pitted dates

½ cup (about 65 g) dried blueberries, dried cranberries, dried cherries, or a mix

1 tablespoon coconut oil, melted

1 teaspoon vanilla extract or seeds scraped from ½ vanilla bean

¼ teaspoon fine-grain sea salt

1 teaspoon finely grated citrus zest

1 tablespoon mixed seeds (such as black and white sesame, hemp hearts, ground flaxseed, and ground chia)

NOTE: Depending on the capacity or strength of your processor, the nuts might need to be ground separately, then moved to a bowl. Then process the dates and dried berries, and either add the nuts back to the machine or combine the two in the bowl by hand.

If your dates are dry to the point of brittle, cover with water from a recently boiled kettle and let stand for 5 to 10 minutes, then drain well before using.

Line a 9 by 5-inch (23 by 13 cm) loaf pan with plastic wrap, laying one sheet of plastic across the length of the pan and one sheet across the width of the pan, so the two form a cross.

In a large, dry skillet over medium heat, lightly toast the peanuts, stirring often, until lightly golden and fragrant, 5 to 7 minutes. Add the sunflower seeds in the last minute of roasting. Transfer to a bowl to cool.

In a food processor fitted with the metal blade, coarsely grind the nut mixture. Add the dates, dried berries, coconut oil, vanilla, salt, and citrus zest and process until the dates are finely chopped and fully incorporated into the nuts, stopping and clearing the sides of the bowl regularly. If needed, drip in warm water, only until the mixture holds together. It shouldn't be overly sticky, just moist enough to compact into a bar. Pulse in the mixed seeds.

Press the mixture into an even layer in the prepared pan. Pull the excess plastic wrap up and over the layer, then press down again to compact and level the top. If possible, place a second loaf pan in the first, weighted with a can. Refrigerate until fairly firm, about 30 minutes, then cut into 9 short bars, each 1 inch (2.5 cm) wide. Wrap each in fresh plastic wrap or waxed paper, then keep in an airtight container at room temperature for up to 4 days, in the fridge for up to 2 weeks, or in the freezer for up to 2 months. (Frozen bars may need to be thawed before eating.)

CHAPTER 4

SUPPERS

When I was sixteen, my summer job was working the front of house for a theater company. When I was scheduled for both the matinee and the evening performances, I'd leave my house just after noon and come home close to 11:00 pm. In the middle of the shift was a dinner break. Depending on the plays slated for that particular day, the break could stretch as long as a few hours, but since the theater was in a different town from where most of us employees lived, we stayed there instead of heading home.

Some of my co-workers would bring their meals. There was one older girl who would ceremoniously pull an assortment of color-coded containers from her bag, like a magician. She'd open each of them, carefully laying it all out . She always remembered a napkin and would often have a book packed in there, too. She took her supper seriously, and to my eyes it seemed a very grown-up thing to do.

I usually bought my supper. The theater was in a tourist town, and the main street had lots to choose from. When the afternoons dragged, dinner plans were a great distraction. My friends and I would conspire over where we'd go and what we'd eat when we were finally off the clock. We'd get sandwiches from the guy at the deli who knew our orders by heart. We figured out that Wednesday had the best special at the diner farther down the road. After a difficult afternoon, we'd share some fries and gravy and call it a meal. I liked mine with gravy *and* ketchup, and my friends kindly allowed it.

Those meals were memorable because at the time we could not imagine anything finer to eat than what was right in front of us. This chapter aims for much the same effect, offering the resounding enjoyment of recipes such as salmon poached in olive oil and served over butter beans and leeks, sweet-hot fried chicken with a gloriously gnarly crust, and a pot of silky braised late-summer vegetables that manages to feel wholesome yet opulent, all at once.

A POT OF
BRAISED VEGETABLES

I live in a region called the Golden Horseshoe. On my branch of the crescent, Lake Ontario is to the north. The lake is broad and blue and, depending on where you stand, without end on the horizon. The Niagara escarpment, a rocky outcropping that carves a jagged, irregular zigzag across the map, is opposite. Then, to the east, there is the river.

The Niagara River flows between lakes Erie and Ontario, over its eponymous waterfalls and through a breath-stealing gorge, an expanse that seems so big, the space it contains feels solid.

Because of this unique geography, this area has a climate made for tender fruit, not just meaning soft fruit, but tender fruit in the official sense—peaches, cherries, pears, plums, and grapes. All around us are fields, orchards, and vineyards, with their imposed geometry of pattern and color on the landscape. Come September, the roadside farm stands are full to overflowing with fruit and vegetables—there's squash, potatoes, tomatoes, corn, beets, cabbage—and we often take Sunday drives, coffees in hand, to load up for the week.

This simple, succulent braise is extraordinarily amenable. On occasion I'll add breadcrumbs fried in olive oil to the herbs at the table; other days I'll forgo the thyme, oregano, and parsley, instead finishing with a dollop of basil pesto or Rustic Salsa Verde (page 269). Or I might scrap the parsley in favor of a small bunch of stemmed lacinato kale, cut into broad ribbons that get stirred through right at the end. Changed a little or as written, the recipe tastes like late summer and the earliest of autumn around here. Even more, it embodies the way I like to cook most—that is to say, in a way that lets the ingredients show off for themselves.

.... *Serves 4 to 6* ....

About 1 pound (455 g) zucchini or other summer squash

¼ cup (60 ml) extra-virgin olive oil, plus more to serve

12 ounces (340 g) fingerling potatoes, cut in halves or quarters lengthwise

2 shallots, sliced

Medium-grain kosher salt and freshly ground black pepper

1 clove garlic, minced

Generous pinch of crushed red pepper flakes

A few sprigs of oregano

A few sprigs of thyme (lemon thyme is ideal)

1 lemon

12 ounces (340 g) mixed tomatoes, stemmed and chopped

Small bunch of flat-leaf parsley, coarsely chopped

Handful of flaked almonds, toasted and then bashed in a mortar and pestle

Parmesan cheese, to serve

. . . continued

A Pot of Braised Vegetables, continued

Slice the zucchini in half lengthwise. If they are woody, scrape out the seeds; if tender, don't bother. Slice the flesh thinly. (If the zucchini is quite slender, I cut them into rounds without splitting first.)

Pop a kettle of water on to heat.

Warm the olive oil in a large, wide, high-sided pan or Dutch oven over medium heat. Tumble in the potatoes, trying to get the cut sides face down so they are in contact with the pan. Cook for around 5 minutes, shaking the pan now and again. Add the zucchini and shallots, then season with salt and pepper. Continue to cook until the vegetables start to become tender, 5 to 7 minutes, flipping and moving them around regularly. Stir in the garlic and crushed red pepper flakes. Pick the oregano and thyme leaves from their stems and add to the vegetables, along with a few gratings of lemon zest. Cook for a minute or so, then scrape in the tomatoes and any juice, and season again. Pour in enough water from the kettle to come three-quarters of the way up the sides of the vegetables, but not covering them. Bring to a boil, then turn the heat down and leave to simmer, stirring once or twice, until the potatoes are soft and the tomatoes have collapsed, 10 to 12 minutes. Check for seasoning.

Spritz with a squeeze of lemon, then sprinkle with more zest, parsley, almonds, and Parmesan cheese. Serve.

LEMON BUCATINI
WITH ROASTED KALE

This slurp-worthy meal can be done in just about 30 minutes, and the bulk of the time is spent waiting as things cook. The kale will mostly manage itself in the oven, as will the pasta in its pot. The sauce takes only moments; half a lemon, peel included, gets whirred in a blender with cream, olive oil, egg, and Parmesan. The last 5 minutes or so—during which time you toss the pasta with the sauce, tweak the seasoning, and perfect the texture, then plate with the kale—leave one with a sense of proficient efficiency. Job done.

Serves 4

Bunch of lacinato kale, tough stems removed

¼ cup (60 ml) extra-virgin olive oil, plus more for drizzling on the kale

Medium-grain kosher salt and freshly ground black pepper

1 pound (455 g) bucatini, linguine, or fettucine

½ lemon (see Note)

½ cup (120 ml) heavy cream

1 egg (see Note)

¾ cup (75 g) freshly grated Parmesan cheese, plus more to serve

NOTE: If there is any concern about the freshness or handling of your eggs, don't use one. The sauce will change in texture, but you can bulk it up with additional cheese and cream.

Since the whole lemon is used, thin-skinned varieties are best. In case one isn't available, cut both ends off a thick-skinned lemon with a small, sharp knife with a thin blade. Stand the lemon up on one end, then run the knife between the pith and the flesh, working your way around. Once the lemon is peeled, turn your attention to the peel itself. Lay the peel against the board, and with the blade parallel to the work surface, trim the pith away from the zest. Discard the pith and proceed with only the zest and flesh. (The interior membranes and seeds are fine.)

Preheat an oven to 350°F (175°C). Pile the kale onto one baking sheet and toss with a bit of olive oil, salt, and pepper. Toss until all the leaves are shining, adding more oil as needed. Spread the leaves out (grabbing a second baking sheet, if needed). Roast in the hot oven until the kale is crisp and starting to shrivel, around 25 minutes, turning regularly. Set the kale aside.

Meanwhile, fill a large pot with water and bring to a boil. Salt the water generously, and drop in the bucatini. Stir the noodles around until the pot comes back to bubbling, then cook for 2 minutes less than the pasta package's directions.

Cut the lemon into wedges and drop it into a blender, including the seeds, with the cream, ¼ cup olive oil, egg, and Parmesan. Set the blender to puree, scraping down the sides of the carafe once, then run the machine again, until the lemon cream is thick and fully emulsified.

Check the bucatini for doneness. It should be al dente, but not raw. If ready, drain, reserving 1 cup (240 ml) of the cooking water. Off the heat, dump the pasta back into the pan, along with ¼ cup (60 ml) of that reserved cooking liquid. Working quickly, pour most of the sauce onto the noodles and toss to combine. Keep turning the noodles into the sauce, adding more sauce and splashes of reserved cooking water as needed, until the sauce looks thickened and glossy, and coats the bucatini. Divide among 4 bowls. Top each with a crackling handful of kale and additional Parmesan, if desired.

SPECIALTY RESTAURANT LENTIL KOFTA CURRY

This curry is named after my father, or rather for a compliment he gave me. Once, when my mother was out of the country, I decided to give her *kofta* (meatball) curry a go, even though I'd not had it in years. My father came to dinner that night, and, after two helpings and a remarkably clean plate, he deemed my efforts not the same as my mother's, but still good enough to be served in a specialty restaurant—in other words, a restaurant that specializes in making one thing very well. It was high praise.

Since then, this curry, now made meatless, has become of my personal specialties, and one of which I'm particularly proud. It is profoundly aromatic, and fills the kitchen with an enticing fug of spice as it cooks. The lentil koftas are hearty while tender, the gravy robust without oppressive richness, and spiced without being spicy.

It is served with cachoombar, a fresh condiment, similar to pico de gallo, but with the addition of cucumber—the base for which can also be stirred into yogurt to make a cooling raita. For both, soaking the onion in lime juice helps tame some of its pungency.

.... *Serves 6 to 8* ....

KOFTAS

1½ cups (300 g) Puy lentils (French green lentils), well rinsed and picked over for stones

3 cups (710 ml) water

2 tablespoons milk

2 tablespoons plain yogurt, Greek-style or regular (page 264)

2 slices fresh white sandwich bread, crusts removed

½ cup (60 g) raw cashews

1 clove garlic, peeled and left whole

Handful of fresh cilantro, leaves and tender stems

Fine-grain sea salt and freshly ground black pepper

Neutral-tasting oil, for brushing

SAUCE

2 teaspoons cumin seeds

1 teaspoon coriander seeds

2 onions, sliced

3 cups (710 ml) water

8 cloves garlic, peeled and left whole

1-inch (2.5 cm) knob of ginger, peeled and chopped

Small bunch of cilantro, leaves and tender stems

Medium-grain kosher salt

2 tablespoons neutral-tasting oil

1 cinnamon stick, about 2½ inches (6.3 cm) long

1 teaspoon garam masala

½ teaspoon ground turmeric

4 green cardamom pods, cracked (see Note)

... continued

½ teaspoon Kashmiri chile powder or cayenne (optional, depending on the heat of the garam masala)

4 plum tomatoes, stemmed and chopped

TO SERVE

Chopped cilantro leaves

Lime wedges

Cachoombar or Tomato Raita (recipes follow)

To make the koftas, combine the lentils with the water in a heavy saucepan. Bring to a boil over medium-high heat, then lower the heat to maintain a simmer. Cook, stirring regularly, until the lentils are just tender, 20 to 25 minutes. Do not overcook; it is best to err on the side of chewy than falling apart.

While the lentils are cooking, whisk the milk and yogurt together in a bowl. Tear the bread into pieces and drop into the milk mixture. Set aside.

Preheat an oven to 400°F (200°C) and line a baking sheet with parchment paper. Brush the paper with a thin film of oil.

In the bowl of a food processor fitted with the metal blade, grind the cashews, garlic, and cilantro into small bits. Once the lentils are tender, drain, then add to the processor with the soaked bread, and any liquid left in its bowl. Pulse to make a coarse puree. Scrape down the sides of the processor, season lightly, then pulse again. Taste, and adjust the seasoning. If there is time, chill the lentil mixture in the fridge, covered, for up to 2 hours.

Roll the koftas, using about 2 tablespoons of the mixture to form each ball. Arrange the koftas on the prepared baking sheet as they are rolled. Once finished, brush each with a little oil, then bake in the hot oven until crusted and brown, 20 minutes.

While the koftas bake, make the sauce (many Indians will call this the gravy). In a large, heavy pan with a lid over medium heat, toast the cumin and coriander seeds until fragrant, around 1 minute. Transfer into a spice grinder or mortar and pestle and process into a powder. Back in the pan, dry roast the onions, stirring often, until the edges are brown and start to curl, 5 to 8 minutes. Add ½ cup (120 ml) of the water to the pan. Scrape the onions and liquid into a blender with the garlic, ginger, cilantro, and a couple generous pinches of salt, then puree.

Turn the heat under the pot to medium-low and heat the oil. Fry the onion paste until brown, 6 minutes or so, stirring all the while. Add the ground spices, cinnamon stick, garam masala, turmeric, cardamom pods, and chile powder and cook for about 1 minute. Stir the tomatoes into the sauce, smudging them across the bottom of the pan to deglaze and darken. Pour in the remaining 2½ cups (580 ml) water and stir well. Raise the heat and bring to a boil, then knock the heat back again to a simmer. Cook, uncovered, and stirring periodically, until the gravy is reduced, tastes cooked, and has split, with the fat separating from the solids, 30 minutes. Drop in the cooked koftas, shake the pan so they sink into the gravy, and turn off the heat. Pop on a lid and let stand for 5 minutes. Adjust the seasoning before bringing the whole pot to the table strewn with chopped cilantro. Serve on cooked basmati rice or with naan (page 124), with lime wedges, and cachoombar or raita.

CACHOOMBAR

Makes about 1 cup (240 ml) . . . .

1 small onion, peeled and diced

Juice from 1 lime, about 2 tablespoons

2 tomatoes, cored and diced

½ English cucumber, peeled or not, diced

1 green chile, minced (optional)

Handful of cilantro leaves

Fine-grain sea salt, as needed

In a medium bowl, stir together the onion and lime juice. Let stand while you get the rest of your ingredients prepped. After a few minutes, add the tomatoes, cucumber, and chile. Chop half of the cilantro and fold into the bowl. Season with salt. To serve, tear the remaining cilantro over the top.

TOMATO RAITA

Makes 2½ cups (580 ml) . . . .

1½ cups (355 ml) plain regular yogurt (page 264)

1 cup (240 ml) Cachoombar (above, before the last of the cilantro is torn over the top)

1½ teaspoons cumin seeds, toasted and ground

A generous pinch of Kashmiri chile powder or smoked paprika

A handful of fresh cilantro, leaves and tender stems, chopped

Stir the yogurt into the cachoombar. Check for seasoning, then finish with the cumin, chile powder, and extra cilantro.

EVERYDAY YELLOW DAL

I'd like to clear up any confusion. Dal is not a soup. In fact, there is a dish called dal soup, and it's different from the dal we're talking about here. Think of dal as similar in use to gravy—in other words, not a side dish or its own course. It is eaten on rice or with flatbreads, or with dry curries, and vegetables; it is meant as part of a meal.

It is the sentimental heart of the meal, even. There is a deep-soul comfort to be found in a bowl of cooked basmati rice, dal, minced sweet onion, salt, and an indecent amount of ghee.

For any dal, lentils must be washed first, thoroughly. This is of paramount importance; those times I've heard people say their dal tastes dusty or too markedly legume-ish, it is usually because the lentils weren't rinsed well enough.

The most common dal I make, the dal I grew up with, is made with split yellow lentils called *moong* (mung), which are actually green lentils with their outer husks removed. Moong is relatively quick cooking when compared to other dals, and even though some cooks use pressure cookers for theirs, it can be made without one.

Dal cooks by absorption, so watch the amount of water in the pot to make sure there is enough to keep things loose and moving (depending on the batch of lentils, the amount of water required for their cooking can vary wildly). As they boil, the lentils will puff up and go soft. I don't feel a need to puree dal by mechanical means; once it is cooked enough, it will become smooth on its own as the lentils lose their structure. Keep stirring in more hot water until it does. When cooked, the dal should be loose enough to drip and puddle from a spoon, never pasty. Again, add hot water, or let the dal thicken, until that descriptor holds true. Dal is tempered when it is finished cooking, which is called *tarka* as both the act of seasoning and the mixture used, usually a combination of spices fried in ghee or oil until bloomed and toasted. It can be a drawer's full of spices, or just one. That's up to you.

Class dismissed.

Serves 4 to 6

DAL

1 cup (225 g) moong dal
(split yellow lentils)

3 cups (710 ml) water

½ teaspoon ground turmeric

Medium-grain kosher salt

TARKA

2 tablespoons ghee or
unsalted butter

1 teaspoon cumin seeds

1 small onion, minced

1 or 2 fresh or dried
whole red chiles

. . . continued

Leaves picked from a small
bunch of cilantro

Fresh lime wedges

Everyday Yellow Dal, continued

To make the dal, in a medium heavy saucepan, cover the lentils with water. Swish the lentils around with your hand, then drain the water through a fine-mesh sieve. Return any lentils from the sieve to the saucepan and repeat, washing, agitating, and draining, until the water runs absolutely clear. It will probably take 7 to 10 changes of water. Pour the 3 cups (710 ml) of water into the pot to cover the lentils. Bring to a boil over medium-high heat, skim any scum that rises to the surface, then lower the heat to maintain a simmer. Add the turmeric and cook until the dal is quite creamy, 45 to 60 minutes. Stir the dal regularly as it simmers or it can catch at the bottom of the pan and burn. If the dal starts to look dry before the lentils are cooked, add hot water (from the tap is fine). Season well with salt.

About 20 minutes before the dal is done, make the tarka. Melt the ghee over low heat. Fry the cumin seeds for maybe 1 minute, until sizzling and fragrant. Add the onion and chile and cook, stirring, until the onion is very soft and translucent, 15 minutes. When the dal is ready, tip the tarka over the dal, stir to partially combine, then sprinkle the cilantro on top. Serve right away with lime wedges and naan (page 124) or over rice.

Tomato Tarka Variation: Melt 3 tablespoons ghee over low heat, then add ½ teaspoon cumin seeds and ½ teaspoon fennel seeds. Fry for 1 minute. Add 1 minced onion and 3 minced garlic cloves and cook for 10 minutes, stirring often. Scrape in 1 teaspoon grated ginger and cook to take away some of its rawness, about 1 minute. Stir in 2 small tomatoes that have been diced, 1 or 2 green chiles split lengthwise, and 2 curry leaves (optional). Fry until the tomato starts to break up, 5 to 7 minutes more. Stir most of the mixture into the cooked dal and let simmer for 5 minutes. Check for seasoning, then tip the remaining tarka over the dal. Garnish with chopped cilantro.

DOG IN A BOG

This is Toad in the Hole, the British classic of sausages baked in Yorkshire pudding, now named after a character in a book I read to my sons when they were small. The batter takes minutes to make, and can be made ahead, as it does best when it is left alone for a while. The sausages get less than 10 minutes of attention, then the batter goes on top of the meat, and all is put away in the oven. An accompaniment of maple-mustard sauce rather than the traditional, and more labor-intensive, onion gravy means that once the pan is in the oven, and the sauce is stirred, I'm free to get on with other things.

.... *Serves 4 to 6* ....

1 cup plus 2 tablespoons (140 g) all-purpose flour

1 teaspoon medium-grain kosher salt

½ teaspoon freshly ground black pepper

Several sprigs of thyme

4 eggs

¼ cup (60 ml) grainy mustard

1 cup (240 ml) milk, warmed

½ cup (120 ml) warm water

8 good-quality banger-style sausages or mild pork sausages

2 tablespoons neutral-tasting oil

¼ cup (60 ml) pure maple syrup

Combine the flour, salt, pepper, and the leaves picked from 2 or 3 thyme sprigs. Set aside.

In a large bowl or biggish pitcher with a pouring spout, beat the eggs until pale yellow and tripled in size. Whisk in 1 tablespoon of the mustard and ½ cup (120 ml) of the milk; add the flour mixture and stir until smooth. Briskly stir in the water and remaining ½ cup (120 ml) milk. Let the batter rest on the counter for at least 30 minutes, and up to 2 hours.

Preheat an oven to 425°F (220°C). In a 10-inch (25 cm) cast-iron or enameled skillet over medium heat, brown the sausages for 5 to 7 minutes, then pour in the oil, and place the skillet in the hot oven for 5 minutes.

Working quickly, remove the skillet from the oven, then place the pan back on the burner and pour the batter over the sausages. Drop in 3 or 4 whole thyme sprigs. Return the skillet to the oven, and bake, without opening the oven door, until the pudding is puffed and deeply golden, around 35 minutes.

In a small bowl, stir the remaining 3 tablespoons mustard into the maple syrup.

To serve, present the pan at the table, strewn with some fresh thyme leaves if you're in the mood for prettiness, and the maple-mustard sauce nearby. Feast.

CLAMS AND ORZO

This is a meal that goes well with improvisation. If you are in a luxe mood, add a splosh of Vermouth or some heavy cream at the finish. On lean days, the saffron and fennel can be shelved; use lager instead of wine, and add handfuls of chopped fresh parsley to the pot when the clams are ready. When the tomatoes are good, throw in some chopped ones with the shallots, in which case let the wine and liquid reduce to about half before adding the shellfish.

.... *Serves 4* ....

8 ounces (230 g) orzo

2 tablespoons mild olive oil

½ small fennel bulb, trimmed and finely diced, plus fronds for garnish

2 shallots, minced

1 clove garlic, minced

½ teaspoon piment d'espelette or crushed red pepper flakes

¼ cup (60 ml) dry white wine

Pinch of saffron threads (optional)

24 manila or littleneck clams, scrubbed

Fine-grain sea salt and freshly ground black pepper

Finely grated zest of 1 lemon

Extra-virgin olive oil or clarified butter (page 259), for drizzling

---

NOTE: The only thing to remember with clams, or any bivalves, is to toss away any ones that are open before cooking (give them a pinch to see if they will shut), then pitch any that remain closed after their steam.

Put a large pot of water on to boil over high heat. When bubbling fiercely, salt the water well, then cook the orzo according to package directions, trimming about 2 minutes off the instructed cooking time. When the pasta is tender but firm at the center, scoop out a mugful of cooking water, then drain the orzo and set aside.

While the pasta is still churning in its pot, get going on the clams. In a Dutch oven or a large, heavy pot with a tight-fitting lid, warm the oil over medium heat. Add the fennel and shallots and cook, stirring, until they start to become soft, about 2 minutes. Stir in the garlic and piment d'espelette and cook for 30 seconds more. Add the wine, which may sputter, along with the saffron. Bring to a boil, then decrease the heat to a simmer for 2 minutes.

Add the clams. Cover and cook, shaking the pan regularly to distribute the heat, until the clams open, 5 to 8 minutes, depending on their size. Discard any clams that do not open. Tip the orzo in with the clams. Use tongs to swirl the orzo through the broth for 1 minute, feeling free to splash in some of the starchy cooking water from the pasta as needed. Check for seasoning; the broth should be light but luscious. Divide among warm serving bowls. Sprinkle with the fennel fronds, finely grated lemon zest, and drops of extra-virgin olive oil. Eat right away.

SLOW-BAKED SALMON
AND BUTTER BEANS

This is a study in texture and restraint. Warmed gently, the fat in the salmon fillet melts slowly, basting the fish in a confit-meets-baked hybrid. The result is salmon that doesn't so much flake as much as it slides into pieces under a fork. The leeks and beans are a silken match to the fish, and the roasted skin adds another layer of texture.

·   Serves 4   ·

1 salmon fillet, about
2 pounds (1 kg), skin on
and preferably center cut

Medium-grain kosher salt and
freshly ground black pepper

1 lemon

¼ cup (60 ml) extra-virgin
olive oil

1 large clove garlic, peeled
and pressed with the side of
a knife but left whole

1 branch fresh rosemary,
maybe 6 inches (15 cm) long,
broken in half

4 leeks, cleaned, trimmed,
and with the white and light
green parts sliced into ¼-inch
(6 mm) rounds

¼ cup (60 ml) water

2 cups (400 g) cooked butter
beans or 1 (15-ounce/425 g)
can, drained and rinsed

⅓ cup (80 ml) crème fraîche

NOTE: Adding the rosemary back to the pan at the end gives a final hit of herbal steam. The twig, and the clove of garlic, can be removed before serving, if desired.

Preheat an oven to 300°F (150°C). Line a rimmed baking sheet with parchment paper.

Season the salmon on both sides with salt and pepper, then place on the baking sheet skin side down. Thinly slice half the lemon and arrange around the fish. Bake until the salmon is almost opaque in the center of its thickest part, 25 to 30 minutes.

Meanwhile, heat the olive oil, garlic, and rosemary in a large skillet over medium heat. When the rosemary begins to sizzle, remove it but reserve for later. Add the leeks to the pan, along with the water and a generous pinch of salt. Cook, stirring often, until the leeks are soft but still brightly green, 5 to 8 minutes. Tip in the beans, and continue to cook for 5 minutes more. Finely grate over a few scrapes of lemon zest, and add a squeeze of lemon juice. Stir gently. Check for seasoning.

Once the salmon is cooked through, remove from the oven and preheat a broiler to high. Plate the beans, then slip a thin spatula between the salmon flesh and skin, lift gently, and let the fish break naturally. Place pieces on top of the beans. After all the flesh has been removed, place the skin under the broiler, flipping once, until brown and sizzling, maybe 90 seconds. Crack the skin into large shards. Sprinkle the salmon and beans with the reserved rosemary sprigs and the crisp skin. Stir lemon juice and zest into the crème fraîche to taste, and serve alongside.

FUSS-FREE ROAST CHICKEN
WITH LEMON AND HERBS

This is the way I taught my eldest son to roast a chicken. It is an immensely forgiving and adaptable recipe, one that gave him a feeling of accomplishment and us an all-over bronzed bird, aromatic and tender, and a very good meal, too.

·· *Serves 4* ··

3½- to 4-pound (1.6 to 1.8 kg) chicken, giblets removed

A few tablespoons clarified butter (page 259) or olive oil

Medium-grain kosher salt and freshly cracked black pepper

1 small lemon, cut into 8 wedges

4 sprigs fresh thyme or rosemary, or a mix

2 cloves garlic, unpeeled but loose paper removed

NOTE: To expedite the cooking process, take the extra step of spatchcocking the chicken, or ask your butcher to do it for you. Using kitchen shears or a sharp knife, cut down either side of the backbone of the chicken and remove it. Flip the chicken to face breast side up, then press on the breastbone with the heel of your hand to flatten. Season the chicken on both sides with salt and pepper, then tuck into a skillet or roasting pan without a rack, skin side up, with the lemon cut in chunks and tossed around and thyme sprigs on top. Roast for 30 to 40 minutes, or until the juices run clear. Rest and carve as above.

If serving more than four or six at the table, opt for two smaller chickens rather than one large one. They will be easier to cook properly.

Bring the chicken to room temperature. Preheat an oven to 450°F (230°C).

Pat the chicken dry thoroughly, both inside and out. Rub the chicken on all sides with the clarified butter. Season the bird liberally with salt and pepper, inside and out. Pop a lemon wedge, 2 thyme sprigs, and the garlic cloves into the cavity. Tie the legs together with kitchen string and truss if so moved, or simply tuck the wing tips behind the back.

Select a pan that is barely larger than the chicken and, if you have one that will fit, place a baking rack inside. (This will allow hot air to get beneath the bird, and the lack of contact with the pan will allow the underside of the chicken to dry roast, rather than boil in its own juices.) Arrange the chicken, breast side up, atop the rack and strew the leaves picked from the remaining thyme in the pan.

Roast the chicken without basting, turning, or fiddling in any way, until the skin is well browned and the juices from the thickest part of the thigh run clear when pierced with a skewer, 50 to 60 minutes. To be certain of doneness, the chicken should have an internal temperature of 165°F (74°C) when checked at the innermost part of the thigh, avoiding bone. Let the chicken rest for 15 minutes before carving. Then serve with the reserved lemon wedges and any collected pan juices.

CHICKEN AND COUSCOUS WITH A PUNCHY RELISH

This is a mostly hands-off dinner that only needs a salad of assertive greens as accompaniment. The chicken gets a head start in the oven, but then finishes up by sharing its pan with the couscous. This way, the pasta laps up flavor from the meat, while getting crispy on top, and in turn, the steam coming up from the couscous keeps the chicken incredibly juicy. An intense slurry of anchovies, garlic, and lemon makes up most of the piquant dressing, with bursts of contrasting sweetness from the raisins.

You'll want a large baking pan that's not much deeper than 2 inches (5 cm). Pyrex and ceramic have the potential to crack when the liquids are added during roasting, so it's best to avoid them this time. The baking dish I use is enameled metal and is 15 inches (38 cm) long, 11½ inches (29 cm) wide, and with a depth of 1½ inches (3.8 cm), but a 13-inch (33 cm) paella pan would be fine. Keep in mind that if the pan is too deep, the sides of the chicken won't brown; if too small, there won't be a lovely crust on the couscous; if too large, the liquid will evaporate before everything is cooked. It's the Goldilocks of baked suppers, but when it's right, it's perfect.

Serves 4, generously

1 whole chicken, about 4 pounds (1.8 kg)

1 tablespoon butter, softened

Medium-grain kosher salt and freshly ground black pepper

1 lemon

Approximately 2½ cups (600 ml) chicken stock or water

4 cloves garlic, with loose paper removed but unpeeled

8 ounces (225 g) large pearl couscous (see Note)

¼ cup (60 ml) extra-virgin olive oil (it needn't be an expensive one but should taste good)

2 to 4 anchovy fillets, rinsed if salt-packed

Generous pinch of crushed red pepper flakes

1½ tablespoons capers, rinsed if packed in salt, drained if packed in brine

2 tablespoons golden raisins or dried currants

A couple of handfuls of flat-leaf parsley, chopped

Pickled caperberries, for garnish (optional)

Preheat an oven to 400°F (200°C) with a baking pan on the lower middle rack.

Pat the chicken dry with paper towels. Rub the butter all over the chicken, making sure to give the back a good coating. Season generously with salt and pepper, inside and out. Position the wing tips behind the back and tie the legs together. Place the chicken, breast side up, on the preheated pan. Roast for 30 minutes.

Meanwhile, stir the juice from ½ lemon into the stock in a small saucepan. Heat over medium-low heat until steaming, then pop in the garlic. Pull from the heat and keep in a warm spot.

. . . continued

Chicken and Couscous with a Punchy Relish, continued

NOTE: I've used a variety of grains instead of the couscous with success—rice blends, bulgur, farro, and all sorts of smaller pastas, from orzo to alphabet shaped, and a mix of all of the above, in an exercise of getting rid of the straggling amounts found in my pantry. Most will cook in the prescribed 30 minutes, but allow some leeway either way, adding heartier substitutions like farro to the pan earlier than you would the couscous, and adding more water as needed.

(I leave it on top of the hot stove, but with the burner off.) After 30 minutes are up for the chicken, pour 1 cup (240 ml) of the liquid into the baking pan, holding back the garlic, and roast for 30 minutes more.

Cut the juiced lemon half into wedges; keep the other half for the relish.

Pull the baking pan from the oven. Sprinkle the couscous around the chicken. Pour the remaining liquid onto the couscous and tuck in the lemon wedges and soaked garlic. Return the baking pan to the oven and continue to roast until both the chicken and the couscous are cooked through, around 30 minutes. If the liquid is absorbed before the couscous is cooked, add more liquid, ½ cup (120 ml) at a time, as needed.

Let the baking pan stand for 10 minutes while you make the relish. Squeeze the (now) roasted garlic into a small skillet. Add the oil and set the pan over medium heat. When the oil is hot, add the anchovies and red pepper flakes. Cook, stirring and breaking up the anchovies and garlic, until they've turned into a grungy paste, 2 to 3 minutes. Add the capers to the pan, and cook for 1 minute more. Stir in the juice from the second half of the lemon, along with the raisins and half of the parsley. Reduce the heat and simmer for 2 minutes, then check for seasoning. Remove the chicken to a board and carve as you'd like. Fluff the couscous with a fork, then arrange the cut chicken on top. Scatter the rest of the parsley over the whole baking pan of chicken and couscous, and serve with the relish.

BEE-STUNG
FRIED CHICKEN

This recipe delivers a cracking, splintering crust, a mix of spices that tickle the edge of the mouth, and succulent meat that's flavorful through and through. It finishes big, with nods to the traditions of Buffalo wings, Nashville hot chicken, and Korean-style fried chicken, by way of a finger-licking, lip-smacking chile butter that coats and catches on the crust, providing an extra hit of heat and sweetness. I'm mad for it, most ideally alongside a crisp green salad (page 185).

While it takes some time, the method for fried chicken isn't burdensome. It is particular, though. There's a dry rub first, then careful dredging and cooking. Mixing flour and cornstarch contributes to the crunch, while using diluted buttermilk slows the browning of the crust, to allow the meat the time it needs to cook, and baking powder helps keep the coating light. There is a glee in the making, and unmitigated joy in the eating. Batter up.

Makes 10 pieces

CHICKEN

1 tablespoon medium-grain kosher salt

2 teaspoons freshly ground black pepper

1 teaspoon smoked or sweet paprika

1 teaspoon dark brown sugar

6 sprigs thyme

2 bay leaves, broken in half

1 fryer chicken, about 3 pounds (1.4 kg), cut into 10 pieces

COATING

1 cup (130 g) all-purpose flour

½ cup (60 g) cornstarch

1 teaspoon smoked or sweet paprika

1 teaspoon medium-grain kosher salt

¾ teaspoon freshly ground black pepper

1½ cups (355 ml) buttermilk, well shaken (page 258)

⅓ cup (80 ml) water

2 teaspoons aluminum-free baking powder

4 cups (1 L) oil, for deep-frying (peanut works best, but vegetable is good)

HOT HONEY BUTTER

3 tablespoons unsalted butter

3 tablespoons honey

2 tablespoons gochujang (Korean hot pepper paste)

½ clove garlic, grated

1 teaspoon gochugaru (Korean ground red pepper powder), cayenne, or crushed red pepper flakes

To make the chicken, with a mortar and pestle, combine the salt, pepper, paprika, sugar, thyme, and bay leaves. Bruise the herbs into the spices, then mix around a bit. In a large bowl, season the chicken with the spiced salt. Refrigerate, covered, for at least 4 hours, and up to overnight.

About 1 hour before you want to begin frying, remove the chicken from the fridge. Set a rack over a rimmed baking sheet.

... continued

Bee-Stung Fried Chicken, continued

NOTE: In terms of double dipping and dredging, more coating sounds like a good idea, but unfortunately, that's not always the case. A thicker crust makes a more solid barrier between the chicken and the heat. That increased distance and the coating's ability to trap steam adds risk; though the exterior looks golden, you might find flabby skin beneath a wet underside of crust and pink spots at the bones. If you choose to double up, keep the layers light, and be sure to check the meat with a thermometer to confirm proper cooking.

While cooking, adjust the heat as needed to maintain the oil temperature around 335°F (170°C)—the initial oil temperature of 350°F (175°C) is to compensate for how much heat will be lost once the chicken hits the fat.

To make the coating, in a wide, shallow dish, stir together the flour, cornstarch, paprika, salt, and pepper. In a bowl, whisk the buttermilk, water, and baking powder together. Remove the thyme sprigs and bay leaves from the chicken.

Using tongs, or one hand for the wet work and one hand for dry, lightly dredge a piece of chicken in the seasoned flour, then dunk in the buttermilk mixture, letting any surplus drip away. Place the piece on the prepared rack, and continue until all pieces have been dipped. Starting with the first piece, coat the chicken again in the seasoned flour. Press and wiggle the chicken around in the dish, then shake off the excess dry mix. The aim is to build up a thin, wrinkled coating. Return the piece to the wire rack and do the same with the rest of the chicken. You can repeat the process and go for a double dip, but it makes for trickier frying (see Note).

Line a large plate with a few layers of paper towels. Preheat an oven to 200°F (100°C). Set another wire rack over a sheet pan and place in the warm oven. In an 8-quart (8 L) Dutch oven with a 12-inch (30.5 cm) diameter, bring the oil to 350°F (175°C) over medium heat. (Or use a deep fryer and follow the manufacturer's instructions.)

While the oil heats, make the honey butter. In a small saucepan set over low heat, warm the butter and honey, swirling to combine. Stir in the gochujang, garlic, and gochugaru. Set aside.

Starting with the legs and thighs, lower half the chicken pieces into the oil, skin side down. Cover and fry for 2 minutes. Open the lid and check for even browning, moving any pieces if needed. Fry for 4 minutes more, uncovered. Turn the chicken pieces over and cook, still uncovered, until the pieces are equally golden on the second side, 6 to 8 minutes longer. Transfer the chicken to the paper-lined plate, rolling the pieces on all sides against the paper to remove any oil. Let stand while you bring the oil back to temperature. Transfer the cooked chicken to the sheet pan in the warm oven and line the plate with clean paper towels. Fry the remaining chicken, drain, and transfer to the oven rack. Leave the chicken in the oven for 10 minutes, after which the chicken should be around 180°F (80°C) at the thickest part of the dark meat. Either toss the chicken with the hot honey butter or drizzle it over the chicken, then have at it.

ZA'ATAR CHICKEN AND ROASTED VEGETABLE SALAD

I appreciate this substantial chicken salad, not just for its taste, but for how it allows a looseness of interpretation. If there are no small beets or parsnips available, substitute a few larger of each, cutting the vegetables down to size. There's also no trouble in swapping in other vegetables that take well to roasting, such as pattypans, fennel, sweet potatoes, carrots, bell peppers, and eggplant. The dish can be made vegetarian by banishing the chicken and giving a similar treatment to slices of griddled halloumi instead, adding them at the same time as the honey.

.... *Serves 4 to 6* ....

CHICKEN AND VEGETABLES

1 tablespoon za'atar, or more as needed

¼ teaspoon ground cumin

1 teaspoon fine-grain sea salt, plus more as needed

½ teaspoon freshly cracked black pepper, plus more as needed

¼ cup (60 ml) mild olive oil

1 small winter squash, such as acorn, seeded and cut into skinny wedges

8 small beets, preferably golden, peeled and quartered

4 baby turnips, scrubbed and cut into quarters

2 parsnips, peeled and cut into chunks

1 red onion

6 chicken thighs, with skin and bone, about 2¼ pounds (1 kg), or 1 small chicken, cut into 8 pieces

Small bunch of thyme

1 tablespoon honey

2 tablespoons white wine vinegar

TO SERVE

About 6 ounces (170 g) salad greens

Extra-virgin olive oil

Flaky sea salt and freshly ground black pepper

½ lemon

¾ cup (180 ml) hummus (page 112), plus more as needed

Chopped roasted almonds or toasted pine nuts

Nubs of honeycomb (optional)

Preheat an oven to 425°F (220°C).

To make the chicken and vegetables, in small bowl, stir together the za'atar, cumin, salt, and pepper.

Pour a thin film of olive oil onto a half sheet pan or a similarly sized shallow roasting pan, then tumble in the squash, beets, turnips, and parsnips. Cut the onion in half through its core, then cut each half into quarters, discarding the papery skin but leaving the pieces attached at the base. Add the onion pieces to the sheet pan. Nudge the chicken pieces into the pan among the vegetables, skin down so the pieces are slicked with oil, then turn right side up. Drizzle the remaining olive oil over all, then dust with half of the za'atar mixture. Give the pan a bit of a

NOTE: The zest and juice of ½ orange makes a fragrant replacement for the vinegar, in which case grate the zest directly over the pan, followed by the juice.

Herbed Yogurt (page 78) is a fine swap for the hummus; its bracing freshness gets on famously with the za'atar and the caramelized vegetables.

shake, sprinkle on the rest of the seasoning, paying particular attention to the chicken. Strew the thyme over the pan, then tuck everything into the hot oven and bake for 50 minutes.

Pull the pan from the oven and anoint the sizzling chicken and vegetables with the honey, letting it trail in a thin, gleaming stream from a spoon held at a height. Spritz on the vinegar by flicking it from the honey spoon. Put the pan back in the oven and bake for 10 minutes more.

To serve, dress the salad greens with a sheen of olive oil, salt and pepper, and a squeeze of lemon juice. Thin the hummus with some warm water to the consistency of barely whipped cream, then spread some on each plate, so it's an uneven base for the salad. Perch the chicken and vegetables on the hummus, and dress with the pan juices, salt, and pepper for good measure. Garnish with the nuts and honeycomb. Eat with a mound of greens on the side.

FIVE-SPICE STEAK

This might smoke up the kitchen, but it is worth it. The five-spice powder is fused to the steak with the blistering heat of the pan, making for a raspy, sizzling crust. It is finished with a quick, flavorsome sauce of herbs, chiles, and rice vinegar, rounded out by toasted sesame oil. The anointing works like a late-addition marinade, not only dressing the meat but also seeming to keep it incredibly soft and tender.

Serves 4 to 6

1 bone-in rib steak,
2 inches (5 cm) thick,
weighing approximately
1½ pounds (680 g)

1½ teaspoons Chinese
five-spice powder

1 teaspoon medium-grain
kosher salt

½ teaspoon freshly
cracked black pepper

2 teaspoons toasted
sesame oil

1 clove garlic, minced

1-inch (2.5 cm) piece
of fresh ginger, peeled
and minced

1 small red chile, stemmed,
seeded, and minced

1 tablespoon unseasoned
rice vinegar

2 teaspoons tamari

1 teaspoon natural cane
or light brown sugar

3 green onions, white and
light green parts only, minced

2 large handfuls of
cilantro, leaves and
tender stems, chopped

Season the steak all over with the five-spice powder, salt, and pepper. Dab on the sesame oil with a brush.

Place a large cast-iron pan over medium-high heat. Once the pan is good and hot, lay in the steak. Let it cook, undisturbed, for 2 to 3 minutes, then check for even color and move the steak around if necessary. Keep shuffling until well browned, 2 to 3 minutes more. Flip the steak, and continue to cook until the second side is equally charred and cooked to your liking. (An instant-read thermometer inserted in the thickest part, without touching bone, should read 120°F [50°C] for medium-rare, and will take approximately 3 to 5 minutes after flipping to the second side.) Set the steak aside and reduce the heat to medium-low.

Add the garlic, ginger, and chile to the skillet and cook, stirring, for 1 minute. Stir together the rice vinegar, tamari, and sugar, then pour it into the pan, scraping up any browned bits and allowing the liquids to reduce, about 1 minute. Scrape the sauce into a small bowl with half the green onions and half the cilantro.

Present the steak whole at the table, or slice across the grain and arrange on a platter. With either, pour some of the sauce over the meat and shower with the reserved green onion and cilantro. Offer the rest of the sauce alongside.

BRAISED BEEF
WITH GREMOLATA

This pot of scorched mahogany chunks in a glossy gravy resides comfortably in between the strict definitions of a stew and a braise, and borrows equally from boeuf bourguignonne and osso buco. It makes for a welcome supper when autumn's chilled evenings arrive. For weekend ease, I usually braise the meat on Saturday, let it cool, covered, and refrigerate it overnight. Then on Sunday I skim and strain the sauce, add the second measure of vegetables, and then leave the pot to calmly bubble and blip, until everything is graciously tender.

.... *Serves for 4 to 6* ....

BRAISE

5 sprigs fresh thyme

Small bunch of flat-leaf parsley

2 small strips orange zest

1 bay leaf

1 cinnamon stick, about 2 inches (5 cm) long

10 peppercorns

4 cloves

4 thick slices bacon, chopped

½ cup (65 g) all-purpose flour

Medium-grain kosher salt and freshly ground black pepper

3 pounds (around 1.4 kg) boneless short ribs or blade or chuck roast, cut into 2-inch (5 cm) cubes

2 large onions, chopped

2 carrots, scrubbed and cut into 2-inch (5 cm) pieces

2 celery stalks, cut into 2-inch (5 cm) pieces

4 cloves garlic, peeled and pressed with the side of a knife, but kept whole

1 tablespoon tomato paste

3 cups (710 ml) dry red wine, such as a Burgundy or Côtes du Rhône

About 3 cups (710 ml) good-quality beef stock

VEGETABLES

4 medium carrots, peeled and cut into chunks

8 ounces (225 g) pearl onions or shallots, blanched and peeled

1 ounce (30 g) dried porcini mushrooms

1 tablespoon butter

8 ounces (225 g) cremini mushrooms, trimmed and cut into halves if small, quarters if large

GREMOLATA

2 cloves garlic, minced

2 tablespoons finely grated lemon zest

Small bunch of flat-leaf parsley, leaves and tender stems, minced

To make the braise. preheat an oven to 325°F (165°C). Tie the thyme and parsley together with kitchen twine. Using a small piece of cheesecloth or a self-fill tea bag, make a bundle of the orange zest, bay leaf, cinnamon stick, peppercorns, and cloves, securing with twine if needed.

In a large, wide, heavy ovenproof pot or Dutch oven over medium heat, cook the bacon, stirring, until almost crisp, 5 to 8 minutes. Remove to a plate. Pour the drippings into a cup,

... **continued**

Braised Beef with Gremolata, continued

NOTE: Ask the butcher for some stewing bones, if possible, to add body and depth to the sauce. Add them with the stock, then remove with the first batch of vegetables, by which point they'll have done their work.

For a more refined dish, strain the braise before adding the second batch of vegetables. Return the meat and liquid back to the pot, along with the fresh carrots, onions and porcini, discarding the original aromatics.

then strain 6 tablespoons back into the pot. Raise the heat to medium-high (the fat should be hot but not smoking).

In a bowl, whisk together the flour, 2 teaspoons salt, and 1 teaspoon pepper. Dredge the beef in the seasoned flour, shaking off any excess. Working in batches without crowding the pan, brown the meat on all sides, 5 minutes or so per batch. Transfer the browned pieces to a large bowl, then continue with the rest of the meat.

Reduce the heat to medium-low. Add the onions, carrots, celery, and garlic to the pot, stirring to coat the vegetables with fat and scraping up any bits stuck to the bottom of the pan. Season lightly with salt and pepper. Sauté until the vegetables are soft and brown, around 10 minutes. Stir in the tomato paste, and cook for another minute. Pour in the wine and bring to a boil. Reduce the liquid by about half, then return the browned meat to the pot along with any accumulated juices and the stock. The liquid should almost cover the meat, but not quite. Pop in the tied herbs and cheesecloth bundle. Bring to a gentle simmer. Cover the pot and place in the preheated oven, and bake until the meat is tender, around 2 hours.

To make the vegetables, uncover the pot, and remove the tied herbs and cheesecloth. Skim any fat from the surface of the braising liquid. Stir in the carrots, pearl onions, and porcini. Return the stew to the oven, partially covered; simmer until the vegetables are soft but not mushy, about 40 minutes.

Meanwhile, melt the butter in a skillet over medium heat. Sauté the cremini mushrooms in the butter until golden brown, 5 to 8 minutes. Stir the mushrooms into the stew, and check for seasoning. In the warm skillet used for the mushrooms, crisp the reserved bacon.

To make the gremolata, combine the garlic, lemon zest, and parsley in a small bowl.

To serve, garnish the stew with the bacon and a sprinkling of gremolata, passing the rest alongside.

MOUSSAKA

My father didn't often cook when I was growing up, so when he did, those times stand out in my memory. I couldn't have been more than ten years old when he made moussaka, the Greek casserole of lamb and eggplant. The word felt exotic in my mouth, *moo-ssaa-KA*, when I said it like my father did, with emphasis at the end. And it looked exotic, too, with its patchwork of vegetables blanketed with an ochre béchamel, the spicy scent of the meat wafting up from further underneath. It was like the shepherd's pie I knew, but far, far more interesting. I remember it tasting familiar, with cinnamon, ground coriander, and clove reminding me of Indian cooking, but then there were other spices, and in proportions that made the flavor more enigmatic.

When I first made this moussaka for my family, my sons were quite young; at the time, they were not fans of fried eggplant. I roasted it instead, in the hope that it would thus sneak past them. The moussaka went down a treat. The method also trimmed an admittedly lengthy procedure and cut out some not-at-all-missed mess and oil. It's what I've stuck with since.

.... *Serves 8 to 10* ....

FILLING

¼ cup (60 ml) mild olive oil

2 medium globe eggplants, sliced lengthwise ¼ inch (6 mm) thick

Medium-grain kosher salt and freshly ground black pepper

1 pound (455 g) ground beef

1 pound (455 g) ground lamb

1 large onion, diced

2 large cloves garlic, minced

1½ tablespoons red wine vinegar

1 teaspoon ground cinnamon

½ teaspoon ground allspice

60 or so gratings of fresh nutmeg, or about ¼ teaspoon ground

¼ teaspoon ground coriander

⅛ teaspoon ground cloves

Leaved picked from 4 sprigs thyme

1 teaspoon dried oregano

2 teaspoons tomato paste

1½ cups (355 ml) crushed tomatoes

½ cup (120 ml) water

Small bunch of flat-leaf parsley, leaves and tender stems, chopped

BÉCHAMEL

3 cups (710 ml) milk

¼ cup (60 g) unsalted butter

¼ cup (30 g) all-purpose flour

½ cup (50 g) grated kefalotyri or Pecorino Romano cheese

60 or so gratings of fresh nutmeg, or ¼ teaspoon ground

Medium-grain kosher salt and freshly ground black pepper

2 eggs, lightly beaten

To make the filling, preheat an oven to 350°F (175°C). Grease 2 baking sheets with a thin coating of oil. Lay the eggplant on the prepared baking sheets, then brush lightly with more olive oil. Season the slices with salt and pepper, then bake until the eggplant is golden and pliable, about 30 minutes. Set them aside, but leave the oven on.

. . . **continued**

Moussaka, continued

In a 6-quart (6 L) Dutch oven or heavy pot with a lid, heat 2 tablespoons of the olive oil over medium-high heat. Add the ground meats to the pan and cook, breaking them up with a spoon, until well browned and quite dry, 10 to 12 minutes. Add the onion and cook, stirring, until the onion is translucent, about 5 minutes more. Stir in the garlic and cook for 1 minute. Splash in the red wine vinegar and turn the heat down to medium. Scrape up any bits stuck at the bottom of the pan and cook until most of the vinegar has evaporated. Chop a third of the eggplant slices into a coarse paste and scrape into the meat mixture. Stir in the cinnamon, allspice, nutmeg, coriander, cloves, thyme, and oregano and cook until fragrant, around 30 seconds. Season with salt and pepper. Make a bit of space at the bottom of the pan and add the tomato paste, smearing and scraping the paste across the hot surface so it cooks and darkens, 1 to 2 minutes. Incorporate the paste into the meat mixture, along with the crushed tomatoes and the water. Bring to a boil, then cover and reduce the heat to a simmer. Let it bubble away, stirring now and again, until the béchamel is ready.

To make the béchamel, gently heat the milk in a glass measuring cup in the microwave, or in a pot on the stove. Either way, it should be just under boiling. Melt the butter in a heavy-bottomed saucepan over medium heat. When fully liquid, whisk in the flour and cook, stirring constantly, for 2 to 3 minutes. Slowly pour in the hot milk, whisking all the while. Continue to cook, stirring, until the mixture comes to a boil and thickens. Stir in the cheese and nutmeg, then taste and season with salt and pepper. Set the béchamel aside for a few minutes.

Check the meat for seasoning; it may need a surprising amount. Stir in the chopped parsley. Now assemble the moussaka directly in the Dutch oven, or spoon the meat into a 9 by 13-inch (23 by 33 cm) baking dish. Lay the roasted eggplant slices in overlapping rows on top of the meat mixture.

Temper the eggs by stirring in some of the warm béchamel, then stir the egg mixture back into the rest of the sauce. Pour this over the meat and eggplant. Bake until the edges are bubbling and the top is well browned, 40 to 45 minutes. Let the moussaka stand for 15 minutes, then serve with simply dressed greens or, preferably, Roasted Red Pepper, Almond, and Feta Salad (page 186).

CHAPTER
5

VEGETABLES & SIDES

When it comes to holiday meals, my family (extended and immediate) is entrenched in a magnificent rut in terms of main dishes. At Thanksgiving, the feast must include a high-heat roasted turkey with apple cider gravy. On Christmas Eve, there will be a braise, preferably short ribs and gremolata, if you please. At Easter there has to be a ham, lacquered with maple and slightly scorched at the edge so the cracklings fracture in the mouth.

I adore every bite of delicious repetition. And so, on those festive occasions, what has me scrolling through websites, dog-earing cookbooks, and trolling the magazine aisle isn't a new way to truss that turkey, but rather the search for brilliant ways to pretty up our vegetables. Side dishes can be the jewels of a dinner, a chance to experiment, to set off those tried-and-true dishes, and to introduce texture and contrast.

It's easy enough to fall back on steamed vegetables with butter, and there is something to say for a really simple platter of tomatoes with olive oil and salt, but when we push that little bit further and grant them a bit of time, a bit of love, side dishes can take a meal from simple to spectacular. This chapter is full of such inspiration, whether it is a holiday or not.

A REFRESHING SALAD WITH CHARRED GREEN ONION DRESSING

If salads had families, meet coleslaw's cousin. Like its kin, this is a salad for barbecues. It makes sense, really, that against the big flavors of smoke, fat, and spice, we need some crunch to enliven the palate. The salad is best because of its combinations. There is a balance of the different sorts of crispness between the supple celery and the assertive radish, while the apple falls between the two. Slice everything, save the lettuces and sprouts, as thinly as you can muster. Shaved wafer thin is where I'd aim, because the textures and flavors seem at their best as such, with it all coming across as ravishingly invigorating. It is wet, but not sopping, and that sounds funny, I know.

Serves 4 to 6

CHARRED GREEN ONION DRESSING

6 green onions

2 serrano or jalapeño chiles

Generous pinch of smoked paprika

½ cup (120 ml) plain Greek-style yogurt, not nonfat

2 tablespoons mayonnaise (page 265)

Small bunch of cilantro, leaves and tender stems

Zest and juice of 1 lime

1 tablespoon agave nectar or honey

⅓ cup (80 ml) extra-virgin olive oil

Fine-grain sea salt and freshly ground black pepper

SALAD

4 heads little gem lettuce or 2 heads Boston lettuce

1 crunchy apple, stemmed, cored, and thinly sliced

1 stalk celery, thinly sliced on the bias

4 baby daikon radishes, sliced as thinly as possible, or a 2-inch (5 cm) piece cut from a larger one

A few handfuls of sprouts (try to include some radish sprouts, or similarly peppery ones)

To make the dressing, heat a large, cast-iron skillet or grill pan over medium-high heat. Cook the green onions and chiles, turning often, until charred all over, 8 to 10 minutes. Let the vegetables cool on a plate, then trim the roots off the onions, as well as any leathery parts of the green end. Stem the chiles and remove the seeds, if desired.

Buzz the green onions, chiles, paprika, yogurt, mayonnaise, cilantro, lime zest, lime juice, agave, and oil in a blender until smooth. Taste, and season with salt and pepper as needed, then cover and chill for at least an hour, to let the flavor develop.

To assemble the salad, break the lettuce leaves off their cores and tear into coarse pieces onto a large serving plate. Arrange the apple, celery, radishes, and sprouts on top of the leaves, and drizzle the dressing over. There will most likely be some dressing left over; cover and keep it in the fridge for up to 3 days.

ROASTED RED PEPPER, ALMOND, AND FETA SALAD

This is not a tossed salad, but rather a composed one. It began its life as an starter with bread, but then became my can't-have-one-without-the-other partner to moussaka (page 177)—the feta and parsley topping is a briny, sprightly combination that balances the richness of that casserole, the lemon juice kicks everything into high gear, and the tender, sweet peppers balance the spice. Still, this salad stands quite nicely beside other roasted and grilled meats, or does quite well on its own.

Feel free to char and peel peppers instead of using jarred, aiming for about 2 peppers per person. This may sound like a lot of peppers, but people seem to always ask for seconds, often thirds, and I prefer to have the provisions to oblige.

Serves 4 to 6

12 ounces (340 g) Greek feta cheese, preferably goat's milk

½ cup (30 g) fresh flat-leaf parsley leaves, coarsely chopped

2 cups (475 ml) jarred whole roasted peppers, preferably piquillo

4 ounces (115 g) blanched almonds (Marconas are nice)

Juice of ½ lemon

Extra-virgin olive oil, for drizzling

Crumble the feta into a small bowl, then stir in the chopped parsley. Tear the roasted peppers into wide strips and arrange on a platter. Sprinkle the almonds over the peppers, followed by the herb-flecked feta. Squeeze the lemon juice over the peppers and drizzle on some really nice olive oil. Serve immediately.

BRUSSELS SPROUT
AND HAZELNUT SALAD

There's no getting around it—separating the individual leaves off of a pile brussels sprouts is fiddly business. That said, the results merit the task; blanched until brightly green and tender, the sprouts are a far cry from the pallid cabbagey-ness often associated with those boiled whole.

Toasted hazelnuts grant a welcome richness; if you happen to have hazelnut oil on hand, use that to replace the olive oil in the dressing.

Serves 4 to 6

1 pound (455 g) brussels sprouts

Medium-grain kosher salt

2 tablespoons whole unpeeled hazelnuts

2 teaspoons extra-virgin olive oil

½ lemon

Flaky sea salt and freshly cracked black pepper

To remove leaves from the brussels sprouts, use a small, sharp knife to trim off the very bottom of the end. The outer leaves should easily come off. Once those are removed, trim again, and remove the next few layers of leaves. Continue, until you are left with the tightly bound center of the sprout; save these for roasting whole another day. You should have a generous 4 cups (280 g) of leaves when all the sprouts have been prepped and stripped.

Bring a large pot of water to a boil, then salt it well. Prepare an ice bath in a large bowl and keep nearby. Blanch the brussels sprout leaves until bright green and tender, 45 to 60 seconds. Using a spider skimmer or slotted spoon, lift the sprouts out of the water and immediately plunge them into the ice bath and leave for at least 5 minutes, to set their color and crunch.

Line a large sheet pan with paper towels. Drain the brussels sprout leaves in a colander, then spread them across the paper towels to dry.

In a small pan over medium heat, toast the hazelnuts until lightly toasted and fragrant. Transfer the nuts to a mortar and pestle and bash to an uneven rubble (alternatively, use a small food processor).

When ready to eat, place the sprout leaves in a large serving bowl or platter. Dress with the olive oil, a few drops of lemon juice, and salt and pepper. Toss to coat, then adjust the seasoning as needed. Garnish with the hazelnuts and serve.

OLIVE AND
ORANGE CAULIFLOWER

I first called this cauliflower rice, but I think it is better served without the comparison to something it is not. It is, instead, a vegetable pilaf of sorts, with the spirit of a salad. The flavors bounce around: the cauliflower mild, bosky, and tasting as a brassica should; briny olives; vinegar for an even higher, clearer astringency; honeyed apricots; and feta's particular blend of fat and salt. It is a dish that is hard to pin down, but strict definitions aren't what's important here.

By the way, if I have some around, I'll use the juice from preserved lemons instead of the vinegar, and add some sliced rind to the mix.

.... *Serves 4 to 6* ....

1 head cauliflower,
cut into florets

⅓ cup (60 g) olives of any
type, pitted and chopped

Fine-grain sea salt and
freshly ground black pepper

2 tablespoons white
wine vinegar

1 shallot, thinly sliced

¼ cup (60 ml) extra-virgin
olive oil

2 oranges

½ cup (60 g) crumbled
feta cheese

¼ cup (65 g) diced dried
apricots (about 10 halves)

½ cup (45 g) sliced
almonds, toasted

Small bunch of chervil
or flat-leaf parsley

A few handfuls of
baby arugula

Working in batches, unceremoniously dump the cauliflower into the bowl of a food processor fitted with the metal blade. Pulse the motor until the florets have been reduced to the size of rice, then tip it all into a microwavable bowl. Cover and cook on high until tender, carefully stirring once with a fork, 5 to 7 minutes. Fold in the olives, then season lightly with salt and pepper.

In a small bowl, pour the vinegar over the shallot. Sprinkle with salt and let sit for a few minutes. Stir in the olive oil, then check for seasoning—remember both the olives and the feta will boost the salt level when everything meets up in the bowl. Slice the top and bottom off one orange so that the flesh is exposed and the orange stands up on a cutting board. Use a knife to remove the peel and pith, working from top to bottom. Cut the orange into thin rings, then fold into the dressing. Repeat with the second orange.

Hold back the oranges and pour most of the dressing onto the cauliflower. Fluff with a fork, then turn the cauliflower out onto a serving dish. Scatter on the orange slices, most of the feta, apricots, almonds, parsley, and arugula, and fork through to mix. Sprinkle on whatever remains and serve.

BROCCOLI RABE
WITH BAGNA CAUDA

This is not a subtle plate of vegetables. The assertive flavor of broccoli rabe is teamed up with an equally assertive dressing based on bagna cauda—a murky, lusty mix of anchovy, garlic, olive oil, and butter. Don't let my description of that Piedmontese classic confuse the message of that sauce, or this combination. The pairing of bold and bold is sometimes precisely what is needed. Sometimes you need to have the volume turned up.

··· *Serves 4* ···

1 pound (455 g) broccoli
rabe, trimmed of tough stems

1 tablespoon extra-virgin olive
oil, plus more for drizzling

Fine-grain sea salt and
freshly cracked black pepper

1 or 2 anchovy fillets, chopped

2 cloves garlic, minced

2 tablespoons unsalted
butter, cold

Preheat an oven to 500°F (260°C).

On a heavy, rimmed baking sheet, toss the broccoli rabe with just enough drizzled oil to get it shining. Season with salt and pepper. Roast in the hot oven until tender and with some singed edges, 7 to 10 minutes, turning once.

While the broccoli rabe is in the oven, warm the 1 tablespoon olive oil, anchovies, and garlic in a small saucepan over low heat. Keep stirring until the anchovies have melted into an aromatic sludge. Whisk in 1 tablespoon of the butter; once that is melted, beat in the remaining 1 tablespoon.

Transfer the broccoli rabe to a serving platter as soon as it is ready. Spoon on some of the dressing, and pass the remainder at the table.

SOUSED TOMATOES

Here is an absolutely beautiful way to treat tomatoes. The slow roasting intensifies their flavor and firms up their texture, and once submerged in chile-dyed, vinegar-zipped, herb-flecked oil, things get even better. Use them as an antipasti, squished onto bread or flatbread; serve as a salad with arugula and lots of Parmesan; or offer beside something that benefits from a contrasting sharpness—grilled and roasted meats or moussaka (page 177). The oil left once the tomatoes are gone can be the start of a vinaigrette, mayonnaise, or marinade, or used as a finishing oil.

·················· *Makes about 3 cups (360 ml) tomatoes, plus flavored oil* ··················

3½ pounds (1.5 kg) medium to large tomatoes, all approximately the same size (see Note)

¾ cup (180 ml) extra-virgin olive oil (one that tastes good on its own)

Fine-grain sea salt and freshly ground black pepper

4 cloves garlic, papery peels removed but left mostly unpeeled and whole

10 sprigs of thyme

5 sprigs of rosemary

1½ teaspoons fresh marjoram or oregano leaves

2 teaspoons minced fresh chives

1 to 2 teaspoons Aleppo pepper, piment d'espelette, sweet or smoked paprika, or a mix

A few splashes of red wine vinegar

NOTE: Tomatoes with a higher ratio of flesh to seed are less likely to collapse upon cooking; Beefsteak, Roma, or paste tomatoes are all excellent for roasting, but Campari and standard vine tomatoes are absolutely fine. When heirlooms are available, I like to experiment with those.

Preheat an oven to 325°F (160°C). Stem and then halve the tomatoes through their equators and arrange cut side up in a shallow, nonreactive baking dish large enough to accommodate them in a single layer without crowding. Pour the olive oil on and around the tomatoes, then season lightly with salt and pepper. Drop 2 of the garlic cloves into the oil, along with half the thyme and rosemary sprigs. Bake until the tomatoes have deepened in color and are collapsed and shriveled, anywhere from 3 to 4 hours, depending on size and ripeness. Carefully remove the tomatoes from the oil and place on a serving dish, or divide among jars for storage.

Peel the remaining 2 garlic cloves and place on a board. Pull the leaves from the remaining thyme and rosemary and add to the fresh garlic. Pluck the roasted herbs and garlic from the oil. Discard those herbs and squish the garlic from its skin onto the fresh stuff. Add the marjoram to the pile and coarsely chop. Add the garlic mixture to the oil, along with the chives and Aleppo pepper. Let the oil steep for 10 minutes, then splash in maybe a tablespoon worth of vinegar. Taste and adjust the seasoning, then pour over the tomatoes. Serve warm or at room temperature, or store, covered and refrigerated, for up to a week or frozen for a few months.

TURMERIC FRIED OKRA

This okra, cut into skinny lengths to expose the interior flesh and never overcrowded in its pan as it cooks, achieves its maximum potential in crunch. I most regularly serve the slivered vegetables as a side to curries, or on top of dal (page 155) and rice with ghee, but they are fairly habit-forming eaten straight from the pan, when they're still blazing hot and crisp.

.... *Serves 4* ....

8 ounces (225 g) okra, stemmed and cut lengthwise into halves

About 2 teaspoons ground turmeric

Neutral-tasting oil, for frying

Fine-grain sea salt

Toss the okra with enough turmeric so that every piece has a light dusting. Set aside.

Line a colander with paper towels. In a wok or similar pan over medium heat, pour in enough oil to make a puddle about 1½ inches (3.8 cm) deep. When the oil is hot (about 350°F/175°C), take a small handful of okra and carefully drop the pieces into the oil. Cook, stirring, until the okra is golden brown and crisp, but not dried out or the flavor will be lost, 60 to 90 seconds. Transfer the fried okra to the prepared colander and season with salt, tossing to coat. Keep frying the okra, in small batches, until all are cooked. Move each batch from the colander to a serving dish before draining the next, and season as you go. Eat right away.

MIND-CHANGING OKRA

I consider it a personal mission to change the perception of okra as damp and slimy. Glazed with soy and caramel-licked at the edges, this okra is one to convert nonbelievers. It is strong enough to stand up to big flavors like roasted meats or can lend some strength to steaming-hot brown rice, for a simple, filling lunch.

.... *Serves 4* ....

2 tablespoons tamari or soy sauce

¾ teaspoon granulated sugar

A few drops of toasted sesame oil

1 tablespoon neutral-tasting oil

1 teaspoon freshly grated ginger

2 cloves garlic, minced

8 ounces (225 g) okra, stemmed and cut thickly on the bias

1 fresh red chile, slit lengthwise and seeded (optional)

Combine the tamari, sugar, and sesame oil in a small bowl.

Set a wok or similar pan over high heat. Add the neutral-tasting oil, and once it is shimmering, fry the ginger and garlic, stirring constantly, until they start to take on color, 1 minute or so. Tumble in the okra and chile, and keep everything moving in the pan for 90 seconds or so. Pour in the tamari mixture. Keep tossing the okra as the tamari mixture boils away and thickens, 2 minutes more. Once the vegetables are tender and glazed, pull off the heat and eat immediately.

GREEN BEANS WITH MUSTARD SEEDS

There's a visual peacefulness in green on green. This combination is based on an Indian green bean *subzi* (vegetable dish). Since a lot of Indian food is eaten with hands, with that intention I would cut the beans into nubs, about the size of the eraser on the end of a pencil, whereas for a knife-and-fork meal, the beans are attractive when left long and simply trimmed.

.... *Serves 4* ....

Fine-grain sea salt

9 ounces (255 g) green beans, trimmed

2 teaspoons neutral-tasting oil

1½ teaspoons black mustard seeds

1 small onion, minced

1 small green chile, stemmed, seeded, and minced, or a generous pinch of crushed red pepper flakes

1 clove garlic, minced

A couple handfuls of baby kale or spinach leaves

Fill a large bowl with ice and the coldest water from the tap. Set aside. Bring a good-sized pot of water to a boil, then salt the water liberally. Blanch the green beans until bright green, then transfer them to the ice water bath.

In a large nonstick skillet or wok, heat the oil over medium-high heat. Fry the mustard seeds, and once they start to pop and fizzle, stir in the onion and chile. Keep cooking, and moving everything around, until the onions are translucent, 5 minutes. Stir in the garlic and cook for 30 seconds. Drain the green beans and add to the pan, and cook the vegetables to tender-crisp, 2 to 5 minutes, depending on how the beans are cut. Fold in the greens, then serve.

ROASTED CARROTS WITH HARISSA AÏOLI AND DUKKAH

The harissa-twirled aïoli that accompanies the carrots has heat and complexity, but with a blend of milder oils, it's not a bodacious personality on the plate. In fact, it plays quite nicely with the mellow sweetness of honey-roasted carrots, especially when those carrots are finished with the mix of nuts and earthy spices that make up the Egyptian spice blend called *dukkah*.

Mayonnaise, which aïoli basically is, can be prepared in a blender or food processor; however, with those methods, the resulting texture is denser than when done by hand. This recipe uses a whisk, but if you'd like the challenge, feel free to use a mortar and pestle. Aïoli is best the day it's made, and I like to keep it out of the refrigerator, so it is advisable to make the mayonnaise while the carrots roast and not much earlier.

A good-quality store-bought mayonnaise can always be used as the base for the aïoli, especially if there is a concern over using raw yolks. Simply stir the garlic, lemon juice, and harissa into ¾ cup (180 ml) of the prepared stuff.

···································· *Serves 4* ····································

3 tablespoons whole hazelnuts, skin on

1 tablespoon sesame seeds, white or black, or a mix

2 teaspoons coriander seeds

1 teaspoon cumin seeds

Fine-grain sea salt and freshly cracked black pepper

12 skinny carrots, trimmed of their tops and scrubbed clean

Extra-virgin olive oil

2 teaspoons honey

¾ cup (180 ml) Harissa Aïoli (recipe follows)

NOTE: The dukkah can be made ahead and stored in an airtight container at room temperature for 3 days.

Preheat an oven to 400°F (200°C) with a rack in the upper third of the oven.

To make the dukkah, in a small skillet over medium heat, toast the hazelnuts until lightly golden and aromatic, shaking the pan often, about 2 minutes. Transfer the nuts to a small bowl and set aside. Repeat the process with the sesame seeds, coriander seeds, and cumin seeds, toasting each separately, then adding to the bowl with the hazelnuts. Let cool completely.

In a mortar and pestle or in a small food processor, process the spices and nuts into an unevenly textured mix. Season generously with salt and pepper.

On a sheet pan, toss the carrots with a light coating of the olive oil and honey, then season with salt and pepper. Roast the carrots, turning once, until browned and tender, 15 to 20 minutes. Arrange the carrots on a serving platter and sprinkle with as much dukkah as you'd like. Pass the aïoli at the table.

HARISSA AÏOLI

Makes about ¾ cup (180 ml)

2 cloves garlic, peeled, halved, and any green germ removed

Fine-grain sea salt

1 fresh egg yolk

¼ cup (60 ml) mild extra-virgin olive oil or neutral-tasting oil

¼ cup (60 ml) peppery extra-virgin olive oil

½ lemon

Freshly cracked black pepper

2 teaspoons harissa (page 274)

Twist a damp kitchen towel into a rope and shape it into a ring on a work surface. Place a stainless steel bowl into the center, so the towel can anchor the bowl as you whisk. In the bowl, sprinkle the garlic with a pinch of salt, then crush the two into a paste with a pestle or fork. Remove half the garlic, reserving it for later.

Stir the egg yolk into the remaining garlic, then add a few drops of the mild olive oil, whisking constantly. Continue to whisk, slowly dripping in oil, until the mayonnaise begins to thicken. At this stage, you can start to incorporate the oil in a thin, steady stream, still whisking all the while. You may need to stop adding the oil every so often, then whisk vigorously to thicken the emulsion, then start again with the oil. Once the mild olive oil is fully blended in, move on to the more rugged one and whisk in. Stir in the lemon juice, and thin the mayonnaise with water, if necessary, to achieve your desired consistency. Check for seasoning, adding salt and pepper and the reserved garlic as needed. Then fold in the harissa paste. Cover and leave at cool room temperature for 30 minutes before using, or refrigerate for up to 2 days.

BAKED IRISH MASH

I am a ship captain's daughter. And while mentioning my father's profession may seem odd in a book about cooking, the fact is that besides my mother and grandmother, the cooks on board those ships were the people who cooked for me most often when I was growing up. On those ships were a couple of cooks per crew, and they made straightforward North American, rib-sticking food, like pork chops, stews, and roast beef. The usual choice of sweets was between ice cream or Jell-O. I was especially fond of a particular cook who wore her hair in two thick braids and introduced me to scalloped potatoes, and served me generous helpings in a soup bowl filled to the brim.

I should explain the circumstances of how I spent a good deal of my childhood on ships. First off, they were freight carriers, the kind that carry things like grain, or iron ore, or coal. My father would usually have a crew of about thirty, on one ship that was "his," traded back and forth with another captain, in a pattern of a couple months on, then some off. The ship would have regular routes it followed, on a set schedule. So, for stretches of summer, or long weekends, or even just a day when my father came through the canal that bordered our city, my mother, brother, and I would join Dad. There must have been times when we missed school, because I remember Mum teaching me a mnemonic device to remember the order of Roman numerals, while sitting in the ship's wheelhouse. (Liquid and Crystal Displays in a Museum.)

The onboard meals were not only sustenance but also a time for the crew to come together, meeting up in the dining rooms just off the galley, three times a day. There was a sense of domestic sociability around those long tables, which helped combat homesickness. Meals were often also a treat: a pizza run in a particular port, or a special dessert on a birthday. In a lot of ways, my time on boats taught me the power of food to bond and comfort.

I am comfortable romanticizing the memory of that braided cook, and assume she knew the swaddling effect a soup bowl's worth of scalloped potatoes has on a small child. It's the same effect I am going for when I make my version of colcannon.

Strictly speaking, traditional colcannon doesn't include cheese and isn't baked. Nonetheless, this recipe came about through necessity one Christmas or Thanksgiving when our guests were running late. Mashed potatoes are notoriously finicky when it comes to reheating, so I added extra cream and butter-slicked greens to some mash I'd already made, then sprinkled on Gruyère for even more insulating richness, and kept everything cozy in a warm oven. When all were assembled, the potatoes came to the table with a crusted top, sizzling edge, and fluffy interior, with the flavor of the onions and greens contributing both texture and vegetal sweetness. It was like a baked potato met up with a spinach gratin, which is to say, a dish that was robust and sumptuous, and very, very good.

. . . continued

Baked Irish Mash, continued

.... *Serves 4 to 6* ....

½ cup (115 g) unsalted butter

2 pounds (910 g) potatoes good for mashing (Yukon Golds or russets, for example)

1 clove garlic, peeled

Medium-grain kosher salt

Bunch of green onions, both white and crisp green parts, trimmed and thinly sliced

½ bunch of kale, stemmed and torn into small pieces, or 1 small Savoy cabbage, shredded (about 4 cups/ 940 ml of either vegetable)

Freshly ground black pepper

¾ cup (180 ml) whole milk or cream

¼ cup (30 g) grated Parmesan or Gruyère cheese

Preheat an oven to 375°F (190°C). Rub the inside of a 2-quart (2 L) casserole with a knob of butter. Place the potatoes, whole and unpeeled, in a large, deep pot. Fill the pot with enough water to cover the potatoes by about 1 inch (2.5 cm). Drop in the garlic and a tablespoon of salt. Bring to a boil over high heat, then reduce the heat to a simmer until the potatoes are cooked through, 30 to 40 minutes, depending on size. Drain the potatoes and return to their hot pot to dry.

While the potatoes are still cooking, melt the butter in a wide skillet over medium heat. Sauté the scallions until soft, 3 to 5 minutes. Add the kale or cabbage to the pan with a generous pinch of salt, and cook, stirring, until the greens collapse and their liquid has cooked away, 5 to 7 minutes. Season well with salt and pepper. Pour in the milk, turn the heat down to low, and keep warm.

If using a ricer or food mill, cut the potatoes in half. If using a masher, peel if desired, and cut into quarters. Mash the potatoes with the implement of your choice, back into their pan. Working quickly, stir the greens mixture into the potatoes and add the cheese. Taste for seasoning, then transfer to the prepared dish. Cool, cover, and store in the fridge for up to a day, or bake right away until the potatoes are piping hot all the way through and the top has some color, 20 minutes (longer if baking from chilled). Let stand for 5 minutes, then serve.

CONFETTI RICE

There are many cultures that have dishes akin to this: the Lebanese mujaddara, Egyptian kushari (koshary), Persian jeweled rice, Indian khichdi (or khichri, depending on where you're from) and pilaus. As one would expect, they start with rice, often with frizzled onions and tender lentils, sometimes with chewy bits of pasta, and usually seasoned with spice and green with herbs. In all cases, these are dishes of festive plenty.

In this rendition there's the weighty, chewy comfort of starch, then there's the bright sweetness of fruit, all against the musky fragrance of cinnamon, coriander, cumin, and clove. There's the spark of pepper mollified by the cool of mint and grassy cilantro. There's a cleaving sharpness, as life must have some to offset everything else, and there's a bit of pampering luxury, too.

A sentimentalist might call this dish a metaphor, but I'll call it a fine supper.

.... *Serves 8 as a side, or 4 as a main* ....

Medium-grain kosher salt

1 cup (115 g) orzo (see Note)

About ¼ cup (60 ml)
mild olive oil

1 cup (100 g)
brown lentils (see Note)

5¼ cups (1.25 L) hot water

1 large sweet onion or
10 shallots, thinly sliced

1 cinnamon stick,
3 inches (7.5 cm) long

¾ teaspoon ground cumin

¾ teaspoon ground coriander

5 whole peppercorns

1 whole clove (optional)

1 cup (200 g) brown rice and
wild rice blend (see Note)

1 bay leaf

½ cup (85 g) golden
raisins (sultanas)

½ cup (70 g) dried currants

Freshly ground black pepper

½ cup (45 g) sliced
almonds, toasted

½ cup (60 g) roasted
pistachios, coarsely chopped

Bunch of mixed herbs, such
as parsley, cilantro, mint,
and dill, chopped

NOTE: I like the nuttiness of brown rice, and the wild rice is a visual boon. However, basmati would make a fine substitution for either, or both.

The cooked orzo, lentils, and rice can be set aside to cool, then covered and refrigerated for a couple of days before they're required.

Put a large pot of water on to boil over high heat to cook the orzo. Once it reaches a rolling boil, add a few big pinches of salt. Stir in the orzo and cook according to the directions on the package for al dente. Drain it in a colander, then toss the pasta in a bowl with enough olive oil to give it a thin coating. (Since we're letting the pasta cool down and sautéing it later, this unorthodox step will keep it from all sticking together.)

Sir the lentils into 3 cups (710 ml) of the water in heavy-bottomed saucepan over medium-high heat. Bring to a boil, then lower the heat to maintain a simmer. Cook, stirring now and again, until the lentils are just tender, around 25 minutes. Drain and set aside.

. . . continued

Confetti Rice, continued

In wide, heavy sauté pan, heat 1 tablespoon or so of the olive oil over medium-high heat. Toss in the onion, and stir around a bit. Lower the heat to medium or medium-low and continue to cook until the onions are deeply colored and a little crisp at their edges, but not scorched, about 15 minutes. Set aside.

Meanwhile, into a medium saucepan with a tight-fitting lid, pour in another tablespoon olive oil. Drop in the cinnamon, cumin, coriander, peppercorns, and clove. Heat the oil and spices over medium heat, stirring occasionally, until the oil is aromatic and sizzling and the spices begin to darken, about 2 minutes. Stir in the rice, making sure all the grains are slicked with the spiced oil and starting to toast. Pour in the remaining 2¼ cups (540 ml) hot water (this is the amount for the brand of rice I like; consult the package instructions for yours in case of discrepancy). Pop in the bay leaf, bring the water to a boil, then turn the heat down to maintain a simmer. Cover and cook until most, if not all, the water is absorbed and the rice is tender. Check the package for timing. Lift off the lid, pluck out the whole spices, if desired, and drain off any remaining water. Off the heat, fluff with a fork and season with salt.

In a large, heavy, enameled cast-iron pot or a large sauté pan, heat a generous tablespoon of olive oil over medium-high heat. When it is shimmering, dump in the cooked orzo and gently break up any clumps with the back of a wooden spoon. Sauté, stirring now and again, until the pasta starts to turn golden in places. Stir in the cooked lentils and toss around until everything starts to get crusty. Tumble the rice into the pan, along with the golden raisins and currants, and fold together. Taste and adjust the seasoning with salt and ground black pepper. Sprinkle half of the almonds and most of the pistachios over the mixture, along with a handful of the herbs. Fold again.

Tip the rice out onto a large serving platter. Top with the caramelized onions, forking them in here and there. Add the remaining almonds, pistachios, and herbs, then serve right away.

FENNEL, CITRUS, AND AVOCADO SALAD

In winter, when we are all in need of some reminder of sunshine, citrus saves the day. Here, two kinds of orange join slices of fennel and avocados in mood-boosting vibrancy against variegated shades of jade.

.... *Serves 4* ....

2 blood oranges

1 Cara Cara or other sweet orange

Fine-grain sea salt and freshly ground black pepper

2 fennel bulbs, sliced wafer thin or shaved on a mandoline, fronds reserved

2 large avocados

Juice from ½ lemon, or 2 tablespoons white wine vinegar

3 tablespoons extra-virgin olive oil or avocado oil

4 handfuls of mâche (also called corn salad and lamb's lettuce)

With a sharp knife, lop both ends off one of the blood oranges, deep enough to reveal the flesh. Stand the orange up on end. Slice the peel and pith away and discard. Over a bowl, cut between the membranes of the orange, to release its segments into the bowl. Squeeze the juice from the membrane and repeat with the second blood orange and the Cara Cara. Season with salt and pepper.

With a slotted spoon or your fingers, lift the oranges from their juice and arrange on a serving plate, then strew the fennel on top. Cut the avocados in half lengthwise and pit. Over the plate, dig into the avocado flesh with a spoon and, with a turn of the wrist, scoop out crescents. Let these drop haphazardly. Add the lemon juice to the collected juices from the oranges, and whisk in 2 tablespoons of the olive oil. Check for seasoning, then pour over the salad. Turn the mâche in whatever dressing films the bowl, then scatter on the plate. Drizzle with the remaining 1 tablespoon of olive oil, pluck any fennel fronds into small pieces, sprinkle over the salad, and serve.

CHAPTER 6

SWEETS, TREATS & SIPS

Sweets are where I started in the kitchen. I can't be sure of the first meal I cooked—though it was possibly something in the toaster oven—but I can tell you about the first cookies I ever made. Or at least attempted to make, with the patient help of my grandmother's friend, who we called Aunty Mary. My teacher had brought homemade chocolate cookies to school, and I was quite certain I could recreate the recipe from memory, with the recruited help of my aunt. I was maybe six years old.

I forgot half the ingredients and I made up the rest. Auntie Mary dutifully followed my instructions, and what we ended up with could have hardly been called cookies. There's a photo of her, valiantly trying, and failing, to scrape the stubborn discs of fossilized sludge off the pan. She's laughing. I'm beside her, sitting up on the counter, delighted, with an ear-to-ear grin.

Every time I make the treats in this chapter, I'm as proud as I was then. Whether baking a comforting apple pie, aromatic with browned butter caramel, or churning a batch of lush, condensed-milk ice cream, or clinking glasses filled with some boozy sip, I feel like I'm conjuring a kind of magic, from the transformation of ingredients to the results—the recipes feel special to make, and to share.

BASIC, GREAT
CHOCOLATE CHIP COOKIES

My obsession with baking chocolate chip cookies started in high school. The recipe resulting from those years of study is one that I've pared back as best I can—there is no need for a mixer, or to get the eggs and butter out of the fridge in advance. With it, it is possible to go from start to cookies in 30 minutes, with little by way of cleaning up.

Even if these cookies required a rigmarole, they'd be worth it. They stay in fattish mounds, with their humped backs shot through with crackles, fudgy without being underbaked, and with a sweetness kept in line by salt.

This recipe works best with bar chocolate that has been chopped, pure chocolate buttons, callets, or fèves. Because they lack the stabilizers used in chocolate chips, these forms of chocolate ooze into the batter during baking, slipping into the cracks and leaving both puddles and rivulets throughout the finished cookies. The irregularity is exceptionally pretty and, in a way, gives the impression the chocolate goes further.

If you have the patience, hold the dough in the fridge overnight and for up to a few days before baking, portioned in scoops and covered. Aging the dough allows for the flour to better absorb the liquids. The flavor will become deeply caramelized and nuanced, and the cookies will have more color, but slightly less spread. I usually bake one tray for immediate gratification, and keep the rest for later demand.

.... *Makes about 28 cookies* ....

1 cup (225 g) unsalted butter, chopped

3¼ cups (415 g) all-purpose flour

1¼ teaspoons baking powder

1 teaspoon baking soda

1½ teaspoons medium-grain kosher salt

1½ cups (320 g) packed light brown sugar

½ cup (100 g) granulated sugar

2 eggs

2 teaspoons vanilla extract

12 ounces (340 g) semisweet or bittersweet chocolate, chopped

Flaky sea salt, for sprinkling (optional)

Preheat an oven to 360°F (180°C). Line 2 heavy baking sheets or sheet pans with parchment paper.

In a medium saucepan over the lowest heat possible, melt the butter. There should be no sizzle, crackling, or pops; let the butter ooze into liquid, without boiling, so minimal moisture is lost. Stir regularly, until the butter is almost completely melted. (This is a good time to chop the chocolate.)

In a bowl, whisk together the flour, baking powder, baking soda, and kosher salt. Set aside.

. . . continued

Basic, Great Chocolate Chip Cookies, continued

NOTE: I prefer baking batches one tray at a time, but two pans can be baked together, one on a rack in the upper third, and one in the lower. Rotate the pans from top to bottom and front to back once while baking.

To make ahead, shape the dough in scoops or logs, wrap tightly, then seal in bags, and keep in the freezer for up to 3 months. Frozen scoops can be baked without defrosting, while logs should be held in the fridge until soft enough to slice. Reduce the oven temperature to 330°F (165°C) and increase the baking time as needed.

Pour the melted butter into a large bowl and whisk in the sugars. The mixture may look like it will seize, but it will relax with a few seconds of stirring. Add the eggs, one at a time, whisking briskly after each addition, but only to combine. Stir in the vanilla. Use a wooden spoon or silicone spatula to stir in the dry ingredients. Once mostly blended, fold the chocolate into the dough until the remaining flour is incorporated, and the dough no longer looks dusty. Bring any stray ingredients up from the bottom of the bowl. Do not overmix.

If the dough seems warm or looks overly glossy, refrigerate for 5 minutes. Then roll into balls using 3 tablespoons of dough for each. Arrange on the prepared pans, leaving 3 inches (7.5 cm) in between each. Sprinkle with sea salt. Bake until the tops are cracked and lightly golden, yet the cookies are still soft at the center, 10 to 12 minutes, rotating the pan halfway through cooking. Leave the cookies on the sheet pan for 2 minutes, then transfer to a wire rack to cool. Continue shaping and baking cookies with the remaining dough, making sure to use a cold sheet pan for each batch.

The cookies can be kept at room temperature in an airtight container for up to 1 week.

Thin and Crunchy Variation: For a thinner, crunchy-through-and-through cookie, use 3 cups plus 2 tablespoons (390 g) flour.

Shiny and Crisp Variation: For a shinier cookie with a crisp surface and edge, decrease the brown sugar to 1¼ cups (265 g) packed light brown sugar and increase the granulated sugar to ¾ cup (150 g).

Whole Wheat Variation: Some or all of the all-purpose flour can be replaced with whole wheat or rye. It will, of course, change the texture and look of the finished cookie, but is worthy of a try.

Nutty Variation: This amount of dough can accommodate ¾ cup (75 g) chopped walnuts or pecans.

WHOLE WHEAT PEANUT BUTTER COOKIES

These are the only peanut butter cookies I make, in accordance with the request of my family, and it is a recipe I've attempted to improve upon, but cannot. They are our end-all peanut butter cookie—chewy, tender-bellied, and crunchily edged. Perfect.

.... *Makes 18 cookies* ....

½ cup (65 g)
all-purpose flour

½ cup (60 g)
whole wheat flour

¾ teaspoon baking soda

½ teaspoon medium-grain
kosher salt

¾ cup (200 g) chunky-style
natural peanut butter
(see Note)

½ cup (115 g) unsalted butter,
softened

⅔ cup (140 g) packed light
brown sugar

⅓ cup (70 g) granulated
sugar

2 tablespoons honey

1 egg, at room temperature

1 teaspoon vanilla extract

Flaky sea salt, for sprinkling

NOTE: Natural peanut butter has a clearer peanut flavor, but the sugared kind is a possibility. The result will be sweeter, more inducing of primary school nostalgia, suggestive of the filling in a chocolate peanut butter cup.

Preheat an oven to 350°F (175°C) with racks in the upper and lower thirds. Use parchment paper to line 3 standard baking sheets and set aside.

In a bowl, whisk together the flours, baking soda, and kosher salt.

In the bowl of a stand mixer fitted with the paddle attachment, cream the peanut butter and butter until light and fluffy, maybe 1 minute. Add the brown and white sugars and honey and beat on high speed for 3 minutes, scraping down the sides of the bowl as needed. Add the egg and vanilla, then mix on medium speed until well blended. Add the dry ingredients to the bowl and stir to just combine. With a spatula, scrape up from the bottom of the bowl to make sure all the ingredients are incorporated, but do not go overboard. Roll the dough into balls, using a generous 2 tablespoons of batter for each. Place on a baking sheet and freeze for 10 to 15 minutes.

Divide the dough among the 3 prepared baking sheets, spacing the balls 2 inches (5 cm) apart. Dip a fork into warm water and use the tines to press the dough balls lightly; once, or if so moved, turn the tines and complete the cross. Freshly dip the fork between pressing each cookie. Sprinkle with sea salt.

Bake for 16 minutes, rotating the pans from top to bottom and front to back once during baking. Cool the cookies on the pans for 2 minutes, then transfer to wire racks to cool completely.

The cookies can be kept in an airtight container at room temperature for a few days.

RHUBARB RASPBERRY RYE CRUMBLE

Behind the house where my mother-in-law grew up is a rhubarb plant that, as I was told by her father, "has been in our family forever." He told me the variety was called Strawberry Rhubarb, and is one that is especially good for baking.

There are four rhubarb plants in the far corner of my own yard, grown from that original. Viewed from the window above the kitchen sink, they form a green, rustling mound, with their built-in parasol of leaves sheltering carmine stems. They thrive beside raspberry bushes also started in my husband's grandparents' garden.

A level of sentimentality for the combination is thus inevitable, yet the pairing of rhubarb and raspberry is undeniably good on the table. I prefer raspberries to strawberries with rhubarb; they seem to stand up to the strident assertiveness of the stalks better, plus I think raspberries take better to baking.

Here the garden's yield is baked to a heady burgundy compote beneath the earthy cover of rye streusel. That topping is almost a shortbread dough, which makes for a buttery complement to the knife-sharp jammy filling.

Serves 8 to 10

STREUSEL TOPPING

½ cup (115 g) unsalted butter, softened

½ cup (100 g) granulated sugar

¼ teaspoon fine-grain sea salt

1 cup (110 g) old-fashioned rolled oats

½ cup (65 g) all-purpose flour

½ cup (50 g) rye flour

¼ cup (20 g) flaked almonds

¼ teaspoon ground cardamom

FILLING

2 pounds (910 g) rhubarb, trimmed and cut into ½-inch (1.3 cm) pieces

1¼ pounds (565 g) raspberries, fresh or frozen

Juice from ½ lemon (about 2 tablespoons)

¾ cup (150 g) granulated sugar (see Note)

¼ cup (28 g) tapioca flour

¼ teaspoon fine-grain sea salt

1 vanilla bean

Vanilla frozen yogurt or whipped cream, to serve

Preheat an oven to 375°F (190°C) with a rack in the lower third of the oven. Line a rimmed baking sheet with parchment paper. Grease a 2-quart (2 L) baking dish with butter.

To make the topping, in the bowl of a stand mixer fitted with the paddle attachment, cream together the butter, sugar, and salt on medium-high speed until fluffy, around 3 minutes. Scrape down the sides of the bowl and turn the speed to low. Sprinkle in the oats, flours, almonds, and cardamom; let the machine

. . . continued

Rhubarb Raspberry Rye Crumble, continued

NOTE: The sugar for the filling may be scant for some tastes; both rhubarb and raspberries are sour, and the amount used here keeps the twang that hits the point at the back of your jaw right below the ear—it's not so much that the muscle clenches, but there's still a twitch. When I eat the filling with the crumble topping, I feel it all evens out, but still, it is a characteristic to know before going in.

run until the dry ingredients are incorporated and the mixture starts to gather into a rough streusel, 3 to 5 minutes, scraping down the bowl as needed. Keep in a cool spot or covered in the fridge while you organize the filling.

To make the filling, in a large bowl, combine the rhubarb, raspberries, lemon juice, sugar, tapioca flour, and salt. Split the vanilla bean down its length, scrape the seeds into the bowl, and then add the pod as well. Fold everything until the tapioca disappears. Tip the fruit into the prepared baking dish, including any collected juices. With clean hands, crumble the streusel over the filling, in haphazard and uneven heaps.

Place the dish on the prepared baking sheet and bake until the juices are gurgling with large bubbles and the topping is golden brown, 50 minutes or thereabouts.

Cool on a rack for 30 minutes before considering eating. Serve warm or cold, with vanilla frozen yogurt or whipped cream.

CARAMEL APPLE PIE

It's hard to resist the urge to get stuck in a pie while it is fresh and hot from the oven, but if you can resist, do. The juices require time to thicken to their sumptuous best, which allows for neater slices when dishing out. For the apples, a mix of tart and sweet baking varieties like Pippin and Golden Delicious, Braeburn or McIntosh are nice. And, by macerating the fruit at room temperature, as is done with jam, then reducing that collected liquid, the filling has that much of a lead toward later lusciousness.

Makes a 9-inch (23 cm) pie

Juice from ½ lemon (about 2 tablespoons)

3½ pounds (1.5 kg) apples

½ cup (90 g) packed light brown sugar

¼ cup (50 g) granulated sugar

½ teaspoon fine-grain sea salt

2 tablespoons unsalted butter

1½ tablespoons cornstarch

¾ teaspoon ground cinnamon

60 gratings fresh nutmeg, or ¼ teaspoon ground

Flour, for dusting

Family-Approved Pie Dough (page 272)

1 egg, beaten with 1 tablespoon water

Coarse sugar, such as Demerara, coarse Turbinado, or sanding sugar, for sprinkling

Vanilla ice cream, to serve

Lightly butter a 9-inch (23 cm) pie pan and set aside. Squeeze the lemon juice into a large, nonreactive bowl. Peel, core, and cut the apples into ¼-inch (6 mm) slices, adding them to the bowl as soon as they are cut. Turn the apples in the lemon juice now and again while you work. Toss the apples with the sugars and salt. Cover and leave at room temperature for at least 1 hour and up to 4 hours, or refrigerate overnight. Stir whenever you remember to do so. If you haven't already, this is a good time to make the pastry.

Set a colander over a large heavy pot. Turn the apples into the colander and let them drain completely. Flip the apples back into their bowl and pour the juice into a liquid measuring cup, taking note of the amount. Melt the butter in the pot over medium heat. Let it brown, swirling occasionally. Add the drained apple liquid and bring to a boil without stirring. Reduce the liquid to ½ cup (120 ml).

Toss the apples with the cornstarch, cinnamon, and nutmeg, until the cornstarch dissolves. Pour the reduced juices over the top and fold to combine. Set aside.

. . . continued

Caramel Apple Pie, continued

On a lightly floured work surface, roll half the dough out to a 12-inch (30.5 cm) round. Drape the dough over the prepared pan and gently ease into place, snug against the bottom and overhanging at the rim. Fill tightly with the apples and the juice, mounding the fruit toward the center. Place in the fridge. Roll out the remaining dough to a 12-inch (30.5 cm) round and either cut into strips for lattice or leave as is. Retrieve the pastry shell from the fridge. Brush the edge of the lower crust with beaten egg, reserving any remaining egg. Place the top crust over the filling, or weave the lattice directly on top of the filling. Press the top and bottom crusts together to seal, then crimp or decorate. Pop the whole pie in the freezer for 15 minutes.

While the pie chills, preheat an oven to 375°F (190°C) with a rack in the lower third of the oven. Line a rimmed baking sheet with parchment paper.

Brush the chilled pastry with the remaining egg wash. Sprinkle with sugar. For solid-top crusts, cut steam vents with either a knife or a small cookie cutter. Set the pie on the prepared baking sheet and bake until the juices are bubbling and the apples succumb to the tip of a knife, 50 minutes or so. If the crust browns too quickly, protect it with a layer of foil.

Remove the pie from the oven and cool on a wire rack for at least 1½ hours. Serve with vanilla ice cream.

WALNUT CHERRY OAT BUTTER TART PIE

The difference between a Canadian butter tart and an American pecan pie is elusive but intrinsic. Butter tarts are as common as doughnuts, maybe more so where I live, available not only at the grocery store, but at the corner store as well, in factory-made and house-made offerings.

Butter tarts don't necessarily have nuts. They are usually smaller than their southern relatives, baked in muffin pans, with high sides that hold a lot of filling, but my version bumps up the tart to full size, as I prefer this ratio of filling to crust.

Here, the filling of brown sugar, eggs, corn syrup, butter, and vinegar comes, once again, from my husband's family. Upon baking, the filling gets an almost honeycomb top with a gelled, glossy underneath. This particular recipe started on his mother's side, but now his father is the tart maker around the holidays.

On my father-in-law's dessert tray, the tarts are offered in variety: some plain, some with walnut, some with raisins, and others with shredded coconut. I've combined and continued the theme, with sour cherries standing in for the raisins, and oats for the coconut (which is not to say that those swaps are irreversible). With this lineup, there is a nice division of duties: the walnut have a tannic interest and snap against the tooth; the oats require the molars, chewy and plain in needed abatement of the richness; the cherries' determined sourness pushes against the thick sugars; and the malt vinegar reinforces that equilibrium.

One more thing: a tart like this benefits from a slick of cold cream, poured or whipped.

.... *Makes a 9-inch (23 cm) pie* ....

TART SHELL

½ recipe Family-Approved Pie Dough, made without egg (page 272)

Flour, for dusting

1 egg white

FILLING

¼ cup (60 g) unsalted butter

1 cup (215 g) packed light brown sugar

3 eggs, plus 1 yolk

½ cup (120 ml) dark corn syrup or pure maple syrup

2 teaspoons vanilla extract

2 teaspoons malt vinegar

¾ teaspoon medium-grain kosher salt

1¼ cups (140 g) walnut pieces, toasted

½ cup (50 g) old-fashioned rolled oats

... continued

Granulated sugar, for sprinkling

⅔ cup (80 g) dried sour cherries

Heavy cream or barely sweetened whipped cream, to serve

Walnut Cherry Oat Butter Tart Pie, continued

Preheat an oven to 400°F (200°C) with a rack in the middle of the oven. Line a standard baking sheet with parchment paper. Grease a 9-inch (23 cm) pie pan and set aside.

To make the tart shell, roll out the dough to a 12-inch (30.5 cm) circle on a lightly floured board. Gently fit in the prepared pan, folding the overhang under itself at the rim to form a nice, high edge. The crust will need to accommodate a generous amount of filling, so keep that in mind. Crimp or decorate as you like, then pop the pastry in the freezer for 10 minutes.

Place the pie shell on the prepared baking sheet, then prick the pastry all over with a fork. Line the pastry with foil and bake for 15 minutes. Keep an eye on it, and with the back of a wooden spoon or silicone spatula, carefully press down any swells as they rise (you'll see the foil bulge). Remove the foil and bake the crust for 10 minutes more, by which time it should be opaque and dry in places. Remove the crust from the oven; brush on a thin coating of the egg white, reserving what remains. Return the crust to the oven to bake for 1 minute more. Set it to one side while you prepare the filling.

Lower the oven temperature to 325°F (165°C).

To make the filling, in a saucepan, melt the butter over medium-low heat. Pull the pan off the heat and stir in the sugar with a wooden spoon or silicone spatula. Briskly beat in the eggs and yolk, then the corn syrup, vanilla, vinegar, and salt. Return to the stove and warm over low heat until the mixture has loosened and is not as gritty as it was to start, about 5 minutes. Once again off the heat, fold in the walnuts and oats.

Brush another coat of egg white on the pastry edge, followed by a glittering sprinkle of sugar. Scatter the cherries across the bottom of the crust and then pour in the filling. Bake until gelled, slightly springy at the center, and with only the faintest wobble, 55 to 60 minutes.

Transfer to a wire rack and cool for at least 3 hours. For it to set properly, the filling must cool completely. Serve at room temperature, rewarmed, or cold, with heavy cream or barely sweetened whipped cream. The pie can be made up to 2 days ahead, kept covered and chilled.

ores. Frozen cranberries may be

	1 mL
milk or sour milk	250 mL
ghtly beaten	1
ble oil	50 mL
	25 mL
rries	250 mL

in bottom of 12 lightly greased
medium bowl. Blend together
ngredients just until moistened.
en about 25 minutes until tops
pletely.

rate, 2.2 g fibre .

erry Tarts
s

h
juice.
berries
s with
Cook
pour

Butter Tarts

¾ c. brown sugar
5 tbsp. melted butter
½ c. syrup.
1 egg
½ tbsp. vanilla & tsp. salt
2 tbsp. vinegar
½ c. currants & raisins
⅛ c. walnuts
½ Mix and fill 3 full tart
tins which have been lined
with unbaked pastry & bake.

Lemon Dreams

2 c. flour   1/8 tsp. salt
⅓ c. butter
Mix & press into 8 x 8" pan. Bake in
oven 325° – 15 min.

ROASTED GRAPES WITH SWEET LABNEH

Truly compelling but dead simple. Sticky fruit, warm cream, crushed cookies, and booze. And it needn't be this fruit, this alcohol, or even these cookies. Grab figs, strawberries, rhubarb, pineapple, or sour cherries. Add herbs and spices to the fruit or the sugar—rosemary, thyme, Chinese five-spice powder, and ground coriander work very well with fruit. Try other alcohols, like marsala, gin, or liqueurs, either before cooking or at the end. Or enlist ginger snaps, meringues, or sugar cookies for crunch.

.... *Serves 4 to 6* ....

LABNEH

Zest from ½ orange, finely grated

⅓ cup (75 g) packed Demerara sugar, plus more for sprinkling

2½ cups (590 ml) labneh (page 262; see Note)

GRAPES

1 tablespoon honey

2 tablespoons grappa

1 pound (455 g) seedless table grapes

Amaretti or shortbread, to serve

NOTE: If you make your own labneh, layer with sugar during its initial straining process.

Preheat an oven to 375°F (190°C).

To make the labneh, rub the orange zest into the Demerara sugar. Fold the labneh into the sugar mixture until lightly veined. If the labneh isn't firm, carefully scrape it into a cheesecloth-lined strainer set over a bowl. Then cover and refrigerate until it is stable enough to form and hold a clean peak (this may only take 10 minutes or up to an hour, depending on how damp the labneh was to start with). Spread the labneh in ripples on an ovenproof plate. Sprinkle with more Demerara.

To make the grapes, thin the honey with the grappa in a large bowl. Snip the grapes into clusters and add to the bowl. Turn the grapes in the syrup, then transfer to a roasting pan with a shallow rim.

Place the grapes and labneh side by side in the hot oven and roast until the grapes start to shrivel and the labneh is set and golden, about 12 to 15 minutes. Carefully set the grapes atop the labneh and spoon the collected pan juices over all. Serve with the cookies, crushed or whole.

COCONUT KHEER WITH BRONZED PINEAPPLE

Kheer, the South Asian milk pudding made with rice, cracked wheat, or translucent strands of vermicelli, is a soothing blanket, creamy and soft with cardamom and vanilla. Here there is a triple dose of coconut, using oil, milk, and shredded flesh; burnished chunks of pineapple, succulent and keen, provide a welcome contrast.

.... *Serves 6 to 8* ....

KHEER

1 cup (200 g) kalijira or basmati rice (see Note)

1 tablespoon coconut oil

½ cup (45 g) ground or shredded coconut, fresh or dried

3 cups (710 ml) unsweetened almond milk

1 (14-ounce/400 ml) can coconut milk

⅓ cup (70 g) natural cane sugar

4 green cardamom pods, bruised (see Note)

1 vanilla bean, split

¼ teaspoon fine-grain sea salt

PINEAPPLE AND TO SERVE

½ cup (100 g) natural cane sugar

1 tablespoon coconut oil or butter

Pinch of fine-grain sea salt

1 small pineapple, peeled, cored, and cut into 8 to 10 wedges

A handful of pistachios, raw or roasted, crushed

Ground cardamom, for sprinkling

NOTE: Granulated sugar can be used instead of the natural cane sugar, but use less because granulated sugar comes across as more aggressively sweet. Using a mix of light brown sugar and granulated sugar will give some of the same toffee-like quality of natural cane sugar.

Kalijira is a fragrant, short-grain rice favored in Bangladesh that is notably suited to rice pudding.

To bruise the cardamom pods, smash them with the side of a knife.

To make the kheer, rinse the rice until the water runs clear. Set a wide heavy saucepan over medium heat, add the coconut oil, and let it melt. Tip in the rice and cook, stirring, until translucent, 45 to 60 seconds. Sprinkle in the shredded coconut and toast for 30 seconds, then stir in the almond and coconut milks, cane sugar, cardamom pods, vanilla bean seeds, the pod itself, and the sea salt. Heat to boiling, stirring, then lower the heat to maintain a simmer. Stirring at regular intervals, cook the rice until the milk is thick enough to suspend the grains, 35 to 45 minutes. Discard the cardamom pods and vanilla bean.

While the kheer is bubbling, give the pineapple its due attention. Sprinkle the cane sugar across a wide, nonstick skillet. Cook the sugar, without stirring, but shaking the pan often, over medium-high heat until the sugar melts and turns golden, 5 minutes. Spoon in the coconut oil along with a pinch of salt, and shake the pan some more until both are incorporated. Carefully lay the pineapple wedges into the caramel, and cook, turning regularly, until the pineapple is heated through, and absolutely lacquered, 3 to 5 minutes more. Serve the kheer with the hot pineapple, any and all juices left in the skillet, some pistachio crumbs, and the tiniest pinch of ground cardamom.

FIG TOASTS WITH BUTTERED HONEY

One night I came home from a food photo shoot with a surfeit of figs that were teetering weightily on the edge of over-ripeness. I was too tired to do much cooking, so I squished the foxy minxes onto slices of hot buttered toast in a rustic, fruited cobblestone. With honey, drops of olive oil, and a healthy amount of salt and cracked black pepper, it was all I could have asked for. The figs, half fleshy and half sandy seeds, melded into the toast's crumb. The butter's baseline, rounded richness was accented by the resiny, throat-warming olive oil.

This is a slightly elevated version of that snack, with the butter and honey, accented with thyme, warmed and thickened. Figs have a great propensity for turning caramel-sweet when met with heat, but here there is the intent to preserve their elusive musk, which is often lost in the process. These toasts make a surprising, sensuous end to a meal, especially with a slice of cheese and a sip of port wine.

Serves 4

2 tablespoons butter

2 sprigs thyme, or 1 or sprig rosemary, plus more for garnish

3 tablespoons honey

Flaky sea salt and freshly cracked black pepper

6 to 8 slices of sturdy, grainy bread

Extra-virgin olive oil, for drizzling

4 to 6 fresh figs

Stilton, to serve (optional)

In a small saucepan over low heat, melt the butter with the thyme. Once the butter is fluid, pour in the honey. Season with salt and pepper and continue to cook, swirling the pot often, until combined and bubbling thickly, 1 to 2 minutes. Set aside.

While the honey and butter are simmering, grill or toast the bread, with a few drops of olive oil brushed on each side. Slice the figs thickly and arrange in mosaics upon the toasts. Use an offset spatula or the side of a blunt knife to squish the figs into the toast, so that the flesh spreads and softens.

Pluck the herbs from the honey and discard. Drip the syrup onto the figs from a height, twirling and circling the spoon so that the honey falls in sweeping arabesques. Season the toasts with more salt and pepper and a few fresh herb leaves. Serve right away, alone or met with a wedge of Stilton at the table.

PLUM MACAROON CAKE

Living where I do, on this peninsula of farmland, there is an abundance of harvest festivals. From the strawberry festival in June to the grape festival in late September, there is almost a weekly community gathering to cheer some yield or another. We fête cherries, garlic and herbs, peaches, tomatoes, and lavender, among so many others, but, oddly, we hop, skip, and jump right past plums in a gross oversight.

The plums here range from yellow with blushed cheeks to full on crimson, to purple and bluest midnight. Some are sweet, others tart, and others almost winelike.

In this cake, this layered business of butter, coconut, and eggy topping, the pointed edges of the plum crescents droop as they bake, while keeping some shape and their luxurious weight. Serve with custard and that's all the celebration I need.

.... *Makes a 9-inch (23 cm) cake* ....

CAKE

1½ cups (190 g) all-purpose flour

½ cup (60 g) shredded coconut (see Note)

2 teaspoons baking powder

½ teaspoon fine-grain sea salt

½ cup (115 g) unsalted butter, softened

1 cup (200 g) granulated sugar

2 eggs, at room temperature

¼ teaspoon almond extract

¼ cup (60 ml) milk

About 1 pound (455 g) red or purple plums (4 or 5 plums), pitted and cut into sixths

2 tablespoons Demerara or granulated sugar

¾ teaspoon ground cinnamon

TOPPING

¼ cup (60 g) unsalted butter, softened

¾ cup (150 g) granulated sugar

2 eggs, at room temperature

2 tablespoons (25 g) almond meal

Seeds scraped from a vanilla bean, or 2 teaspoons vanilla extract

¼ teaspoon almond extract

½ cup (60 g) shredded coconut (see Note)

Confectioners' sugar, to dust (optional)

Preheat an oven to 350°F (175°C). Grease a 9-inch (23 cm) cake pan with a removable bottom or a springform pan with butter.

To make the cake, whisk together the flour, coconut, baking powder, and salt in a bowl. Set this dry mix aside.

In the bowl of a stand mixer fitted with the paddle attachment, cream the butter and granulated sugar on medium-high speed for 5 minutes. Scrape down the sides of the bowl and beat for 2 minutes more. Decrease the speed to medium-low and add the eggs, one at a time, beating well after each addition. Add the almond extract and turn the speed down to low. With the mixer still running, add half the dry ingredients to the wet, followed by all the milk, and then the rest of the dry ingredients. Mix until combined, scraping down the bowl once or twice. Transfer the batter to the prepared pan, coaxing it into the edges with a spatula or the back of a spoon. The batter will look distressingly scant. Press on. Stand the plums in rings in the batter, up on their ends. The fruit will shift inward during baking, so arrange them nice and close to the edge of the pan, and do not cluster too many at the middle. Combine the Demerara sugar and cinnamon in a bowl, then sprinkle across the fruited Stonehenge. Bake for 50 minutes.

While the cake bakes, make the topping. Whisk the butter, sugar, eggs, almond meal, vanilla bean seeds, almond extract, and shredded coconut in a pitcher with a pouring spout. Working quickly, remove the cake from the oven and pour the mixture over the hot cake. Return the cake to the oven and bake until the topping is puffed, evenly golden, and set, 25 to 30 minutes more.

Cool the cake completely, in its pan on a wire rack, before serving. Serve as is, or dusted with some confectioners' sugar. The cake can be kept under a dome or loosely wrapped in its pan at room temperature for 3 days.

BLUEBERRY POPPY SEED
SNACKING CAKE

While baking as a discipline requires a degree of exactitude, cakes such as this one are immensely forgiving when it comes to substitutions. You have leeway in swapping in other fruit, or nuts, or flavors, or doing as I do, and using this recipe as a loaf cake, or in miniature rounds and squares (as pictured at right). This cake is especially endearing in blocky shapes destined for packing, for travel, and for giving away. In all cases, tailor the baking times to the size of the cake, checking for doneness with a tester and a gentle push at its center—it should bounce back from the prodding, and the sides of the cake should pull away from the sides of the pan.

············   *Makes an 8-inch (20 cm) cake or four 2-inch (5 cm) miniature cakes*   ············

2 cups (255 g) all-purpose flour

2 tablespoons poppy seeds

1 teaspoon fine-grain sea salt

1 cup (225 g) unsalted butter, softened

1¼ cups (250 g) granulated sugar, plus extra for sprinkling

4 eggs, at room temperature

Seeds scraped from a vanilla bean, or 2 teaspoons vanilla extract

2 tablespoons crème fraîche (page 261) or sour cream

Juice and finely grated zest from ½ lemon

1 cup (170 g) blueberries, fresh or frozen

Preheat an oven to 300°F (150°C) with a rack in the middle of the oven. Butter an 8-inch (20 cm) round cake pan and line the bottom with parchment paper. Butter the parchment paper.

Whisk together the flour, poppy seeds, and salt; set aside.

In the bowl of a stand mixer fitted with the paddle attachment, cream the butter and sugar for 8 minutes on medium-high, scraping down the bowl and beater regularly. Decrease the speed to medium and add the eggs, one at a time, scraping down the beater after each, and then beating well. The batter may look to have curdled, but it will smooth out once the dry ingredients are added. Add the vanilla. With the mixer on low speed, beat in half the flour, then the crème fraîche, lemon juice and zest, and then the last of the flour. Do not overmix. Fold in the blueberries by hand, making sure to get all the way down to the bottom of the bowl. Scrape the batter into the prepared pan, smooth the top, and sprinkle with granulated sugar.

Bake the cake for 80 to 90 minutes, rotating the pan halfway through, until a skewer inserted in the center comes out clean.

Transfer the cake to a wire rack to cool for 30 minutes in its pan. Then unmold and cool completely. The cake can be kept at room temperature for 4 days, loosely covered or under a dome.

BLOOD ORANGE STOUT CAKE

Sticky, sharp, sweet, and spiced, this gingerbread-meets-marmalade cake is a vibrant addition to a winter afternoon. If you cannot find golden syrup, use a light honey in its place.

.... *Makes a 10-inch (25 cm) cake* ....

CANDIED ORANGES

1 cup (200 g) granulated sugar

1 cup (240 ml) water

2 blood oranges, sliced into rounds horizontally, peel and all, each around ⅛-inch (3 mm) thick

CAKE

1 cup (240 ml) stout

1 cup (240 ml) unsulfured molasses or buckwheat honey

½ cup (120 ml) golden syrup

1½ tablespoons ground ginger

1 teaspoon ground cinnamon

½ teaspoon ground black pepper

¼ teaspoon ground cloves

2 tablespoons grated fresh peeled ginger

1½ teaspoons baking soda

4 eggs, at room temperature

1 cup (220 g) packed dark brown sugar

¾ cup (175 ml) neutral-tasting oil

2½ cups (320 g) all-purpose flour

1 teaspoon fine-grain sea salt

¼ cup (50 g) chopped candied ginger

Sweetened sour cream, to serve

To make the candied oranges, combine the sugar and water in heavy pan. Bring to a boil, stirring, then lower the heat to a simmer. Add the orange slices and cook until soft and almost translucent, 15 minutes or so. Set aside.

Preheat an oven to 350°F (175°C) with a rack in the lower third of the oven. Grease a 10-inch (25 cm) springform or conventional cake pan with butter. Line the bottom with a round of parchment paper; line the sides with a strip to form a collar. Butter the parchment paper.

To make the cake, combine the stout, molasses, golden syrup, ground ginger, cinnamon, pepper, and cloves in a large, heavy saucepan over medium heat; bring to a boil. Off the heat, stir in the fresh ginger and baking soda, being careful because the mixture will bubble robustly, almost doubling in size. Cool to room temperature.

Whisk the eggs, brown sugar, and oil together in a pitcher, then pour into the stout mixture. Whisk to combine. Sprinkle the flour, salt, and candied ginger on top, then beat until smooth. Rap the pot against the counter to release any trapped air.

Arrange the orange slices across the bottom of the prepared cake pan, overlapping only enough to make a solid layer, and with some slices climbing the sides of the pan. Reserve the syrup. Carefully pour the batter over the oranges. Bake until the middle of the cake has swelled and puffs back when touched, and a cake tester inserted in the center comes out clean, 50 to 55 minutes.

While the cake bakes, boil the remaining cooking liquid from the oranges until it is reduced to the consistency of maple syrup.

Cool the cake in its pan on a wire rack for 20 minutes, then invert onto a serving plate. Remove the parchment paper. Carefully poke holes in the cake with a thin skewer, then brush most of the syrup on the top and sides. Serve warm or fully cooled, alone or with sweetened sour cream. Drip the remaining syrup on the slices, if desired.

Store the cake under a cake dome at room temperature. It will keep for up to 5 days, becoming even more moist as it sits, and in my opinion it is at its best after a day or two. Alternatively, wrap tightly in a double layer of plastic wrap and freeze for up to 1 month.

Glazed Variation: To gussy up this cake, whisk 1 cup (160 g) confectioners' sugar with the seeds scraped from a vanilla bean in a small bowl. Add blood orange juice or water, a tablespoon at a time, until the mixture is pourable but still quite thick. Spoon the glaze over the cooled cake. Let set completely before slicing.

WHISKEY SELF-SAUCING PUDDING CAKES

To make this miraculous invention of cake and sauce, you stir together a simple batter and spoon it into a buttered baking dish. Then you pour a watery syrup, in this instance a caramel one, over the top of the unbaked cake. Yes, *over the top*. It *will* resemble a sludge-covered bog. Remain steadfast.

In the oven, all will be made right. As it bakes, the modest batter grows, rising above the murky darkness of the liquid, to become a cake that is pleasantly solid, with a crumb that reminds me of rough-knit wool. And that syrup, so unceremoniously displaced, will sink and ooze its way down, around and through the cake, ending thickened and clinging to the sides of the dish and puddled at its bottom. The final effect is akin to a glimpse of a tawny silk slip peeking from beneath the hem of a tweed skirt, something soft beneath something heavy, with magic in the contrast.

.... *Makes 6 individual cakes* ....

SYRUP

2 tablespoons unsalted butter

½ cup (90 g) packed light brown sugar

⅛ teaspoon medium-grain kosher salt

1 cup (240 ml) water

CAKES

6 tablespoons (85 g) unsalted butter, softened

1 cup (130 g) all-purpose flour

1 teaspoon baking powder

¼ teaspoon medium-grain kosher salt

4 ounces (115 g) pecans, toasted and ground into meal with a food processor

2 eggs, at room temperature, lightly beaten

½ cup (90 g) packed light brown sugar

¼ cup (60 ml) milk

2 tablespoons whiskey

Seeds scraped from a vanilla bean or 1 tablespoon vanilla bean paste

Heavy cream, to serve

To make the syrup, in a small saucepan over medium heat, melt the butter. Stir in the brown sugar, salt, and water. Bring to a boil, then lower the heat and simmer for 5 minutes. Set aside.

Preheat an oven to 325°F (160°C).

Grease six 1-cup (240 ml) ramekins or similar oven-safe cups with butter. Arrange the ramekins on a baking sheet and set aside.

To make the cakes, melt the butter in a saucepan over medium heat. Cook until the butter begins to brown and smell toasty, around 5 minutes, swirling often. Off the stove, leave the butter to cool, stirring occasionally—it will continue to darken as it sits.

In a small bowl, whisk together the flour, baking powder, and salt. In another bowl, stir the browned butter into the ground pecans, eggs, brown sugar, milk, whiskey, and seeds from the vanilla bean, then incorporate the dry ingredients. Do not overmix.

NOTE: These cakes can be fancied up with roasted grapes (page 229); roasted figs; sliced apples sautéed in butter, sugar, and cinnamon; or a handful of Spiced Candied Nuts (page 139), bashed into gravel in a mortar and pestle.

Leftover cakes should be wrapped and stored in the fridge, then rewarmed in the microwave. Use a low setting and heat in 20-second bursts until the caramel is once again liquid.

Divide the batter among the prepared ramekins. Give the syrup a stir, if needed, then carefully pour some over the back of a spoon onto each of the cakes. It will look like a mess, but don't worry. Bake until the cakes are puffed and set, with dry, glistening crusts and syrup bubbling around the edge of the dishes, about 30 minutes. Remove from the oven and cool for 5 minutes before serving with cream passed alongside.

AN UNCOMPLICATED CHEESECAKE

A cheesecake's preparation is rife with dangers. Too-cold ingredients, over-beaten batters, temperature changes during and after baking, and insufficient resting time can cause cracks, pocked and spotted tops, and clammy centers.

To keep out of such harm's way, start with truly room temperature ingredients for the filling (the ones for the topping should be cold). Beat the cheese until absolutely, completely smooth, with repeated and attentive scraping down of the bowl and beaters. Only mix the eggs until incorporated, don't let them gain volume, then bang the bowl against the counter to release any trapped air. Pour the custard into a partly baked shell and then send it to the oven, doubly wrapped in foil but without a water bath. No multiple cooking temperatures, just a long, low bake, and a slow cooling-down process.

The finish is sublimely velvety, a cake that maintains the dairy's lactic tang and brightness. It's a cake that makes friends.

For serving, the cheesecake stands quite handsomely alone, or garnish with a generous spoonful of Pickled Strawberry Preserves (page 111, especially good with fruit simply macerated overnight but not cooked), Twangy Blueberry Sauce (page 245), or even Golden Honey Elixir (page 62), passing extra at the table.

.... *Makes a 9-inch (23 cm) cheesecake* ....

CRUST

5 ounces (140 g) digestive biscuits, crushed in a food processor (see Note)

2 tablespoons granulated sugar

3 tablespoons unsalted butter, melted

CHEESECAKE FILLING

2 pounds (910 g) cream cheese, at room temperature

1⅓ cups (270 g) granulated sugar

Pinch of fine-grain sea salt

4 eggs, at room temperature

⅓ cup (80 ml) sour cream (not nonfat), at room temperature

⅓ cup (80 ml) heavy cream, at room temperature

Seeds scraped from 1 vanilla bean, or 2 teaspoons vanilla extract

TOPPING

⅔ cup (160 ml) sour cream (not nonfat), cold

⅔ cup (160 ml) heavy cream, cold

2 tablespoons confectioners' sugar

½ teaspoon vanilla extract

Preheat an oven to 325°F (160°C) with a rack in the lower third of the oven. Wrap a 9-inch (23 cm) springform pan with a double layer of aluminum foil, shiny side out.

To make the crust, use a fork to combine the crushed digestive biscuits, sugar, and butter in a bowl. Press the crumb mixture across the bottom of the prepared pan, then place the pan on

. . . continued

An Uncomplicated Cheesecake, continued

NOTE: Find digestive biscuits wherever British foods are sold, or use the same weight of graham crackers if digestives can't be found.

    I often swap a Mediterranean-style, full-fat yogurt for the sour cream in both the cake and the topping. Since brands vary wildly on consistency, I'm reluctant to promote the replacement as foolproof, but I mention it as a possibility.

a rimmed baking sheet. Bake until barely toasted, 8 to 10 minutes. Set aside to cool.

While the crust cools, prepare the filling. In the bowl of a stand mixer fitted with the paddle attachment, beat the cream cheese on medium-high speed until fluffy and smooth, 4 minutes or so. Stop the machine, scrape down the sides of the bowl, and beat for 1 minute more. Turn the speed to medium-low and gradually add the granulated sugar and salt. Continue beating until the mixture is creamy and free of lumps, scraping down the sides of the bowl as needed, 3 to 5 minutes more. Add the eggs, one at a time, beating well after each addition. Scrape down the bowl and beater after each egg. Add the sour cream, heavy cream, and vanilla, and beat for 2 minutes. Remove the bowl from the stand mixer and knock against the counter a few times to release any trapped air; let the filling stand for a couple of minutes to give any bubbles a chance to rise to the surface.

Pour the filling into the cooled crust, then run the tip of a thin knife between the filling and the edge of the pan, to a depth of about ½ inch (1.3 cm). Bake without opening the oven door until the cheesecake is firm at the edges and still has a lazy wave at the center if jiggled, about 1 hour and 15 minutes. Turn off the oven, leave the door slightly ajar, and let the cheesecake rest for 15 minutes. Then transfer the cheesecake to a wire rack to cool to room temperature. Remove the foil, then refrigerate the cheesecake for at least 4 hours. It can then be covered with plastic wrap and stored for up to 3 days.

To make the topping, in the bowl of a stand mixer, beat the sour cream, heavy cream, confectioners' sugar, and vanilla to soft peaks. Spread the cream over the cold cheesecake; return to the fridge to set for 90 minutes.

To serve, run a thin offset spatula between the cake and sides of the pan and remove the sides. Slip the offset spatula beneath the bottom crust and slide onto a serving plate. Let stand for 20 minutes, then slice with a hot, wet knife.

TWANGY BLUEBERRY SAUCE

I would like to vanquish gummy fruit sauces, the ones that are halfway to jam without any of jam's good qualities and instead are an oversweet sludge. Fruited sauces can be easy and quick—this one is—while delivering an unencumbered taste of blueberries. Half the berries make up the oozing foundation of the sauce, while the other half are only barely cooked. The combination results in bursting fruit delicately bound by a velvety liquid, and the balsamic vinegar stands up to cooking, with a perfumed acidity that suits blueberries and brings out their depth.

The sauce is brilliant as a cloak for ice cream and cheesecake (page 243), and to pour on yogurt, pancakes, and waffles, or to use as the start of a blueberry vinaigrette.

Makes about 2½ cups (625 ml)

3 cups (510 g) fresh or frozen blueberries, preferably wild

¼ cup (50 g) granulated sugar

2 teaspoons tapioca flour

1 tablespoon best-quality balsamic vinegar or port wine

NOTE: If you are feeling fancy, infuse the berries with a small sprig of fresh thyme or rosemary or an Earl Grey tea bag while cooking. Remove before serving or storing.

Tumble half the blueberries into a saucepan over medium heat. Cook, stirring, until the berries start to release their liquid, about 1 minute. Stir the sugar and tapioca flour together in a small bowl, and add to the saucepan. Continue to cook, stirring now and again, until the fruit begins to split and the juices become thick and glossy, 3 to 5 minutes. Add the vinegar and cook for another minute, stirring all the while—the sauce will quickly turn sticky. Turn off the heat, fold in the reserved berries, and set aside to cool in the pan. Give a stir every few minutes. Use the sauce right away, or cool to room temperature, cover, and refrigerate until needed for up to 1 week. Enjoy cold, warm, or hot.

VIETNAMESE COFFEE ICE CREAM

Indians make something they call espresso, but it's unlike any espresso you'd see in Italy; it's actually closer to a Greek frappé, a bold brew of instant coffee whipped with an enthusiastic amount of sugar, and then combined with hot water and milk.

I've been a longtime fan of that coffee, so when I was first introduced to the Vietnamese version, a drink with very much the same uncompromising intensity, I was sold. When I decided to freeze it, well, then I was lost.

This is my full-stop favorite ice cream. A voluptuous mix of evaporated milks and cream gets infused with ground coffee, then chilled, churned, and swirled with caramel. Easy peasy, that's that, and you're left with an ice cream worthy of any and all accolades.

Makes about 1 quart (1 L)

1 (14-ounce/400 g) can evaporated milk

1 (14-ounce/400 g) can sweetened condensed milk

1½ cups (355 ml) heavy cream

2 ounces (60 g) coffee beans, ground (see Note)

Seeds scraped from 1 vanilla bean, or 2 teaspoons pure vanilla extract

Generous pinch of fine-grain sea salt

Espresso Caramel and/or Candied Cacao Nibs (recipes follow)

NOTE: Grind regular or decaffinated coffee beans to a medium grind. For a milder, rounded flavor, use 2 tablespoons of instant espresso powder or 3 tablespoons instant coffee powder instead of ground beans.

Chocolate fudge can take the place of the caramel.

Combine the evaporated milk, condensed milk, cream, coffee, vanilla, and salt in a saucepan set over medium heat. Cook, whisking often, until the mixture begins to steam. Remove from the heat and let steep for 20 minutes.

Using a fine-meshed strainer or a standard strainer lined with cheesecloth or a coffee filter, strain the liquid into a bowl. Cover and chill for at least 3 hours, but preferably overnight. Freeze according to your ice cream maker's directions.

Spoon a third of the ice cream into a lidded storage container. Smooth the top, and pour over a few tablespoons of the caramel in long stripes. With the tip of a knife, lightly marble the caramel into the ice cream. Layer in half of the remaining ice cream, splatter with more caramel, then swirl again. Repeat the layers once more, ending with a drizzle of caramel. There will be caramel left over, so cover and refrigerate it for later. Cover the ice cream and freeze for at least 6 hours. Enjoy as is or sprinkle the ice cream with Candied Cacao Nibs just before serving.

. . . continued

CANDIED CACAO NIBS

Makes approximately ½ cup (125 ml) ·························

2 tablespoons
granulated sugar

½ cup (45 g) cacao nibs

½ teaspoon unsalted butter

NOTE: Making the caramel and coating the cacao nibs goes fast, taking maybe 5 minutes total; be sure to have everything ready by the stove, and don't leave the pan unattended at any point.

Line a baking sheet with parchment paper.

In a wide, heavy skillet over medium heat, warm the sugar for a minute, without stirring. Scatter the cacao nibs over the sugar and leave the pan undisturbed until the sugar begins to melt. With a wooden spoon or silicone spatula, quickly stir the cacao nibs into the liquid sugar, incorporating any unmelted sugar as you go. Once most of the sugar has coated the nibs, remove the pan from the heat and quickly stir in the butter. Immediately spread the cacao nibs onto the prepared baking sheet, pressing them into an even layer with the back of the spoon or spatula. Leave to cool.

Break the cacao nibs into tiny clusters by hand. Store in an airtight container at room temperature for up to 1 month.

ESPRESSO CARAMEL

Makes about ⅔ cup (150 ml) ·····································

½ cup (105 g) packed
dark brown sugar

2 tablespoons unsalted butter

2 tablespoons corn syrup,
honey, or glucose

¼ teaspoon fine-grain
sea salt

¼ cup (60 ml) heavy cream

¼ to ½ teaspoon finely
ground espresso beans
or espresso powder

½ teaspoon vanilla extract

NOTE: Leftover caramel can be used on pound cake or ice cream, or stirred into a milkshake or warm milk. Any and all of these can be made all the more enticing with a share of whiskey.

In a heavy saucepan over medium-high heat, heat the brown sugar, butter, corn syrup, and salt, stirring until the butter has melted. Pour in the cream and espresso powder. Bring to a boil, whisking until the mixture is smooth and the sugar dissolves. Lower the heat and simmer, undisturbed, for 1 minute longer. Remove from the heat and stir in the vanilla. Set aside to cool, stirring occasionally. If you are making this ahead of time, cover and refrigerate until needed, then rewarm gently before using.

RHUBARB ROSE GIN GIMLET

A nearby distillery makes a rose gin, and the Christmas they released their first batch, I went a bit overboard giving it as gifts. One of my favorite cocktails had long been a rhubarb gimlet, and during that gin-filled holiday, I started making fancied-up ones with frozen garden rhubarb, rose water, and Prosecco. It's now *the* favorite.

Gimlets are classically shaken with ice and served in a cocktail glass, but I go rogue and reach for a Collins or Old Fashioned glass instead, depending on how icy I want it to be. I tend to like this with a lot of ice, so it is cold enough to cause a shiver.

For the gin, steer clear of anything that will be at odds with the syrup; London Dry is a good match.

·· *Serves 8* ··

RHUBARB SYRUP

½ cup (100 g) sugar

12 ounces (340 g) rhubarb, chopped into chunks

½ cup (120 ml) water

2 pieces lime zest, each 1 inch (2.5 cm) wide

COCKTAILS

Rose water

8 lime wedges

Ice

16 ounces (500 ml) gin

8 ounces (250 ml) Prosecco or Cava

NOTE: Spread the cooked rhubarb on a digestive biscuit or sugar cookie, or eat it with Greek-style yogurt, Glazed Sesame Oats (page 51), and a pour of rhubarb syrup.

To make the syrup, sprinkle the sugar over the rhubarb in a heavy saucepan. Macerate at room temperature for 30 minutes, stirring regularly. Add the water and lime zest, with a few gentle stirs. Bring to a boil over medium-high heat, then lower the heat to maintain a simmer until the rhubarb has collapsed and the juices are thick, about 12 minutes. Discard the lime zest, then strain the syrup into a clean pitcher through a fine-meshed strainer—fork through the solids to release any trapped juice, but resist the temptation to press on the stalks or the syrup will be irrevocably clouded. Set aside the rhubarb for another use (see Note). If there is more than 1 cup (250 ml) syrup, return it to the saucepan and reduce over low heat until it is 1 cup, then cool. Refrigerate the syrup until cold.

To make each cocktail, in the glass of your choice, stir 1 ounce (30 ml) rhubarb syrup with a few drops of rose water. Squeeze in the juice from a lime wedge, then drop in the rind. Add a handful of ice, pour 2 ounces (60 ml) of gin over, and give everything a spin with a swizzle stick or spoon. Top up with 1 ounce (30 ml) of Prosecco. Cheers.

Ginger Gimlet Variation: Replace the lime zest in the syrup with a 1-inch (2.5 cm) knob of ginger, unpeeled and sliced into quarters. Omit the rose water and use ginger ale (page 250) instead of the Prosecco to provide some bubbles.

LIME GINGER ALE

I will, almost always, pick limes over lemons in drinks. (Iced tea is the only exception that comes to mind.) Here, added to a tongue-tingling ginger ale, the acidity of the lime is like the spark that lights the fuse of a firecracker.

The ginger bug is a natural starter for sodas, and maintaining it is similar to caring for a scoby (the starter) when making kombucha, a vinegar mother, or a sourdough starter for bread. With daily feedings it will start to bubble and smell sweetly fermented.

Makes about 2 quarts (2 L)

2 ounces (60 g) fresh ginger, grated

½ cup (100 g) natural cane sugar

2 limes, zest cut into 1-inch (2.5 cm) strips, plus the juice, about ¼ cup (60 ml)

7½ cups (1.8 L) filtered, nonchlorinated water

½ cup (120 ml) strained Ginger Bug (recipe follows), or ⅛ teaspoon active dry yeast

In a heavy saucepan, combine the ginger, cane sugar, zest, and 1 cup (240 ml) of the water. Bring to a boil over high heat, stirring often. Reduce the heat and simmer for 10 minutes. Set aside to cool completely.

Strain the cooled mixture into a pitcher with a pouring spout, pressing down on the solids to extract all the juice. Using a funnel, pour the syrup into a clean 2-liter plastic bottle. Add the lime juice, the remaining 6½ cups (1.56 L) water, and the ginger bug or yeast. Screw on the cap and give the bottle a shake. Set the bottle aside to ferment at room temperature for 48 hours. Unscrew the cap and check the progress. If you are satisfied with the carbonation, store in the fridge right away. If not, reseal and leave to develop further, checking its progress periodically. Bottles with yeast will be ready faster than those made with the bug, which can take up to 72 hours.

Store the ginger ale in the fridge for up to 1 week, but be sure to open the bottle daily to release excess pressure.

GINGER BUG

Makes about 2 cups (475 ml)

3 ounces (85 g) fresh ginger, about a 6-inch (15 cm) piece

5 tablespoons natural cane sugar

2 cups (475 ml) filtered, unchlorinated water

Grate a 1-inch (2.5 cm) piece of ginger. Measure out 1 tablespoon, grating more if needed. In a clean, 2-cup (475 ml) jar, use a nonmetal spoon to stir the ginger and 1 tablespoon of the sugar into the water. Cover the jar with a piece of cheesecloth secured with a rubber band. Set in a spot outside of direct sunlight for 1 day, and then feed again with 1 tablespoon each of fresh grated ginger and sugar. Repeat for 4 more days (5 total). When ready, the bug will be bubbly and give off a faintly funky but not unpleasant odor. There should not be any visible mold. Strain and use the bug as needed, continuing to feed it daily at room temperature, or once a week if kept in the fridge. Let refrigerated bug warm up before using.

PALOMA WITH CHAAT MASALA

When I was a kid, I wasn't the apple-a-day type; rather, my brother and I had our daily grapefruit (half). In the mornings, there would be two bowls, a hemisphere of fruit in each, segments freed from their confines by the work of my mother and one of those bent citrus knives. We were allowed white sugar on top. Once the fruit was done, we'd squeeze the remaining juice from the peel into our bowls, and then tip said bowls to our lips and slurp.

On occasion, my mother would peel the grapefruit, separate the segments by hand, and then open each segment along its seam with her thumb, to pull the pith away from the flesh. We'd be given these supremes as she revealed them and, instead of sugar, we'd dip them in bowls of *chaat masala* (snack spice in Hindi).

I've never gotten over grapefruit seasoned with spiced salt and have brought the combination to my adulthood, often as a snack, but sometimes as a cocktail.

The traditional Mexican Paloma is made with grapefruit soda, and there are really good and vivacious ones around. That said, there's a better chance I'll have a grapefruit in the house than soda these days, so I've included instructions for both versions.

.... *Serves 2* ....

¾ cup (180 ml) freshly squeezed grapefruit juice plus 2 tablespoons agave nectar, or ¾ cup (180 ml) grapefruit soda

1 lime

½ teaspoon fruit or regular chaat masala (see Note)

Ice

8 ounces (250 ml) tequila, 100 percent agave, preferably aged

Sparkling water or club soda (only if using fresh juice)

Sliced citrus—rounds or wedges—or zest, for garnish

NOTE: Fruit-specific and regular chaat masalas can be found in Indian markets and online. I like chaat masala best on grapefruit, sliced apples, and wedges of watermelon. If you can't track down either masala, make a spiced salt instead, using flaky sea salt, freshly ground black pepper, ground cumin, ground ginger, and Kashmiri chile powder or cayenne.

Divide the grapefruit juice or soda between 2 highball glasses. Squeeze the juice from half a lime into each glass, and divide the chaat masala between the two. Top with ice, then tequila, and the sparkling water, if using. Garnish with citrus slices or zest. Give a good stir, then bottoms up.

STAPLES

I consider these recipes the complement to the ingredients I stock in my pantry. They cover everything from churning butter (which I don't do often) to making ghee (which I do), to salad dressings and condiments, to a master recipe for a pie dough that is as forgiving as it is adaptable.

CULTURED BUTTER

You may never need to make your own butter, but there is a sense of empowerment in knowing that you could. Cultured butter differs from sweet (regular) butter by having a fermented base, which results in a slightly tangy, hazelnut finish.

Makes about 1½ to 2 cups (375 to 500 g) butter and 2 cups (480 ml) buttermilk

2 cups (480 ml) crème fraîche (page 261)

2 cups (480 ml) heavy cream, not ultra-pasteurized

½ teaspoon flaky sea salt (optional)

Chill a metal strainer and a food processor bowl with its metal blade in a freezer for 20 minutes. Once chilled, pour in the crème fraîche and heavy cream, and whizz until the mix has separated, about 3 to 5 minutes. Stop a few times during processing to scrape down the sides of the bowl and to check on how things are progressing; the liquid will first look whipped, then grainy, then finally split. Place the cold metal strainer over a bowl and line with a double layer of cheesecloth hanging over the rim. Pour the contents of the processor into the strainer and let it drain for a few minutes. Gather the cheesecloth into a bundle, then squeeze tightly to expel as much liquid as possible. Save the buttermilk, covered and refrigerated, and use as you would store-bought.

Unwrap the butter and place it into a clean bowl. Pour about ½ cup of ice water into the bowl on top of the butter. Use a spatula or your hands to knead and press any remaining buttermilk from the solids, then drain the bowl. Repeat the process of rinsing, kneading, and draining,

until the water remains clear. Dry the butter thoroughly on a clean, lint-free kitchen towel, then knead and dry again on the towel. The drier the butter is, the longer its shelf life. Sprinkle the butter with salt, then knead to incorporate. Roll the finished butter into logs wrapped in parchment paper or transfer to a covered dish, then refrigerate for up to 1 month.

Sweet Variation: Simply follow the same instructions, replacing the crème fraîche with an additional 2 cups (480 ml) of heavy cream.

BUTTERMILK

If you need more buttermilk than your butter-making endeavors yield, then you can make a quick version, which is basically soured milk. It will not be as thick as store-bought.

Makes 1 cup (240 ml)

1 tablespoon lemon juice or white vinegar

1 scant cup (225 ml) milk (low-fat or whole)

Pour the lemon juice into a liquid measuring cup. Add enough milk to make 1 full cup (240 ml). Stir and leave for about 5 minutes at room temperature. Stir and check; once it has noticeably thickened, it is ready to use.

CLARIFIED BUTTER, BROWNED BUTTER, AND GHEE

The difference between clarified butter, browned butter, and ghee is basically time; all are pure forms of butterfat and have much higher smoke points than regular butter. They start with butter that's melted, then heated until the water evaporates and the milk solids separate from the fat. Ghee and browned butter are cooked longer, so that the milk solids caramelize and brown, giving a nutty aroma and flavor.

With any, the quality of the butter used will directly correlate to the qualities of your result. Fresh, homemade, cultured butter (page 258) is a divine choice, and closest to what is often used in India for ghee. Store-bought, European-style butter, with its higher butterfat content, will have a slightly greater yield than American-style butter.

Makes about 1½ cups (375 ml)

1 pound (455 g) best-quality unsalted butter, cut into chunks

Line a strainer with a double layer of cheesecloth, then set it over a bowl (if you have a superfine strainer, the cloth isn't necessary). Bring the butter to a boil in a heavy-bottomed saucepan over medium-high heat, which should take about 3 minutes. Reduce the heat to medium-low and simmer. The butter will foam, then subside. Once it has subsided, stop at this point for clarified butter and strain, but for browned butter and ghee, continue cooking until the butter foams a second time and the milk solids begin to take on color. Pull the pan from the heat and skim off any remaining foam. As is, you have browned butter. Pour the melted butter through the strainer and what drains out is ghee; discard the solids. Transfer the liquid to a sealable container.

Both clarified butter and ghee can be kept, covered, at cool room temperature. However, I prefer to keep my clarified butter in the fridge, where it will be fine for a few months. I sometimes refrigerate ghee, but not always, and feel comfortable with keeping it for about 1 month without chilling. Any foam skimmed from the butter can be used to dress cooked vegetables or to enhance savory oatmeal (page 45).

COMPOUND BUTTERS

Use compound butter to garnish cooked meats and vegetables, in baked goods, to finish sauces, or simply as an oomph-packed spread. I've even used it to make spectacular biscuits (page 32).

Makes about ⅔ cup (150 ml)

What follows are loose guidelines for making a compound butter.

Anchovy Butter: ½ cup (225 g) unsalted butter; 4 to 6 anchovy fillets, mashed; 1 clove garlic, minced; ½ teaspoon finely grated lemon zest; fine sea salt and freshly ground black pepper

Chile Garlic Butter: ½ cup (225 g) unsalted butter; 3 tablespoons minced flat-leaf parsley; 2 cloves garlic, minced; ½ teaspoon crushed red pepper flakes or 1 small fresh red chile, minced; 1 teaspoon finely grated lemon zest, fine sea salt and freshly ground black pepper

Curry Butter: ½ cup (225 g) unsalted butter; 1½ to 2 tablespoons curry powder (not curry paste); 1 tablespoon mango chutney, such as Major Grey's; 1 teaspoon minced cilantro leaves; salt and freshly ground black pepper

Harissa Butter: ½ cup (225 g) unsalted butter, 2 tablespoons harissa (page 274), 1 tablespoon minced flat-leaf parsley, 1 tablespoon minced mint, salt and freshly ground black pepper

Jam Butter: ½ cup (225 g) unsalted butter, ¼ cup (50 ml) jam or marmalade, finely grated citrus zest to taste

Maple Butter: ½ cup (225 g) unsalted butter, ¼ cup (60 ml) Grade B maple syrup, ⅛ teaspoon freshly grated nutmeg

Pesto or Tapenade Butter: ½ cup (225 g) unsalted butter, 2 tablespoons pesto or tapenade, finely grated lemon zest to taste, fine sea salt and freshly ground black pepper

Sweet Fennel Pollen Butter: ½ cup (225 g) unsalted butter, 1 teaspoon fennel pollen, 2 teaspoons honey, 2 teaspoons finely grated grapefruit zest, and ¼ teaspoon minced fresh rosemary

Mix the flavorings into softened butter, then transfer to a container and refrigerate to firm up. Alternatively, shape the butter into logs with parchment paper, label, and chill or freeze in a sealed freezer bag.

CLOTTED CREAM

I have a weakness for cream tea, of which cream scones are a part, and clotted cream is a must. Clotted cream, also known as Devonshire cream, is made by cooking cream slowly over low heat, so that the milk fats rise to the top of the liquid. Those solids are then skimmed and kept as a sweet, dense spread with about 64 percent butterfat. This metamorphosis can take place over a steam bath or indirect heat, but a low oven will do trick. Since the oven will be on so long, I usually make a large batch; however, because clotted cream has a frustratingly short shelf life, it is good to plan on giving some away, or to have a tea party on the calendar.

Oh, and even though the buttermilk scones (page 54) are not the traditional partner, they get along just fine with this clotted cream.

Makes about 2 cups (480 ml)

4 cups (1 L) heavy cream, not ultra-pasteurized

Preheat an oven to 150°F (65°C). Pour the cream into a wide ceramic baking dish and cover with foil. Bake until thickened with a skin on top, 10 to 12 hours. Cool completely on a rack at room temperature, then cover with plastic wrap and chill until fully set, 8 hours or so. Carefully skim the clotted cream off with a spoon, and transfer to a clean jar; it is now ready to use. Clotted cream can be kept, refrigerated, for 3 to 4 days. The cream left in the pan can be strained, then used as you would half-and-half.

CRÈME FRAÎCHE

Crème fraîche is like a richer, slightly pluckier version of sour cream. Its high butterfat content makes it more stable when heated, and it can be whipped like heavy cream. It establishes a needed counterpoint to sweet desserts; in mashed potatoes, it is divine.

Makes a generous 2 cups (500 ml)

2 cups (480 ml) heavy cream, not ultra-pasteurized
2 tablespoons cultured buttermilk (page 258)

Combine the buttermilk and cream in a clean, nonreactive container. Cover and leave on the counter until thickened to your liking, anywhere from 12 to 24 hours depending on the temperature of the room. Store in the refrigerator for up to 2 weeks.

LABNEH

This Middle Eastern fresh cheese couldn't be simpler to make—strain some yogurt for a day and there you have it. It can be kept voluptuous and softly spoonable, or drained to the consistency of cream cheese. With its pleasant tang, labneh is traditionally served dressed with olive oil and spices alongside flatbread, but it can be used as a spread or dip, savory or sweet. I often use cold labneh in place of cream cheese, sour cream, crème fraîche, or Greek-style yogurt.

And about Greek-style yogurt: traditionally, Greek yogurt and labneh are similar, and the terms are often used interchangeably. From my understanding, while both begin with yogurt, labneh is strained further, to a denser result. What's more, many manufacturers use thickeners in their Greek-style yogurt production and I sometimes find the texture off-putting, especially when the yogurt is used in large quantities.

Makes approximately 3 cups (710 ml)

¾ teaspoon fine-grain sea salt for savory uses, ⅓ teaspoon for sweet

1½ quarts (1.4 L) full-fat plain yogurt, made from cow's or goat's milk or a mixture

Set a super-fine nylon strainer over a deep bowl. Stir the salt into the yogurt and scrape the mixture into the prepared strainer. Cover and refrigerate and let the yogurt drain for between 8 and 24 hours, or until the labneh has reached the desired consistency. Alternatively, set a nonreactive metal strainer over a bowl and line with a few layers of overhanging cheesecloth. Stir the salt into the yogurt and scrape the mixture into the prepared strainer. Either cover and refrigerate as is, or for faster draining, tie the ends of the cheesecloth securely to put pressure on the yogurt. Remove the strainer from the bowl. Push a hook or the handle of a wooden spoon through the knot on the cheesecloth. Suspend the bundle over the bowl in the refrigerator, then leave to drain as before.

Scrape the labneh into an airtight storage container and store in the fridge for up to 4 days. Discard the whey.

Sweet Uses:

As a creamy protein-rich base for smoothies.

Alongside roasted peaches (page 51) or to top a breakfast cobbler (page 53).

Make frozen labneh. Strain, without hanging, for 8 hours. Stir in enough honey to make it slightly too sweet, ⅓ to ½ cup (80 to 120 ml), and the seeds scraped from 1 vanilla bean. Chill for an hour. Freeze in an ice cream maker according to the manufacturer's instructions.

Beat with an equal amount of heavy cream and fold into lemon curd. Serve with blackberries and crushed gingersnaps.

Savory Uses:

Strain until quite firm, then form into balls. Coat in minced tender herbs (parsley, mint, cilantro) or spices (paprika, za'atar, sumac) and serve with crackers. Marinate plain balls in olive oil, garlic, chiles, and herbs, as you would bocconcini or feta.

Spread on toast, with gravlax (page 115) or beneath roasted beets with chermoula (page 122) or salsa verde (page 269).

Dollop on a plate, cozy up two halves of a hard-cooked egg or still-hot roasted potato chunks. Sprinkle liberally with dukkah (page 198).

Swirl into a shallow bowl, top with black-eyed peas, diced avocados, pico de gallo, and torn cilantro leaves. Splatter with lime juice, olive oil, and Mexican-style hot sauce. Eat with tortilla chips.

Serve underneath a chopped olive salad or mixed pickled vegetables.

Whirl with peas and lemon, as in Blitzed Ricotta with Peas (page 114).

NUT MILK

Soaking nuts before blending is imperative to a smooth, creamy result. Even more than textural concerns, soaking starts the germination process of the nut, breaking down the natural enzyme inhibitors and thus making the maximum nutrients accessible to our bodies.

Makes about 1 quart (1 L)

1 cup (115 g) raw nuts (hazelnuts, almonds, cashews, pistachios, walnuts)

6 cups (1.5 L) filtered water, 2 cups (0.5 L) cold and 4 cups (1 L) hot

Pinch of fine-grain sea salt

1 tablespoon agave syrup, maple syrup, or honey (optional)

In a large bowl, soak the nuts in the 2 cups (0.5 L) cold water at least overnight, or for up to 24 hours, at room temperature.

Drain the nuts and discard the liquid. In the carafe of a blender, combine the nuts, the 4 cups (1 L) hot water, salt, and sweetener if using. Blend until absolutely smooth, 2 to 3 minutes. Line a strainer with a nut milk bag or with a double layer of cheesecloth, with the ends overhanging. Set the strainer over a bowl. Pour the nut mixture through the cheesecloth or into the bag and allow

to drain. (If you are using cheesecloth, it may be necessary to pour the milk in batches. Once drained, twist the ends of the cloth together to put pressure on the nut solids, extracting as much liquid as possible. Dispose of the nut pulp, then transfer the milk to a sealable container. Store in the fridge for up to 3 or 4 days, and shake before using.

NOTE: Add vanilla extract or vanilla paste for, you guessed it, vanilla nut milk.

RICOTTA

Sweet and mild, ricotta is one of the easiest cheeses to make at home, no special equipment required. Use all milk with no cream for a lower-fat ricotta, or when making paneer (see variation below).

Makes a generous 2 cups (500 ml)

6 cups (1.5 L) whole milk, not ultra-pasteurized

**2 cups (480 ml) heavy cream,
not ultra-pasteurized**

**⅓ cup (80 ml) fresh lemon juice,
plus more as needed**

½ to 1 teaspoon fine-grain sea salt (optional)

Line a strainer with a double layer of cheesecloth and set it over a bowl. Heat the milk and cream in a heavy 4-quart (4 L) pot over medium heat. Let the mixture warm slowly until it reaches 200°F (93°C), using an instant-read or candy thermometer to keep track of the temperature, and stirring occasionally. Do not boil. Pull the pot off the heat and stir in the lemon juice and salt. Leave, undisturbed, for 10 minutes. With a slotted spoon, check the mixture. If it does not look mostly curdled, add another tablespoon of the lemon juice and wait a few more minutes. Put back over gentle heat if the pot feels cold. Once curdled, use a slotted spoon to transfer the large curds to the prepared strainer. Pour the remaining curds and whey through the strainer. Let drain until the ricotta has reached the desired consistency, up to 2 hours. Transfer the ricotta to a sealable container and keep chilled for a few days or up to a week, depending on the freshness of the dairy used.

Paneer Variation: Paneer is a fresh Indian cheese that can be treated like tofu. Prepare as above, using all milk. Rinse the curds under cool water before draining. Twist the ends of the cheesecloth together to form a tight ball. Squeeze out as much whey as possible, then tie the bundle shut. Leave in the strainer to drain for 10 minutes. Transfer the bundle to a shallow dish with the knotted end to one side; then place a cutting board or plate on top, with a heavy can or another weight on top of that. Leave on the counter for 30 minutes or longer, until the cheese is dry enough to cut cleanly, or place the whole rig in the fridge for an even firmer finish. Store paneer wrapped in the fridge for up to 2 days.

YOGURT

For what feels like every night of my early childhood, though I know it can't be so, the oven light illuminated our kitchen come darkness because my mother was making yogurt. In the same bowl always, a heavy ceramic brown one, with a small plate placed on top as a lid. The oven light kept the milk warm, thereby encouraging the bacterial process, while we all slept. I have a very specific memory of that bowl, cold and slick with condensation from the fridge, and the sound of the plate pushed away from the rim, and the strange sort of pleasure there was in breaking the pristine surface of the yogurt with a spoon.

My mother always made plain yogurt; we'd eat it with curries as is, or as raita (page 153), or as dessert with coarse sugar on top. The yogurt that follows can be flavored before setting; stir honey, maple syrup, vanilla, espresso powder, or cocoa into the hot milk and starter yogurt, then add to the pot as detailed below.

Be sure to always use plain yogurt to start a fresh batch.

Makes 1 quart (1 L)

1 quart (1 L) milk, skim or whole

2 heaped tablespoons plain yogurt, with active cultures

Pour hot water into a 1-quart (1 L) heatproof jar. In a large, heavy pot, carefully heat the milk to 185°F (85°C) over medium heat, stirring. Pull the pot off the heat and let the milk cool to 115°F (45°C); it will feel warm to the touch. Pour some of the milk into a 1-cup (240 ml) liquid measure, and stir in the yogurt. Once smooth, stir the yogurt mixture into the pot of milk. Empty the water out of the jar that was warming. Pour the milk into the jar, cover, and wrap in a kitchen towel. Place the jar into a (cold) oven with the interior light on (not necessary for stoves with pilot lights). Leave the jar, undisturbed, until the milk has set, up to overnight. Whisk the yogurt before chilling for at least 4 hours to firm. The yogurt can be kept, covered and refrigerated, for up to 2 weeks.

NOTE: You can make the yogurt entirely in its cooking pot, in which case a Dutch oven is perfect. Cover the starter and milk mixture and tuck the entire pot in the oven to set. Whisk and pour into storage containers, then refrigerate as above.

MAYONNAISE

Mayonnaise is like butter; you can buy a good-quality one at the store, which I often do, but now and again, it is rewarding to make your own. Consider this an excuse to fiddle with the choice of acid (think orange juice jolted with champagne vinegar) and oils (ponder a blend of light olive oil and peanut oil).

Makes ¾ cup (175 ml)

1 egg yolk

2 teaspoons fresh lemon juice

1 teaspoon Dijon mustard

Fine-grain sea salt and freshly ground black pepper

¾ cup (175 ml) mild olive oil or neutral-tasting oil

In a medium bowl, whisk together the egg yolk, lemon juice, mustard, and a pinch each of salt and pepper. Still whisking, start dripping in the oil, in the tiniest of droplets at first, and then in a thin, trickling stream as the mixture emulsifies. Once all the oil is incorporated, which will take enough beating for your arm to tire, check for seasoning and use right away, or cover and refrigerate for a few days.

NOTE: Since the eggs are uncooked, use only the freshest farm eggs possible, or use yolks that have been pasteurized.

BASIL BUTTERMILK DRESSING

Think of this on fat wedges of summer tomatoes, or on avocado and cucumber. Keep the consistency thick and spread on grilled corn, or use as a condiment on burgers, BLTs, and club sandwiches.

Makes a generous 2 cups (500 ml)

½ cup (120 ml) mayonnaise (page 265)

2 tablespoons full-fat plain yogurt (page 264) or sour cream

2 teaspoons apple cider vinegar

2 tablespoons minced shallot

2 tablespoons chopped fresh basil

1 cup (240 ml) well-shaken buttermilk (page 258)

1 tablespoon honey

Fine-grain sea and freshly ground black pepper

¼ teaspoon smoked paprika

In a bowl, stir together the mayonnaise, yogurt, vinegar, shallot, and basil. Stir in most of the buttermilk and all the honey. Check for consistency, and add more buttermilk if needed. Taste, then season with salt, pepper, and paprika. Cover and refrigerate for an hour before using, to allow the flavors to blend and develop. Store any leftover dressing in the fridge and use within a couple of days.

CITRUS MISO TAHINI DRESSING

Tear up some kale, add a sliced apple and a handful of nuts and seeds, pour on this dressing, and there's a salad I'd happily eat daily. Or, use this dressing as a dip for raw carrots, on any kind of cooked broccoli rabe or broccolini, or on a baked sweet potato, still hot and steaming.

Makes 1 cup (240 ml)

1 clove garlic, peeled

⅓ cup (80 ml) white (shiro) miso

⅓ cup (80 ml) tahini, stirred

Juice from a medium to large orange, plus more as needed

Fine-grain salt and freshly ground black pepper

Honey (optional)

Fresh lemon juice or rice vinegar (optional)

Water, toasted sesame oil, or extra-virgin olive oil (optional)

In a mortar and pestle, pound the garlic into a paste. Stir in the miso and tahini, then most of the juice from the orange. Taste, season with salt and pepper, and taste again. Here's where you'll have to decide how best to proceed. Fiddle with the dressing until there is a pleasing balance of fat and acid. You'll have the urge to smack your lips when it's right. You should taste the orange—give it a boost if necessary with more of its juice and maybe a scant spoon of honey. If the dressing tastes flat, add lemon juice or rice vinegar. The ideal consistency is that of pouring cream; stir in some water, or little drops of either of the oils, until it runs easily off a spoon. Store any leftovers covered in the fridge for a few days.

BANG-UP BLUE CHEESE DRESSING

As silly as it sounds, blue cheese dressing is an art more than a science. There are variables to consider and balance, ones that can't be pinned down to hard and fast rules: the pungency and the moisture of the cheese, the astringency of the particular lemon that's juiced, the consistency of the sour cream. So please simply use what follows as a guideline to steer you in the right direction.

For the cheese, I gravitate toward a Stilton or Roquefort, or something similarly pungent, so there's that much more bang for the quantity of cheese. Also, I have a weakness for cayenne-based sauces partnered with blue cheese—it's a cheese that benefits from a vinegary sting, a lip-prickling heat. And while we're on the topic of hot sauce, I don't mix the hot sauce into the dressing. I'm not fond of the pinkish shade it dyes everything, but that's also a taste preference. Keeping it instead in dribs and drabs across the salad perforates the dressing's richness.

Makes about 1 cup (240 ml)

½ cup (120 ml) mayonnaise (page 265)

¼ cup (60 ml) Greek-style yogurt or sour cream

¼ cup (60 ml) well-shaken buttermilk (page 258)

1 tablespoon white wine vinegar

1 teaspoon honey

1 tablespoon minced fresh chives

4 ounces (115 g) blue cheese, crumbled

Freshly cracked black pepper

Cayenne-based hot sauce, crushed red pepper flakes, or chile oil to serve

Get out a bowl and mix together the mayonnaise, yogurt, most of the buttermilk, and all the vinegar and honey. Fold in the chives and blue cheese, then season with pepper. Taste, then tweak the seasoning for your taste. You can use the dressing right away, but I think it improves after a day in the fridge, after the flavors have a chance to settle. The dressing will thicken as it sits, but can be thinned with a few drops of water. Serve with a dash of hot sauce. Keep any leftover dressing in an airtight container in the fridge and use up in a few days.

SHAKEN SESAME DRESSING

While minced garlic, ginger, or chiles would surely be welcomed to the party, I usually leave them out, so getting this dressing together is purely a measure-and-shake affair. Use it on a salad of thinly shredded cabbage and carrots, a cool plate of cucumber and soba noodles, or alongside Salad Rolls (page 75).

Makes about ⅔ cup (160 ml)

2 tablespoons tamari

2 tablespoons natural cane sugar

2 tablespoons unseasoned rice vinegar, preferably brown

A few dashes of fish sauce (optional)

2 tablespoons avocado oil (or any neutral-tasting oil)

2 tablespoons toasted sesame oil

Combine all the ingredients in a jar. Screw the lid on tightly and shake well, until the mixture looks thick and the sugar dissolves. Taste and adjust for seasoning, adding more sour (vinegar), salty (tamari or fish sauce), or sweet (sugar) as needed. Let the dressing sit for a few minutes before using. Keeps well in its jar in the fridge for up to a week.

counter for 10 minutes for the flavors to really start waking up, or cover and refrigerate for up to 4 hours, then bring it back to room temperature before using. It is best used the day it is made.

RUSTIC SALSA VERDE

There is more than one salsa verde; the Mexican, made with tomatillos, and the Italian, which is straight-up herbs. Try this on a burger (page 92) or splashed onto hummus (page 112), or use to marinate fresh bocconcini. You'll be hooked.

Makes around ½ cup (120 g)

1 lemon

½ cup (30 g) chopped fresh flat-leaf parsley

1 tablespoon capers, rinsed if packed in salt, drained if in brine, then coarsely chopped if large

2 anchovy fillets, minced

1 heaped teaspoon Dijon mustard

½ cup (120 ml) extra-virgin olive oil

¼ teaspoon crushed red pepper flakes

Flaky sea salt and freshly ground black pepper

With a peeler, cut the zest from the lemon, then slice into the thinnest strands you can manage. (If you have a julienne peeler, use that instead.) Set the zested lemon aside.

In a small bowl, combine the parsley, capers, anchovy fillets, and lemon zest. Stir in the mustard, then juice from the lemon, followed by the olive oil in a steady stream until you have a loose, chunky vinaigrette. Check the balance of acid to oil, adjusting if needed. Season to taste with red pepper flakes, salt, and pepper. Let stand on the

PICKLED JALAPEÑOS WITH GARLIC AND ORANGE

Pickles require faith. Commitment. They work on their own schedule, and while you might set things in motion, that is where your influence both begins and ends.

What you put in the jar is acrid and overblown, eye-twitchingly sour. From there, the pickle takes care of itself as it sits in the fridge. That time under glass is transformative. The jalapeños are hot, of course, but it is a heat that builds, rather than knocks you flat at the get-go. The vinegar mellows and becomes muted; its acridity is tinged with a floral note from the orange. That orange is what is most remarkable; it underscores the agave nectar, with a brightness that brings out the chiles.

Makes a 1-pint (475 ml) jar

1½ cups (355 ml) apple cider vinegar or white vinegar

½ cup (120 ml) water, preferably filtered

1 tablespoon medium-grain kosher salt

1 tablespoon agave nectar or granulated sugar

2 cloves garlic, peeled and sliced

12 fresh jalapeños, stemmed and sliced

4 pieces orange zest cut stem to end from a navel or Seville orange, each strip about 1 inch (2.5 cm) wide

In a heavy saucepan, combine the vinegar, water, salt, and agave nectar. Drop in the garlic. Bring this brine to a boil over medium-high heat, swirling regularly. Lower the heat to the barest simmer while you sort out the jalapeños.

Pack the jalapeño slices tightly in a clean glass 1-pint (475 ml) jar, tucking in the orange zest between the layers as you go. Pour the brine over the jalapeños until covered. Let cool to room temperature, then seal and refrigerate. The pickles can be used after 1 day, but they are really something special after 1 week. Treat and use as you would any opened jar of commercially produced pickles—in other words, they'll last a long time, and you'll find a whole bunch of uses for it.

NOTE: Since these pickles are raw and unprocessed, they end up crunchier than store-bought ones. I know some prefer a tender chile, in which case simmer the jalapeños in the brine for 1 to 2 minutes before transferring to jars.

Use a splash of brine spooned from the jar in vinaigrettes and salad dressings, especially ones with creamy bases (Charred Green Onion Dressing, page 185), or to perk up a cocktail—it is an effective addition to a Paloma with Chaat Masala (page 252).

FAMILY-APPROVED
PIE DOUGH

My mother taught me to put an egg yolk in pie dough, adding richness and a hint of elastic strength, and making the pastry a dream to work with. (I keep the white around for an egg wash before baking whatever pie I've made.)

Pie crust recipes will often have similar ingredients and proportions. The fact is, there's a pretty set ratio of flour to fat because the flour will only be able to take a certain amount of fat before it starts to weep all over the oven. Usually it is the method that differentiates, and mine shares a good deal of theory with biscuit making—My Best Biscuits (page 32) covers the logic in detail.

Something to keep in mind: Laminated dough swells forcefully when baked. Consider rubbing the butter into smaller pieces when forming the dough, and ignore the rolling and folding step when making a pie with a raised, intricate edge—in which case, divide the dough in two before the first rest. There will be less puff, but the decorations will stay neat.

Makes enough for 2 pie shells or 1 double-crust pie, each 9 inches (23 cm) in diameter

2½ cups (320 g) all-purpose flour

**2 teaspoons granulated sugar
(for sweet crusts only)**

1 teaspoon medium-grain kosher salt

**1 cup (225 g) unsalted butter, cold
and cut into large dice**

1 egg yolk

1 teaspoon apple cider vinegar

Ice water

In a large, wide bowl, whisk the flour with the sugar and salt. Scatter the butter over the flour. With the pads of your fingers, squish each cube of butter into thin flakes, in a motion similar to dealing cards off the top of a deck. Toss the butter into the dry ingredients as it is flattened, so that it is kept coated on all sides. Once all the butter has been squashed, chill the mixture for 30 minutes.

Stir the egg yolk with the vinegar in a 1-cup (240 ml) liquid measure, then add enough ice water to make ¼ cup (60 ml) total. Drizzle the liquids over the flour and butter mixture, then, with a butter knife, start stirring the wet into the dry. After a few stirs, abandon the knife and use your hands or a spatula to pick up stray flour and press it into the damp pockets of dough. Continue collecting the dough together in this way, pushing and smearing the mass against the bowl. This will not only incorporate the flour but also create long sheets of fat within the dough in a lazy-person's version of *fraisage*, a classic pastry technique. If the dough seems dry, stingily drip in more ice water as needed. Once the lion's share of the flour is incorporated, fold the dough onto itself a few times, trapping any remaining flour in the folds. Cautiously pat out the dough in between each fold, and shift the bowl a quarter turn so that the dough isn't always folded the same way. The dough should be together, albeit raggedly, with visible pieces of butter.

Tip the dough onto a work surface and shape into a round. Wrap with plastic wrap. Once sealed, press firmly, so that the film is good and tight and the dough looks like it could burst from its wrapping. I feel this binding helps the dough in the end, encouraging the dry ingredients to fully absorb the wet. Refrigerate for 30 minutes.

Lightly flour a work surface, a rolling pin, and both sides of the unwrapped dough. Roll the dough into a long rectangle. Dust off the excess flour and fold into thirds, like a business letter. Turn the package 90 degrees and roll out again, flouring the board, rolling pin, and dough as needed. Brush away loose flour, then fold as before. If ever the dough gets too warm, cover and chill before proceeding. Turn the package a final time and roll the dough into a rectangle double the length of its width and cut in two. Shape the pieces into rounds, wrap snugly with plastic wrap, and chill for at least 1 hour, and up to 2 days, or freeze for up to 1 month. For frozen dough, defrost in the fridge before using.

Whole Wheat Variation: Up to about ¾ cup (85 g) whole wheat flour can be swapped in for the same amount of white, though the crust will not be as flaky. Use whole wheat pastry flour if you can.

Sour Cream Variation: For an especially delicate crust, use 2 tablespoons sour cream or whole-milk yogurt instead of the egg and vinegar.

Eggless Variation: Omit the egg (keeping the vinegar) and make up the extra liquid with more ice water.

Lard Variation: Substitute lard for the same amount of butter; lard will make for a finer, more fragile crust. A mix of butter and lard— say, ¾ cup (170 g) butter to ¼ cup (60 g) lard—will give the best of both worlds.

Sweet Variation: Use up 2 tablespoons sugar for a shell destined for a sour or mild filling (such as lemon curd or labneh).

Cheese Variation: A few tablespoons of a grated hard cheese, such as Parmesan, Pecorino, or aged cheddar, gives extra personality to quiche or vegetable tarts. Grind in some black pepper, too.

HARISSA

This North African spice paste is one I adore unreservedly. Rub it on chicken before roasting or toss with roasted sweet peppers, eggplant, and chickpeas. I eat it with eggs, add it to hummus, and spread it on pitas stuffed with koftas (page 151).

Makes about 1½ cups (355 ml)

1 tablespoon cumin seeds

½ teaspoon coriander seeds

Olive oil, as needed

2 fresh hot red chiles, stemmed, seeded, and chopped

1 shallot, sliced

6 cloves garlic, minced

1½ teaspoons sweet paprika

1½ teaspoons cayenne

Small bunch of cilantro, leaves and tender stems

Small bunch of flat-leaf parsley, leaves and tender stems

1 cup (240 ml) canned crushed tomatoes, preferably fire-roasted

1 cup (240 ml) water

Medium-grain kosher salt and freshly ground black pepper

Juice from ½ lemon

Honey

Extra-virgin olive oil (it needn't be expensive, but it should taste good)

In a heavy saucepan over medium heat, toast the cumin and coriander seeds until fragrant, 90 seconds or so, tossing often. Transfer the seeds to a mortar and pestle and, once cooled, pound them into a powder.

In the same saucepan, get a tablespoon of oil nice and hot, still over medium heat. Sauté the chiles and shallot until caramelized and intensely aromatic, 8 to 10 minutes, stirring all the while. Stir in the spices from the mortar and the garlic, paprika, cayenne, cilantro, and parsley; cook for 30 seconds more. Pour in the tomatoes and water and season generously with salt, pepper, and the lemon juice. Bring to a boil, then reduce the heat to a simmer. Maintain that gentle bubbling until the mixture is thickened and reduced, stirring often, about 1 hour.

Check the seasoning, adding honey if the tomatoes had some edge. Remove from the heat and blend with an immersion blender until smooth. Transfer the harissa to a clean jar, pour some extra-virgin olive oil over the back of a spoon so it floats on top of the paste, then cover and refrigerate. Use right away, replenishing the olive oil cap as needed, for up to 1 month.

ACKNOWLEDGMENTS

This book's existence is due to a whole cast of folks to whom I am immeasurably grateful.

To Aaron Wehner and everyone at Ten Speed Press. Emily Timberlake, you are the editor every writer wishes to have. You brought finesse and elegance to this book. Thank you for *The Hobbit*, for Wes Anderson films, for being the captain of the team, and for being a gin drinker to boot. Emma Campion, when I heard that you were to work on this book, I could have pinched myself. (I totally did.) To have your talent involved was an honor. Thank you for your vision. Nami Kurita, thank you for your input and execution on the design, and all your diligence. To the marketing and publicity team, Lorraine Woodcheke, Michele Crim, Daniel Wikey, and Ashley Matuszak, I take enormous comfort in the knowledge that you've got my back. Thank you for believing in this book.

Robert McCullough, you are a mentor and my friend. Your guidance, faith, and humor helped me become an author.

And to everyone else on the Canadian side of publishing who works with Robert at Appetite by Random House: thank you for giving me a home in my home country. Laura Cameron, you are an absolute doll. Cathy Paine, Josh Glover, Jennifer Herman, Lindsey Reeder, and Jordan Fenn, superstars all, you make this whole business into a party.

To Julie van Rosendaal, for not only your support and encouragement, but also for introducing me to Robert in the first place. You started this, really.

Thank you to Janine Vangool, for giving me an early break.

Many, many thanks to those who ran these recipes through their paces: Yossy Arefi, Tim Robison Jr., Ashley Denton, Alana Chernila, Sarah Kieffer, Martha Coleman, Kelly Novitski, and John Krussi. I owe you.

The generosity of your effort, groceries, comments, and time was a gift, and you were my collaborators. And another thanks to Yossy for the chocolate, and for that beautiful little bowl of yours.

To Michael and Anna Boekestyn, for the harvest reports and the strawberries.

To Tiffany Mayer, for comparing notes and for the lunches. To Linda Crago, for your commitment to the food you grow and the people you feed. And for the tomatoes.

To Ashley Rodriguez, for the company through so many steps of the way, with your clear-eyed commitment to your own work. And to Sara Forte, for sharing your experience and advice as openly as you do your friendship. Aran Goyoaga, thank you for dukkah, your perspective, your energy, and the example of your hospitality. You've taught me more than you know.

To Heidi Swanson, for always making time, and for being a consistent source of inspiration.

To Molly Wizenberg, for writing the first food blog I ever read, and for setting the standard so high. And thank you, Molly, for a conversation that made me feel like this was possible.

To Tara Austen Weaver, for not letting a little thing like the width of a continent and a number of time zones stand in the way of kindred spirit.

To Michèle Rice, for being there at the start, and being here still.

To Michael and Christa Krause—and the girls, Arleigh, Kennedy, Trevi, and Brylee—for being enthusiastic tasters and important friends.

To Nikole Herriott, for being my usual sounding board and my sometimes partner-in-crime. Thanks for bostocks, bubbles on the stoop, and that first spoon from LH. Meet you in the back house.

To Jason Hudson, for saying things as they are, for your strength and reassurance, for sending the best mail, and for never feeling too far away.

Thank you, thank you, April Spires, for being my sparkling best for all these years.

To my family: the Powells, the Malhotras, the Ralphs, and the O'Bradys.

To my nephews. Aidan, for being my second with the chocolate chip cookies and for baking them on your own. Jackson, for giving great compliments.

To my grandmother, Jaishri Malhotra, for trips to the library, making eggs, and putting up with my nonsense (and calling me on it just as much). You are missed.

To Tom and Sandra, for butter tarts and sharing with me that cake recipe. Thank you for welcoming me into your family with such open arms and never feeling like in-laws.

To my father and mother, Benjamin and Geeta. For making the choices you did, your hard work, and the opportunities both allowed me. Thank you for all your help, and thank you for being better cooks than I will ever be.

To my Benjamin and William, my fine lads. You are at the center of everything. You are funnier, wilder, more mischievous, curious, brilliant, and all-get-out wonderful than words can say. You are a greater adventure than I could have ever imagined, and I cannot wait to see what you two do next. Thank you for showing me the infinite possibility of this world.

And to Sean. For the idea to start a blog in the first place, and for your belief in me. It is not only that I wouldn't have written this book without you, it is that I couldn't have. I love you.

Finally, I am forever indebted to the readers of *Seven Spoons*. You changed my life.

INDEX

Appetite by Random House® is a registered trademark of Random House LLC

Published by arrangement with Ten Speed Press

Library and Archives of Canada Cataloguing in Publication is available upon request

ISBN: 978-0-449- 01630-5
eBook ISBN: 978-0-449-01631-2

Design by Nami Kurita

Printed and bound in China

Published in Canada by Appetite by Random House®, a division of Random House of Canada Limited, a Penguin Random House Company

www.penguinrandomhouse.ca

10 9 8 7 6 5 4 3 2 1

appetite
BY RANDOM HOUSE

Penguin
Random
House